ECOLOGICAL STATES

A volume in the series
The Environments of East Asia
edited by Ann Sherif and Albert L. Park

A list of titles in this series is available at
www.cornellpress.cornell.edu.

ECOLOGICAL STATES

Politics of Science and Nature
in Urbanizing China

Jesse Rodenbiker

Foreword by Albert L. Park

CORNELL UNIVERSITY PRESS   **ITHACA AND LONDON**

Thanks to generous funding from the Luce Foundation and the Institute for Chinese Language and Culture, Renmin University of China, the ebook editions of this book are available as open access volumes through the Cornell Open initiative.

First published 2023 by Cornell University Press

Library of Congress Cataloging-in-Publication Data

Names: Rodenbiker, Jesse, 1983– author.
Title: Ecological states : politics of science and nature in urbanizing China / Jesse Rodenbiker, foreword by Albert L. Park.
Description: Ithaca : Cornell University Press, 2023. | Series: Environments of East Asia | Includes bibliographical references and index.
Identifiers: LCCN 2022038029 (print) | LCCN 2022038030 (ebook) | ISBN 9781501768996 (hardcover) | ISBN 9781501769009 (paperback) | ISBN 9781501769023 (pdf) | ISBN 9781501769016 (epub)
Subjects: LCSH: Ecology—Political aspects—China. | Human ecology—China. | Power (Social sciences)—China.
Classification: LCC JA75.8 .R64 2023 (print) | LCC JA75.8 (ebook) | DDC 304.20951—dc23/eng/20221101
LC record available at https://lccn.loc.gov/2022038029
LC ebook record available at https://lccn.loc.gov/2022038030

For Akira

Contents

Foreword

In the face of climate change and environmental crises in the twenty-first century, "ecology" has become a popular stand-in for laying out a new pathway for sustainable living. Ecology, as a scientific term, focuses on the relationship between living organisms, and as such, it has been deployed as a tool to rethink the ways humans should approach and treat nature. Governments talk about ecology as a panacea for national and global environmental issues—something to reverse the destructive pathways of modern civilization by promoting environmental protection and a more harmonious relationship with nature. Since 2012, ecology has figured prominently in the Chinese Communist Party's (CCP) campaign "to build a new ecological civilization." This campaign has been a top-down drive to reconstruct landscapes, built environments, and people's habits and culture in the pursuit of developing a more green society. Green development for ecological civilization has been imagined and articulated by the CCP as a vehicle for overcoming environmental degradation without compromising or sacrificing material prosperity for the citizens of China, but it has given way to dispossession, displacement, and rupture in both human and nonhuman worlds.

In *Ecological States*, Jesse Rodenbiker points out that the pursuit of ecological civilization has been a way to construct right relationships with nature. In this quest for building a new relationship with nature, who gets to define "right" relationships? That is, who has the power to determine the definition of ecology, how that definition plays out between humans and nonhumans, and the appearance and shape of ecological civilization? *Ecological States* carefully interrogates these questions. In so doing, it becomes a platform to shine light on the politicization of the process to build an ecological civilization in China. It draws attention to the ways in which the Chinese state has turned ecological civilization into a vehicle for governing, exercising and reinforcing state authority in people's daily lives through techno-scientific knowledge and practices. As such, *Ecological States* powerfully reminds readers that there is nothing "depoliticized" in ecology and that building an ecological civilization is far from a simple neutral process to save the environment.

Any top-down, state-led campaign is not a monolithic process in which people are simply bystanders. *Ecological States* makes this quite clear by carefully laying out how the CCP's policies have shaped and influenced the lives of its citizens. Through ethnographic research, it highlights how people on the ground have navigated these policies and demonstrates the indeterminacy of any policy regardless of the power of the state. In studying how ecological civilization as a state policy was formed and the impact this has had on the public, *Ecological States* is a valuable tool to historically and materially ground the meaning of ecology and its connection to state power. It makes visible the dynamics and infrastructure of authority behind drives to build ecological civilizations in order to show that it is never, and will never be, a simple process to protect the environment without domination and control.

—Albert L. Park

Acknowledgments

Making a book is a collective endeavor. My debts and gratitude for all involved in the making of this one run deep. First and foremost, I thank the people of China for sharing their insights and experiences with me. Without the generosity of those who opened doors to their homes, government offices, and research facilities, this project would not have materialized. From environmental scientists, government officials, and urban planners to everyday citizens and ecological migrants, all who participated in this project have my utmost gratitude.

Along the way, I have been fortunate to have some of the best colleagues one could wish for. At University of California, Berkeley, where this project began, mentors and colleagues provided inspiration and support. You-tien Hsing has always been a model of intellectual rigor for me. She fostered my work in geography along with generous support from Jake Kosek, Nancy Peluso, and Michael Watts. While at UC Berkeley, I benefited from writing groups and workshops, including those organized through the Center for Chinese Studies, Global Metropolitan Studies, Left Coast Political Ecology, and the Institute of East Asian Studies. I appreciate support from UC Berkeley colleagues including Alexander Arroyo, Teresa Caldeira, Phillip Campanile, Sharad Chari, Ying-fen Chen, Renee Elias, Greg Fayard, Thomas Gold, Paul Groth, Gillian Hart, Camilla Hawthorne, Adam Jadhav, Laurel Larsen, Chris Lesser, Peiting Li, Kan Liu, Yan Long, Juliet Lu, Annie Malcolm, Bridget Martin, Jeff Martin, Tim McLellan, Chris Mizes, Kevin O'Brien, Meredith Palmer, Will Payne, Nicole Rosner, Lana Salman, Ettore Santi, Kristin Sangren, Nathan Sayre, Tobias Smith, David Thompson, Alessandro Tiberio, Erin Torkelson, Shu-wei Tsai, Mollie Van Gordon, Alex Werth, Jenny Zhang, and Leonora Zoninsein, many of whom provided feedback on chapters or otherwise fueled intellectual conversations. Adam Liebman, Kristen Looney, Jean Oi, Lisa Rofel, and Tomo Sugimoto provided helpful comments and questions on chapters in progress. Geospatial librarian, Susan Powell, and Chinese collection librarian, Jianye He, helped locate archival material through means only they know. Before I arrived in Berkeley, Ina Asim, Daniel Buck, Bryna Goodman, Lionel Jensen, John Kronen, and Yizhao Yang provided guidance and encouragement.

Support for conducting fieldwork in China and concentrated writing time were instrumental to this project. At Sichuan University Department of Land Resource Management and School of Public Administration, Liu Runqiu provided key support, as did Yu Chao, Cao Qian, and Dong Huan. For their support, I thank Hu Zhiding formerly of Yunnan Normal University School of Geography and Tourism, Yang Shuo at the Yunnan Institute of Environmental Science, Peter Edward Mortimer at the Kunming Institute of Botany, and colleagues at Tsinghua Urban Planning and Design Institute. Du Yiran assisted with transcribing interviews. Numerous institutions provided indispensable grant and fellowship support for fieldwork, including the Social Science Research Council, Fulbright-Hays Program, Confucius China Studies Program, as well as UC Berkeley's Center for Chinese Studies and Institute of International Studies. A grant from the Chiang-Ching Kuo Foundation for International Scholarly Exchange supported the early writing stage. A Postdoctoral Research Fellowship with the Cornell Atkinson Center for Sustainability and Department of Natural Resources and the Environment at Cornell University provided time and resources for further developing the manuscript. The Institute for Chinese Language and Culture at Renmin University supported the illustration program and Open Access publication. Portions of the book previously appeared in research articles with the *Annals of the American Association of Geographers, Geoforum,* and *International Journal of Urban and Regional Research.* I am grateful to the managing editors of these journals Kendra Strauss, Harvey Neo, and Fulong Wu, as well as anonymous reviewers, for their feedback. The American Council of Learned Societies and Henry Luce Foundation Program in China Studies, Woodrow Wilson International Center for Scholars, and Princeton University's Paul and Marcia Wythes Center on Contemporary China provided fellowship support for the completion of the book manuscript.

Over the years, I have presented parts of this book at conferences, universities, and research centers. I am grateful to conference participants at annual meetings of the American Association of Geographers, Association of Asian Studies, Dimensions of Political Ecology, International Association of China Planning, Nordic Geographers Meeting, and the Royal Geographical Society–Institute of British Geographers. The arguments presented here benefited from critical and encouraging audiences at Barnard College and Columbia University (Architecture and Urban Studies), Chulalongkorn University (Cultural Studies), Cornell University (Natural Resources and the Environment), Guangzhou University (Geographical Sciences), Hohai University (National Centre for Resettlement), National University of Singapore (Geography), National University of Taiwan (Geography), Norwegian University of Science and Technology (Geography), Princeton University (Ecology and Evolutionary Biology and Public and International Affairs), Rutgers University (Geography and Human Ecology), Sichuan University (Public Administration and Land Resource Management), South China Normal University (Geography), Southwest Forestry University (Geography and Ecotourism), Stanford University (Shorenstein Asia-Pacific

Research Center), State University of New York at Buffalo (Environment and Sustainability), University College London (Bartlett School of Planning), University of Pittsburgh (Institute for Chinese Studies), and University of Sydney (China Studies Centre).

I found vibrant intellectual communities at Cornell University, Princeton University, and Rutgers University. Yan Bennett, Raymond Craib, Priscilla Ferreira, Nate Gabriel, Aaron Glasserman, Jenny Goldstein, Qian He, Junming Huang, Qing Huang, David Hughes, Mazen Labban, Preetha Mani, Pamela McElwee, Robin Leichenko, Melanie McDermott, Paul O'Keefe, Victoria Ramenzoni, Åsa Rennermalm, Kevon Rhiney, Louisa Schein, Laura Schneider, Mi Shih, Kevin St. Martin, Julia Teebken, David Wilcove, Willie Wright, Yu Xie, and Jerry Zee have been gracious and convivial interlocutors. I thank cartographer Mike Siegel for producing the maps and figures for the book. My deep appreciation goes to Yue Du, Clifford Kraft, D. Asher Ghertner, Paul Nadasdy, Wendy Wolford, Emily Yeh, and John Zinda, who provided critical feedback on the full manuscript during a book workshop at Cornell University.

Cornell University Press Environments of East Asia series editors Albert Park and Ann Sherif believed in this project from the beginning. They provided enthusiastic support and valuable feedback. Editor Emily Andrew saw the importance of the work and welcomed the manuscript to the press. Editor Alexis Siemon shepherded the book through production alongside Karen Laun. Scott Levine designed the cover illustration. Special thanks go to these editors and the staff at Cornell University Press, as well as Anna Ahlers and Tim Oakes who provided incisive comments on the manuscript.

Heartfelt acknowledgements are due for my family. My parents, Harold and Bonnie, offered unyielding moral support. Jake, Jordan, and Josh provided fraternal camaraderie and frequent reminders of other meaningful activities. Rain interrupted writing whenever she pleased with dog kisses.

My daughter Akira grew and changed alongside this project. She accompanied her single father for long-term fieldwork abroad—no easy task. Not only did she learn a new language during kindergarten and first grade in China, but she proved to be an indispensable research partner. Her presence kept me grounded. Her strength and creativity continue to inspire me. I dedicate this work to her, with love.

Finally, for support in all matters, from the intellectual to the mundane, I thank Andrea Marston. During fieldwork, her visits from antipodes were sources of renewal. During writing, she volunteered countless hours to read drafts, discuss the ideas that fill these pages, and offer encouragement. I am grateful for her brilliance, support, and enduring love without which this book would not have come to fruition.

ECOLOGICAL STATES

ECOLOGICAL STATES

Ecology has become a means through which to express and constitute state power in China. In 2012, the Chinese Communist Party (CCP) wrote "ecological civilization building" into the party constitution. In 2018, it was written into the Constitution of the People's Republic of China with amendments that emphasized conservation and a "scientific outlook on development." These amendments included ideological messages that building a beautiful China, maintaining the purity of the ruling communist party, and creating an "ecological society" were crucial to sustainable development. A nationwide environmental campaign organized around strategic policies to build an ecological civilization (*shengtai wenming jianshe zhanlüe zhengce*) became a key pillar of China's party-state. Alongside the reorganization of party-state ideology and national policy over the last decade, the state introduced myriad techniques aimed at optimizing green governance and urbanization, such as ecological redlines and New-Type Urbanization planning, which initiated a new phase of urban-rural coordination.

Contrary to news media and scholarly accounts, the ecological civilization building paradigm did not originate from President Xi Jinping who came to power in 2012. Even though the scientific knowledge and techniques guiding ecological civilization building emerged through the work of China's scientists and state planners engaged in global ecological and socialist thought, Xi is the figure most closely associated with the ecological turn. Xi Jinping Thought

(*Xi Jinping sixiang*) was enshrined in the Nineteenth Party Congress in 2017 during a three-hour speech in which Xi articulated a vision for sustainable development. In the speech, Xi emphasized nature aesthetics and nation-building through the theme of "beautiful China." A beautiful China, Xi claimed, is a nation that is "ecological and civilized" and "ensures global ecological security."[1] To become a "fully modernized socialist country by 2035," Xi vowed to develop "ecological goods to meet people's growing demand for a beautiful environment," promote green development, protect the environment, and improve society.[2] The scope of ecological civilization building is vast, crossing an array of governmental policies. It epitomizes a socio-technical imaginary aimed at balancing economy and environment by optimizing biophysical nature, urbanizing rural society, and improving the aesthetic character of China's landscapes.[3]

From forest restoration to nationwide projects aimed at urbanizing millions of rural citizens,[4] there are significant tensions between the multiple aims of a vision that directs environmental protection, social transformation, green development, and national beautification. How did ecology come to take on such an all-compassing role in China's environmental governance? How did socio-environmental improvement, civilizational progress, urbanization, and a national aesthetic come be articulated in relation to ecology? What logics undergird the state's vision for sustainable development? How do these logics shape techniques of socio-environmental governance? How are China's citizens affected by a state that wields ecology for governmental ends? How do everyday people act under state programs, which routinely displace and resettle millions in the name of social and environmental optimization?

Expressions and constitutions of state power in relation to ecology are at the heart of the present work—as are their effects in shaping society and space. Ecology is not merely the study of relations between living organisms and physical environments, but also a multimodal signifier within and through which nested relations between the state, society, and nature articulate. This book details how the state wields ecology to govern and within this context how society encounters and counters state power. The early chapters focus on relationships between ecology and state power. They engage environmental scientists, urban planners, and government officials as they define logics underlying the state's vision of green governance and deploy techniques to bring it to fruition. The latter chapters focus on how relationships between ecology and power shape domains of social conduct and uneven social trajectories. They follow everyday people, villagers, and resettlement migrants—often referred to as "ecological migrants"—as they struggle to survive and thrive among transformations introduced by the state in the name of sustainable development.

My central argument is that the Chinese state wields ecology to shape nature, society, and space. As such, ecology mediates power relations, fields of social action, and unequal subject positionalities within China's citizenry. The chapters are grounded in extensive fieldwork with scientists, state planners, and everyday people. The following section provides context through a rural citizen's experiences of two state environmental campaigns.

Zhang's Tale of Two Environmental Campaigns

"First the government told us to fill in the lake to make farmland, now they are taking our farmland and turning it into wetlands," exclaimed Zhang Jian, a villager living on the outskirts of Kunming, the provincial capital of Yunnan Province. The municipal government had recently zoned Zhang's village land within an ecological protection area as part of their urban-rural comprehensive plan. Afterward, the buildings and the village houses that surrounded Zhang's land were on a timeline for demolition. Zhang lost access to his farmland, which was transformed into an aestheticized ecological protection area that attracts hundreds of urban tourists daily. He was concerned about the rapid transformations underway and his future. But this was not the first time Zhang experienced rapid socio-environmental transformation as the fulcrum of state-led modernization. The first was during the Maoist period (1949–76) when rural land productivity became central to socialist modernization. Zhang's reflections on two state environmental campaigns elucidate continuities and ruptures in how the Chinese state governs nature, society, and space.

In the summer of 2014, we spoke in an abandoned courtyard in the shade of a willow tree where, before the Maoist period, a Buddhist temple stood. Once central to social life, the temple was targeted during the Cultural Revolution (1966–76) campaign to "destroy the four olds" (posijiu), which changed the significance of the building. Old customs, old culture, old habits, old ideas of the precommunist era were to be replaced. The temple came to represent something anachronistic—out of sync with a new form of modernity—and therefore in need of transformation. It was torn down. Villagers converted the space into a school with a concrete courtyard, formed by four rectangular two-story barrack-styled buildings. Now under state efforts to build an ecological civilization, beautify China, and urbanize millions of rural people, this rural infrastructure once again became out of sync with the state's vision of modernity.

Zhang likened Xi's campaign to build an ecological civilization with Mao Zedong's campaign to transform the countryside. In 1965, Mao initiated a state campaign to "study agriculture from Dazhai" (*nongye xue dazhai*). Dazhai is a village in eastern Shanxi province that produced an abundance of agricultural goods in the early 1960s. Dazhai became a national model for how diligent labor and social mobilization can transform the environment and increase agricultural yields. Mao exhorted peasants to study Dazhai's example in their efforts to turn unproductive land into agricultural land. He famously referred to the modernist enterprise as "conquering all under the sky" (*rending shengtian*). This adaptation of a Confucian phrase has often been translated for Western audiences simply as conquering or warring against nature.[5] But for Mao the phrase meant overcoming a historically specific form of subjugation, both feudal and colonial, symbolically embodied within the process of cultivating collective agency to shape the natural world and achieve utopian communism.[6] Regardless of interpretation, the project of increasing the sum total amount of agricultural land was undoubtedly as much about modernist state building and the performance of proper politics as it was about overcoming environmental limitations through harnessing social powers.

During Mao's campaign, Zhang was a laborer and a performer in his village's performing arts troupe called the Fill in the Lake Brigade. His work unit was stationed in south Kunming, alongside hundreds of others. They were assigned the massive environmental engineering project of transforming portions of Lake Dian, the largest high plateau lake in the province, into farmland. The project was Kunming's local interpretation of the nationwide campaign to study agriculture from Dazhai. Achieving this feat of human-induced environmental change entailed backbreaking manual labor with minimal mechanized machinery to enclose parts of the lake with agricultural fields (*weihaizaotian*).

As part of the propaganda performance troupe in the Fill in the Lake Brigade, Zhang's tasks were twofold. During the day he pulverized rock with handheld tools and piled them into the lake. If Zhang transported enough fill, he obtained ration cards for his labor exchangeable for lunch and dinner. If he failed to move enough rocks, he would go without food for the day. At night, regardless of whether he ate or not, Zhang performed song and dance alongside the propaganda troupe. Their nightly performances to labor units communicated party-state ideology and campaign maxims. Zhang referred to his efforts to entertain and raise morale through performing state-sanctioned messages as spreading Maoist Thought (*Mao Zedong sixiang*). Zhang remembered his role in this campaign with great pride.

Smiling, and donning the face of a performer, he rose from his seat in the open courtyard and began singing a song from his days in the performance troupe. Involuntarily, it seemed, his limbs recognized the rhythm and swayed along. His body followed suit. He began to sing and dance as if performing for an audience. Zhang's voice retained a youthful vibrato as he sang a slogan from the campaign:

> Dazhai's sorghum is tall.
> Dazhai's rice is long.
> Their children are all so strong.
> Move the mountains to make farmland.
> Change the sky to alter the land.

The song lyrics echoed maxims from Mao's environmental campaign to mobilize social powers and human capacities to transform the earth in an effort to increase agricultural output. Performances such as this reveal how the campaign doubled as a theater to advance state interests and communicate ideology.[7] Even though this time was challenging for many Chinese citizens, including Zhang, he relished memories of his youthful exploits in song and dance. He felt assured that his labor, his artistic expression, and his sacrifices helped strengthen his country.

Resting from his performance, Zhang talked about how proud he was to remember (*huixiang*) his role in the campaign, which resulted in more than thirty-three square kilometers of new land formations in the 1960s. I was intrigued to hear this, as none of the reclaimed land grew crops well; agricultural gains on the reclamation site were minimal. Moreover, the process of reclaiming land drastically degraded the aquatic conditions effecting plant life in the inner part of Lake Dian (*caohai*). Over the decades following Deng Xiaoping's reform-era modernization drive, often referred to as the "long 1980s" (more or less from 1978 to 1992), the reclaimed land became the site of urban development. Environmental conditions worsened after decades of urbanization during which industrial and urban wastewater were dumped directly into the lake. Urban sprawl came to encompass the filled-in land. This reclaimed land now houses the Yunnan Ethnic Minorities Museum, Yunnan Ethnic Minorities Village, and several ecological protection sites that portray the natural world and romantic images of rural life side by side. Urbanization coupled with aesthetic representations of rural life spatially overlay this former site of agricultural modernization.

As Zhang spoke with me, he and his fellow villagers were again at the forefront of an environmental campaign as momentous on a national scale as Mao's. They now encountered state efforts, under Xi, to build ecological civilization. Building ecological civilization, or what is sometimes translated as "ecological civilization construction" (*shengtai wenming jianshe*), is a key contradiction in terms.

The Chinese word *jianshe* means to build, construct, or to develop. Ecology, on the other hand, is generally considered the study of relations between organisms and their physical environments—less something to be built than a relation existing in nature. In popular terms, however, ecological civilization building is often used to reference state conservation projects. The state issued a number of ecological protection land designations, deemed as crucial to building ecological civilization, in the early to mid-2000s. There are now more than thirty different types of ecological protection land designations that span national, provincial, and municipal levels.

In 2012, ecological protection land designations covered more than 15 percent of national territory.[8] Given subsequent state efforts to expand protected areas, ecological protection zones cover at least 20 percent of China's national territory.[9] The state claims 25 precent of land has already been zoned for ecological protection.[10] The number of types and total areal coverage keep rising annually, which makes tabulating the number of ecological protected areas and the percentage of the national territory they occupy an exercise in chasing the Red Queen.[11]

Each protected area, to varying degrees, is enrolled in political economies of ecological construction.[12] Political-economic activities related to ecological construction are mechanisms not only of shaping biophysical relations in nature but also for governing people. As land is incorporated into ecological protection projects, the state endeavors to relocate people living in newly made protected areas into resettlement housing (*anzhifang*). Government officials and planners refer to this as "ecological migration" (*shengtai yimin*)—the uneven process of displacement and resettlement experienced by those whose land and housing are incorporated into state conservation projects. The political economy of ecological construction revolves around displacement, resettlement, and conservation-oriented development. These are state techniques aimed at optimizing relationships between nature, society, and space.

For Zhang, the confluence of state conservation efforts at the municipal government level and the state drive for urbanizing the rural population brought significant changes. Zhang had participated in agricultural production and rural industry throughout his life. Although his labor and social life changed over time, he nonetheless remained intimately tied to rural land and community. In the socialist period, he worked the land with his rural commune and acted in the village performance troupe. During the 1980s, with the decollectivization of farmland, Zhang began to sell surplus products on the market. With the growth of rural industry, he worked in the local township-village enterprise (TVE), a shift commonly referred to as "leaving the soil but not the countryside" (*litu bulixiang*). Many other rural citizens at that time began working in city factories. Their rural land, housing, and communities, however, remained crucial social safety nets. Migrant laborers could return from cities to a rural house with access to farmland. After the closure of his local TVE in the 2000s, Zhang returned to agricultural work. He grew seasonal vegetables and flowers, which he sold on the market. Like many rural citizens, Zhang's relations to rural land and community were central to his life. With the establishment of an ecological protection area and municipal government plans to resettle village residents into high-rise apartments, however, Zhang and his village comrades were set on a new trajectory.

Urbanization, Environmental Science, and State Power

In 2011, at least insofar as most citizens came to live in urban areas and were designated urban residential status, China became predominantly urban. Urbanization did not happen spontaneously. China's urbanization is the product of ongoing state efforts, including municipal territorial extension,[13] rural-to-urban migration, and agricultural industrialization, which prompted movement of (predominantly rural) flexible labor to factories in major cities. Urbanization in China is as much about controlling mobility and marketization as it is about economic migration. In the current moment, the state portrays urbanization of rural people as necessary to optimizing socio-natural relations and fostering a more equitable society.[14]

The historical roots of economic disparity between urban and rural people can be traced back to feudal relations, the urban-biased socialist pricing system,[15] and household registration policies called *hukou* that kept people geographically bound to either rural or urban locales.[16] The hukou system is a geographical control mechanism that defines citizens' access to space—either "urban" (nonagricultural) or "rural" (agricultural)—as well as place-based social welfare benefits. Urban hukou holders have historically received disproportionately high benefits, which contribute to stark inequalities. Xi's urbanization efforts aim to reclassify millions of rural hukou holders as urban citizens and resettle them in urban spaces. Changing hukou status, depending on local context, can come with benefits, such as health care and educational services. But as rural people officially take on urban residential status, the social fabric of rural communities transform and individuals forfeit rural housing and use rights to rural land.

Land is one of the last remnants of postsocialist China's great capitalist transition. It is not only many rural people's most valuable asset, but also embodies material possibilities for land-based production and economic security. While all land in China is socialized, urban land is controlled by municipal government hierarchies and other state institutions. Use rights to rural land are distributed to villagers for building homes, farming, and developing collective enterprises. Rural land in close proximity to cities is of high value, which makes the politics of land control in municipal regions contentious.[17] State efforts to urbanize rural people are equally fraught.

When Xi became president, he outlined a plan to urbanize 100 million rural people, which he called the "100 million people" issue.[18] It is the first part of a long-term green modernization plan, which aims to urbanize 250 million citizens by 2025.[19] According to the plan, one of the primary mechanisms through which urbanization should occur is through the resettlement of rural citizens, especially in three types of cities within China's central and western regions: provincial capitals, prefectural cities, and county-level towns.

I conducted the fieldwork and research for this book in three southwestern cities, which correspond to each of these urban categories: Kunming (provincial capital of Yunnan Province and prefectural-level city), Chengdu (provincial capital of Sichuan Province and prefectural-level city), and Dali (county-level town in Yunnan Province) (figure 1). I also conducted interviews in Beijing. During fieldwork, from 2014 to 2018, I utilized multiple research methods, including interviews, archival work, field observations, and photovoice focus group discussions. For a discussion of research methods in this study see the appendix.

To direct this new phase of urbanization, Xi called for coordinating planning and development of urban and rural areas.[20] The National New-Type Urbanization Plan (2014–20) marked a new phase in urban-rural coordination by incorporating rural planning within the municipal government's planning processes, which government officials referred to as "comprehensive urban-rural planning."[21] The state's New-Type Urbanization Plan stipulates that 20 percent of all municipal regions (*shiqu*) be zoned for ecological protection.

At this point, it is crucial to clarify key geographical facets related to China's municipalities and ecological protection zoning. First, municipal regions are subprovincial territories corresponding to areal units that contain multiple urban districts and extensive rural areas. Municipal governments have come to exert hierarchical control over townships within their jurisdiction. Townships oversee administrative villages within which there are any number of "natural" villages.[22] Second, when I use the term *ecological protection areas*, I am referring to "ecological redlines" (*shengtai hongxian*), "ecological protection areas" (*shengtai baohuqu*), and "urban ecological control areas" (*chengshi shengtai kongzhiqu*) within municipal regions. I simplify them with a single term because one of my findings is that, despite extensive Chinese-language literature that details their

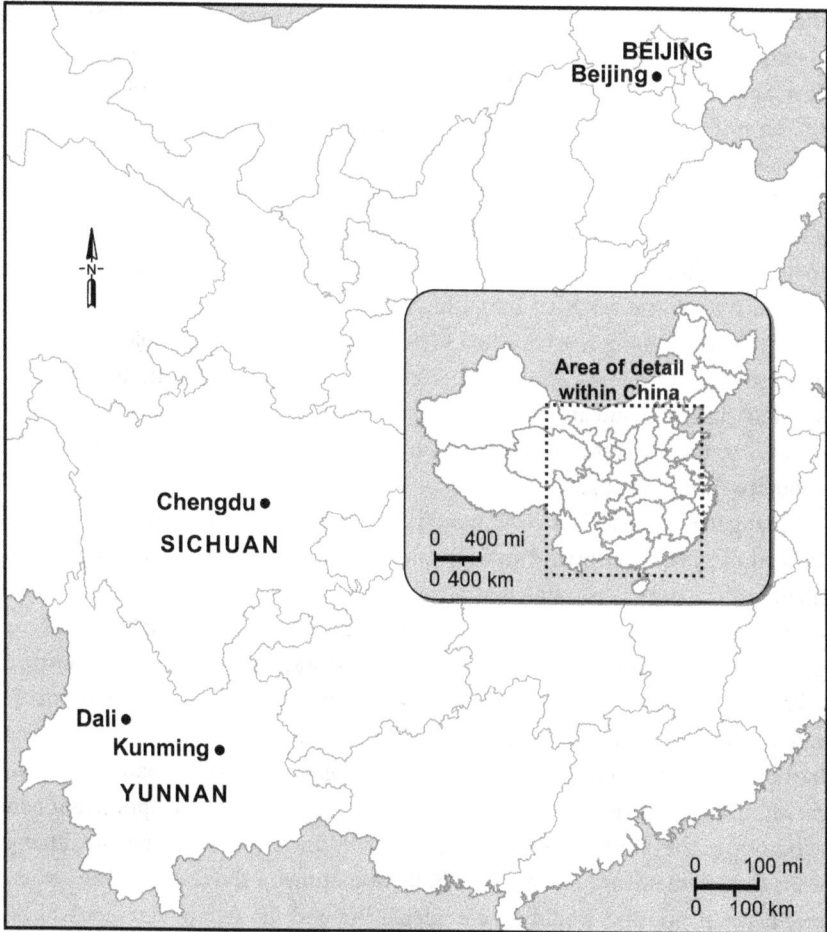

FIGURE 1. Map of research sites.

policy differences, for municipal state planners they serve the same function and are treated in the same way. When I use the term *ecological protection site*, I am referring to a particular site within an area zoned by the municipal government for ecological protection.

Since this self-styled New-Type Urbanization Plan emerged, ecological protection areas have sprung up across municipal regions throughout China, particularly on peri-urban village land like Zhang's on the outskirts of Kunming. By peri-urban, I mean porous areas of transition between urban and rural land uses, classifications, or characteristics that are proximate to municipal regions. In Kunming alone, there are more than one hundred spatially distinct peri-urban ecological protection areas. Over 200,000 peri-urban villagers were displaced in their making. For a municipal region with a population of six million, this is a substantial subset of people—roughly 3.3 percent of the regional population. Similar numbers are applicable to Chengdu with a population of more than fifteen million and Dali with a population of 650,000. Zhang is one of these peri-urban villagers.

After Zhang's village land was incorporated into the urban-rural comprehensive plan and zoned within an ecological protection area, he not only lost access to his agricultural land, but was also notified by the local government that village residents would be resettled into a high-rise resettlement complex being built nearby. There, Zhang was expected to become a fully "urban" subject. But how and on what terms was Zhang to become urban? How would he be compensated for his rural land and housing? What would urban life be like for him? The answers to these questions remained elusive. In his uncertainty, Zhang thought about his future through his past.

Zhang felt that Mao's environmental campaign had been turned on its head. Instead of making farmland out of water, Zhang's farmland was dredged and filled with water. The municipal government, in conjunction with a private developer, transformed Zhang's former farmland into an artificial wetland for treating urban wastewater. The ecological restoration landscape emphasized botanical features, which symbolized beautification and environmental purification. Not merely an aesthetic symbol, the treatment wetland was designed to harbor effluent pollutants thereby mitigating pollution in Lake Dian. Moreover, the site attracts tourists who come to witness state-led ecological optimization in action from the comforts of pristinely manicured walkways. Meanwhile, Zhang waits for resettlement housing to be built. Sometime in the coming years, when resettlement housing would be completed, he and his fellow villagers will be asked to relocate into one of the spatially concentrated high-rise housing units. In the eyes of the state, such transformations are crucial to green urbanization and making a beautiful China.

Urbanization, according to state development plans, is key to shifting China's political economy away from manufacturing and toward a service-oriented economy driven by domestic consumption. The transition to a service-oriented economy is gradual.[23] Manufacturing remains the bulwark of China's economy. Yet spurring domestic spending is crucial to continuing economic growth with a bourgeoning middle-class. The proliferation of ecological construction projects and leisure-oriented ecological protection sites are indicative of this political-economic transition. With a national average of two domestic trips annually and many more locally, domestic tourism has become important to China's transitioning economy.[24] Within this context, peri-urban sites offering natural and rural aesthetics welcome urban tourists to environs close to home. Through the processes of ecological protection zoning and urban-rural comprehensive planning, Zhang's agricultural land was transformed into one of these sites.

Zhang's experience, although potentially isolating for him, is far from isolated. Millions of rural citizens across China, like Zhang, find themselves in a political bind as they confront state logics and techniques aimed at shaping their conduct. With his farmland turned into a wetland, Zhang awaited ecological migration. How will Zhang and rural citizens like him navigate state projects of environmental protection and urbanization? As millions of China's rural citizens are enrolled in environmental campaigns to conserve nature and urbanize the countryside, it is hard to overstate the relevance of this question to their everyday lives.

Zhang was uncertain of how he will navigate the transitions underway. And the question for him was an unsettling one. He felt proud to work on Mao's environmental campaign to fill in the lake. But after the elation of singing, dancing, remembering the past, being reminded of the present and trying to forecast his future, his face fell. He expressed feelings of reluctance at the prospect of forfeiting his rural home and moving into an urban high-rise. Would Zhang make sacrifices for the new environmental campaign as he did for the first?

In considering how these environmental campaigns intersected with his life, Zhang articulated each as logically opposed to the other. In the first, the local government, in their implementation of central state imperatives, spearheaded a massive campaign to fill in Lake Dian. A key logic of the campaign was to create more arable land in effort to foster agricultural modernization. The current campaign, wherein Zhang's farmland was requisitioned by the municipal government, is orchestrated around building ecology and restoring a landscape degraded, in part, through the first campaign. Although Zhang experienced each campaign as thoroughly different from the other, Mao and Xi's approaches to governing natural and social worlds share common logics.

Mao's logic entailed mobilizing social forces and state powers to shape the natural world and modernize the country. It was avowedly anticapitalist and anticolonial. Mao came to power on the heels of war. The People's Republic of China (PRC) was founded in 1949 after China's Communist Party triumphed in civil war against the US-backed Guomindang. That war was preceded by World War II and a "century of humiliation" wrought by European, American, and Japanese colonial powers. Xi's logic exhibits significant continuity with Mao's, particularly regarding the notion of mobilizing social forces and state powers toward environmental transformation and modernization. Xi's logic is anticapitalist insofar as it espouses a model of sustainable development and economic production that counters the deleterious environmental effects of global capitalist forces. Perhaps most important, the current campaign fundamentally continues the ideological message that the state can scientifically orchestrate modernist social and environmental improvement. Both espouse visions of technical triumphalism over nature (much like elsewhere in the world). And both propose the application of socio-environmental models across regional contexts, even when they may not be appropriate for local conditions. Yet there are also key shifts in how these logics are articulated and the role of environmental science within state governance.

During Mao's rule, environmental science embodied tensions between Soviet-inspired anti-Mendelian Lysenkoist science (that precipitated the disastrous Great Leap Forward famine),[25] and Green Revolution–era agricultural science that modeled pest management for the world while creating new agricultural crop strains.[26] Environmental campaigns, during Mao's reign, were models of technocratic triumphalism. But the fraught negotiations between "reds" and scientific "experts" throughout these campaigns reflected their dual functionality as motors of modernization and theaters for performative politics. Principally for Mao, environmental campaigns projected the achievements that could be brought to fruition through the mechanization of *correct* political thought and action. Politics were front and center, part and parcel of state efforts to govern society and nature.

A key difference, under Xi, is that logics espoused by environmental scientists, instead of being explicitly political, contribute to naturalizing technocratic socio-environmental models of governance. I use the term *eco-developmental* to refer to the logics that undergird state techniques of governing nature, society, and space. These logics, in the contemporary period, revolve around complex systems science thinking, socio-environmental modeling, and a political narrative of sustainable developmental progress. Central to Xi's green modernization campaign, and highly consequential to the lives of millions of rural citizens across China, like Zhang, is the notion that state scientists and planners can optimize socio-natural relations. And that scientific optimization is essential for societal improvement and sustainable development.

For the state, attaining ecological civilization entails totalizing systems science techniques aimed at bringing about steady-state equilibrium in the biophysical world and optimized socio-spatial relations. The logic of this endeavor is advantageous to state building as it solidifies the role of the state within a unitary scientific paradigm.[27] In the current moment, the state supports a totalizing systems science approach to socio-environmental management in effort to build an "ecological society." Ecological society is presented, by the state and key environmental scientists, as the natural endpoint of green modernist progress. Efforts to create an ecological society are explicitly framed as righting the environmental wrongdoings of the Maoist era and subsequent development-first approaches of the 1980s through the early 2000s.[28] During the reform era, scientists advanced arguments that urbanizing the rural population was integral to a sustainable future. These logics have become central to socio-environmental governance under Xi. Hence, ecological civilization building reflects continuities with the socialist modernization drive, but also departs from socialist-era logics as ecology now figures centrally in the articulation and naturalization of state models for sustainable development and civilizational progress.

Every civilizational story demarcates who is within and outside the boundaries of civilization. China has a long history of civilizational narratives dating back to the first dynasties. In dynastic China, those who lived outside the boundaries of China's empire were referred to as "barbarians" (*huren* or *yemanren*). Barbarians were portrayed by the imperial state as operating without capacity to reason and without culture. The Chinese word for culture (*wenhua*) is literally the transformation (*hua*) that comes through writing and language (*wen*). Those outside of Chinese civilization, were imagined as barbarians ignorant of China's cultured forms of expression. They were framed as the relational other vis-à-vis the imperial population. Narratives of barbarian outsiders served the imperial state project of unifying the population around a shared sense of belonging. The specificity of imperial narratives, within which social groups were either within or outside the civilizational vision, changed throughout dynastic history. Civilizational boundaries, therefore, ebbed and flowed with the boundaries of empire.[29] In the present, the state's civilizational story is tethered to ecology and its myriad situated and contradictory meanings.

In China, or anywhere else for that matter, ecology is far from apolitical.[30] Ecology is embedded within and constitutive of the very workings of state power and socio-spatial organization across contexts. By way of comparison, science figures centrally in expressions and constitutions of state power across global contexts. Ethnology, for instance, was central to the formation of US territorial power from the late nineteenth into the early twentieth centuries. Counterintuitive as it may seem, ethnology was crucial to framing Native Americans as so-called noble savages—a social category closer to a primordial state of nature and therefore outside the bounds of civilization.[31] Ethnologists were at the heart of the US scientific understanding of its civilizing mission. Ethnological science, therefore, was central to the US colonial project, in that it justified the state's acquisition of land and resources that had not been made productive by so-called uncivilized societies. The US conservation movement and establishment of national parks further advanced state land territorialization efforts and Native American dispossession.[32] Analogously, ecology was integral to social Darwinist and nativist expressions underlying the eugenics movement in fascist Germany, which precipitated Nazism and the second world war.[33] Therefore, as states the world over draw on science in constituting power, it is imperative not to simply villainize China as an outlier in the global gambit.

Articulations of science and nature are distinct in any given historical, social, and political contexts. Who and what relationships are deemed "natural"? Who is civilized or—in other words—outside of and in control of nature? The answers to these questions lie in particular expressions and constitutions of state power in relation to science and politics of nature. In contemporary China, ecology has come to figure centrally in articulations of state power.

Under Xi's regime, ecology mediates the articulation between state power and a differentiated citizenry navigating environmental governance. It mediates how everyday people act, organize, or even resist incorporation into the state's civilizational vision. I theorize this articulation of power through the multidimensional framework of ecological states.

Ecological States

I define ecological states as expressions and constitutions of state power in relation to ecology. Ecology is not only a scientific discipline related to process-pattern relationships in the world but also a multimodal signifier that has become enrolled in a political narrative of socio-environmental change, human manipulation of nature, and the role of the state in governing sustainable development. In this framing, ecology is a situated universal with multiple logics. By *logics* I mean ways of knowing nature that order how it is to be acted on.[34] Eco-developmental logics undergird China's national sustainable development narrative, which projects an apex of biophysical, governmental, and aesthetic achievement. At their core, eco-developmental logics hold that state intervention will produce ecological equilibrium in the biophysical world, a modern society, and an aesthetic sublime in physical landscapes. Therefore, I anchor ecological states within key modes through which state power, society, and nature articulate—the biophysical, governmental, and aesthetic.

Biophysical

First, and perhaps most immediate when considering ecology, is the study of biophysical relations. Across iterations of ecology, ecological states refer to relations between biotic organisms and abiotic components constituted through the comingling and interaction of compounds in totalizing systems. Since the late twentieth century, the term *ecosystem* was used to describe the interactions between organisms and physical environments linked through nutrient cycles and energy of the Chinese state in building ecological civilization .

states in nature.

brium states entails mechanistic approaches to managing

approaches to nature define, measure, and operationalize

physical relations with the express purpose of optimizing them. Underlying this logic, is the understanding that if nature is appropriately altered it will exhibit desired relations and effects. Nature, in this sense, is modular. It can be modeled and operationalized for specified ends. According to a mechanistic logic, if the appropriate application of science and technical intervention is applied, then desired outcomes in nature will result in a predictable machine-like fashion. Mechanistic approaches to nature can be distinguished from other human-nature relations, such as state simplifications of nature, which James Scott argues have been central to modernist state governance.[36] In contrast, mechanistic logics of governing nature hold biophysical relations as external natures—distinct and separate from the human—but also manageable through human interventions. Humans, as biotic entities, are crucial within the calculus, not only as exceptionally agential organisms, but also as entities ascribed their own natural qualities.

Human natures, as Raymond Williams argues, are linked to historically specific ideas of nature and innate human qualities.[37] Ideas and meanings of nature, however, are malleable. They change in different historical and epistemological contexts depending on how claims on nature are expressed and made generalizable, not only to the biophysical world, but also to social groups. Human natures (or other forms of nature, for that matter) take shape through historical processes of scientifically knowing and defining nature. Processes of defining human natures inevitably demarcate social differences. In chapters 1 and 2, I show how China's natural and social scientists articulate ecology in relation to biophysical natures, as well as malleable human natures categorized in terms of urban and rural difference. Logics derived from ecological thought define techniques for altering and ultimately improving biophysical and human natures.

For scholars of science and technology, such as Donna Haraway, objects of knowledge are not objective reflections of universal realities, but agential forces that derive from social, historical, and political contexts.[38] Scientific logics, therefore, need to be situated in the context of their articulation. Ecology has been wielded across global contexts to propel nativist ideology in early twentieth-century Germany,[39] eugenics movements across Latin America,[40] and US colonial expansion.[41] Ecology, like all sciences, is always social and political.[42] So is sustainability, which takes on different meanings across social and historical contexts.[43]

many key scientists involved in defining sustainable development in China were engaged in global attempts to negotiate socialist thought with ecological thought. Given the longstanding resonance between ecology and socialist thought and the challenges for socialist states to balance industrial production with its multiscalar environmental effects, the issue of remaking socialism in relation to ecology resonated globally.[44] As chapter 1 illustrates, ecological thought in China developed over a century of global scientific exchanges across Marxian political economy, botany, systems science, urban ecology, and ecological economics. China's scientists, from the 1920s through the present, shaped ecology as a form of science organized around questions of how to optimize biophysical relations and foster civilizational progress. For Mao, the peasantry figured as the vanguard of modernization, revolution, and industrialization. This logic was informed by a stage-oriented social evolutionary reading of Marxian political economy. The scientific logics that predominated the 1980s socialist reform period, however, articulated the role of the peasantry no longer as the vanguard of socialist revolution, but as closer to an "original" or "primitive" form of ecology (*yuanshi shengtai*) and therefore outside the folds of ecological civilization. Eco-developmental logics, such as these that project stage-oriented societal trajectories, emerged through the reasoned argumentation of natural and social scientists. Their arguments took shape synchronously with civilizational narratives of sustainable development, state-directed urbanization, national aestheticization, and societal optimization. These scientific logics, however, are not uncontested.

Notable Chinese scientists offer alternative formulations of ecology, sustainable development, and the role of rural society. One alternative, for instance, posits traditional rural lifeways and small-scale agricultural production as models for sustainable development.[45] Such logics, however, do not predominate in state policy and action. While China's debates are richly varied, I focus on delineating logics that have become central to serving governmental ends.[46] My genealogy, therefore, focuses on how eco-developmental logics emerged in relation to expressions and constitutions of state power from the rise of Mao to the present.

Governmental

I refer to governance or, in other words, that which pertains to the governmental, in two senses. The first relates to techniques aimed at governing nature, society, and space. I define *techniques* as political technologies that target spatial organization, relations in nature, and populations. For Michel Foucault, forms of knowledge and practice produce political techniques of power and spatial orientations aimed at governing populations—what he calls "biopower."[47] Power, in this sense, refers to a multiplicity of forces that shape socio-natural configurations and physical spaces.[48] Modern subjects come to know and understand themselves, their societal roles, and realms of possible actions within this field of power. Governmental power, therefore, operates through disciplinary modes of "acting upon the actions" and interests of subjects and "conducting the conduct" of populations.[49] In detailing eco-developmental logics and techniques, I focus on disciplinary expressions of power and knowledge, as well as forms of technical action that materialize through them.[50]

The second sense of governmental relates to "states," as in the institutions, actors, and ruling entities enrolled in practices of governance. In China, this includes institutions that span central and local jurisdictions, state scientists and planners, as well as the party-state. Ecology, I contend, has become instrumental to expressions of state power—ideologically, territorially, and within banal bureaucratic formations. Eco-developmental logics define the role of the state as the builder of an ecological form of civilization. In other words, an ecological civilization is to be brought into being through state intervention. Ecological civilization building, therefore, is an inherently future-oriented governance project.

According to state modernization plans from the Nineteenth National Party Congress of 2017, ecological civilization will be attained by the year 2050; the People's Republic of China centennial is October 1, 2049. Such timelines portray temporal logics of attaining a desired state of modernist achievement through state techniques of socio-environmental optimization. Not merely a discursive enterprise, state techniques that derive from eco-developmental logics are key to the reproduction of state power. As I discuss in chapters 2 and 3, ecology has become central to extending the territorial reach of the local state and producing landscapes that reflect the state's vision of socio-natural optimization. Eco-developmental techniques, such as ecological restoration, are geared toward transforming biophysical relations in nature, beautifying the landscape, and producing a modern urban society from one that has been predominantly rural. How state scientists produce and read historical ecological records is shaped by how they imagine restoration landscapes and visualize landscape beautification and purification, as I have detailed in chapter 2.

Chapter 3 illustrates how municipal bureaucrats' conservation planning techniques strengthen their control over rural land surrounding cities. I use the term *ecological territorialization* to refer to the ecological protection and urban-rural planning processes through which opportunistic municipal government officials incorporate rural land and housing under their control. The emergence of these territorializing processes marks a new phase in, what You-tien Hsing calls, the "urbanization of the local state."[51] State scientists and municipal planners discuss ecological protection zoning not only as a technical process of optimizing bio-physical relations in nature, but also as means to foster an ecological society. As the second half of the book attests, however, the societal actions and outcomes that emerge from ecological civilization building projects do not neatly fit the state's eco-developmental imaginary.

Although state scientists and planners deploy techniques aimed at mechaniz-ing nature, and optimizing society and space, their mechanistic techniques don't simply produce mechanistic outcomes. Despite the veneer of a centrally orches-trated environmental governance effort, there is a great deal of indeterminacy to the processes involved. The interplay between the exercise of state power in relation to ecology and social actions is filled with contradictions, refusals, and creative reworkings. The final three chapters highlight forms of counter-conduct; that is, the ways that people struggle with and against governmental processes aimed at conducting society.[52] In highlighting forms of counter-conduct, I stress that citizens do not merely internalize ecological expressions of power aimed at producing an ecological society.[53] Instead, society actively exercises capacities in relation and counter to eco-developmental logics and techniques aimed at con-ducting human conduct. In doing so, individuals and communities transform their lives in relation to governmental forces.

There is an array of social trajectories contingent on the myriad ways people navigate state environmental governance. By *trajectories*, I mean the differenti-ated socioeconomic and spatiotemporal pathways through which people navi-gate state power. How society transforms in relation to a state wielding ecology to govern depends on how people act not only in relation to expressions of state power, but within the context of preexisting unequal social positionalities and emergent power relations. Therefore, trajectories are shaped by already existing socioeconomic positionalities and environmental conditions, as well as the poli-tics of counter-conduct. The exercise of individual and collective actions, within this context, produces myriad social trajectories.

Trajectories are also shaped by the ways social differences come to be defined and contested. Eco-developmental logics define distinct roles within China's citizenry. They categorically ascribe high value (*suzhi*) to urban people and low value to rural people. Within the ideological vision of ecological civiliza-tion building, China's future is urban. The past is rural. Urban populations are modern and civilized. The nature of the rural citizenry, in this vision, is back-ward and uncivilized. In these ways eco-developmental logics reify urban-rural difference and rural deficiency.[54] They hold that the nature of rural people and their inherently malleable value can be improved through rational state-led urbanization.

Although the urbanization of the rural population is often heralded as the end of China's villages,[55] rural lifeways do not simply disappear but transform in relation to how society responds to a state wielding ecology to govern. Society exercises power within this eco-developmental milieu—at times in line with the state's vision, but often in ways that counter it. For instance, many rural people do not simply accept government terms for resettlement or embrace the prospect of becoming urban. Instead, they harness individual and collective powers for their own ends.

In some instances, rural people facing conservation-oriented displacement and resettlement individually or collectively mobilize to maximize rural land and housing compensation capital. In doing so, they utilize the state's resources in ways unintended by state planners. As I discuss in chapter 4, rural people navigate the politics of valuation and compensation to reorient their relationships to land, housing, and labor. Many strive to maximize resettlement compensation capital, which they utilize as they see fit. Some balk at the prospects of living in urban resettlement housing. Instead, they use compensation capital to lease land outside their original village and continue farming elsewhere. Others move into new agrarian sectors or otherwise act outside state prescriptions for planned urbanization. While the aims and outcomes for individuals differ, and some also readily accept and benefit from moving into new urban environs, I illustrate how the aspirations of rural people facing ecological migration take shape in relation to the volumetric politics of land and housing valuation and compensation. In ways such as these, social navigations of state environmental governance remake constellations of power, albeit unevenly.

Aesthetic

In the context of a state wielding ecology to govern, citizens draw on alternative understandings of ecology for their own ends. They do so through banal spatial practices, which aesthetically express the rural as ecological. Chapter 5 details rural citizens' spatial practices of aesthetically representing what I call a "rural-ecological sublime" in villages being incorporated into ecological protection areas. Politics of nature infuse, not only state governance, but also the ways rural citizens remake rural spaces and meanings. The aesthetic senses they cultivate, at times align with and at other times counter eco-developmental logics.

I consider aesthetics as shared senses and material forms through which things in the world are spatialized, visualized, or associated with beauty. Aesthetics is inseparable from politics and power relations. Jacques Rancière theorizes aesthetics as the "distribution of the sensible"—a shared perception and sensibility in the arrangement of space.[56] D. Asher Ghertner, drawing on Rancière and Foucault, argues that the aesthetic terms within which senses become shared are central to rationalities of rule and the operation of government.[57] As these scholars attest, politics operate within and through shared aesthetic senses. The role of the Chinese state in the aesthetic vision of building an ecological civilization and a beautiful China is that of a technical manager intervening to optimize socio-natural relations and beautify the landscape.

In a related philosophical vein, the "aesthetic state" was articulated by Friedrich Schiller in 1795 as a mode of politics that incorporates aesthetics into state governance.[58] Schiller's notion of the aesthetic state was expounded on by Republican-era thinkers, like Zhang Jingsheng who considered aesthetics as key to revolutionizing postimperial China into a "beautiful society" and forming a national, albeit authoritarian, "government of beauty" (*mei de zhengfu*). The aesthetic state was also discussed by late-imperial philosopher Kang Youwei who articulated the science of beauty and aesthetic education as central to national modernization and the creation of a moral society.[59] While acknowledging Schiller's, Kang's, and Zhang's insights into how political rationalities operate through aesthetics, I depart from their romanticist and enlightenment tendencies. Instead, I detail how aesthetics and power articulate not only in relation to expressions of state power but also in expressions of social difference and politics of nature.

I propose two contrapuntal aesthetic sublimes that figure prominently in China's state-society interplay—an eco-developmental sublime and a rural-ecological sublime. An eco-developmental sublime underlies aesthetic expressions of state power. It operates via two interweaving aesthetic registers. Ecology as pristine natural object and ecology as technically enhanced natural object. A pristine natural landscape, in this sense, is one that looks "natural," without trace of human activities (even though the appearance of pristine nature is created through extensive human interventions). Since the imaginary of pristine nature does not include humans, the state cultivates this aesthetic sensibility through removing people and human activities from landscapes and altering them to appear natural. An aesthetically pleasing natural landscape, therefore, is something "civilized" humans can produce. It is a technical form of beauty created through rational scientific management, intentional landscape engineering, and aestheticization. Semiotic gestures of ecology as pristine and optimized nature are visually emplaced, for instance, in ecological protection areas and resettlement housing. Through ecological construction efforts, the state endeavors to transform landscapes that previously supported agriculture and rural housing into those that express an eco-developmental sublime. In place of rural land-scapes, the state produces scientifically optimized landscapes, such as treatment wetlands, artificial waterfall parks, and spatially concentrated housing facilities. In these ways, eco-developmental aesthetics appear as landscape beautifications and improvements on nature and society through the urbanizing-cum-civilizing of the rural population.

Within this context, rural people produce a counter-aesthetic through spatial practices that remake the rural in relation to ecology. They produce a rural-ecological sublime for their own socioeconomic benefit as they navigate uneven displacement from land and housing, and to maintain senses of their rural past. As I discuss in chapter 5, this aesthetic is particularly prevalent in rural-themed restaurants and guesthouses (*nongjiale*) within and on the borders of ecological protection areas. Rural citizens' spatial practices portray rural-ecological natures in the built environment, cuisine, music, art, and tourist-oriented service provisioning. In these sites, villagers, much like natural and social scientists, represent rural nature as closer to primitive ecology (*yuanshengtai*). Doing so reifies urban-rural difference. Yet, their spatial practices also portray rural people as intimately tied to land and multigenerational environmental stewards. In producing a rural-ecological sublime, villagers actively aestheticize politics of nature and difference in the landscapes of their own displacement.

Spatial practices of rural representation and the lived experiences of displacement are contingent on historically conditioned forms of social difference. Drawing on Brandi Summers's work on aesthetics and politics of difference,[60] I advance "differentiated aesthetic emplacement" as a survival strategy for the poor to profit from performing rurality and as a way of inhabiting space and maintaining lifeways for rural elites. As people navigate environmental governance and state urbanization efforts, inter-rural class differences shape the aesthetic politics of displacement and forms of counter-conduct.

Some citizens resist state governance through confrontational forms of counter-conduct. Chapter 6 highlights the role of what I call "infrastructural diffusion" in delimiting forms of counter-conduct and maintaining authoritarian rule. The chapter details partial destruction of village housing by demolition bureaus, coercive demobilization by street-level police, militarized uprooting of guerrilla agriculture, and digital erasure. These infrastructural expressions of state power diffuse counter-conduct. Infrastructure, in this sense, refers both to the built environment and forms of social organization. In theorizing the former, I draw on Julie Chu's insights into how citizen-state struggles play out through infrastructure, particularly aesthetic politics of infrastructural disrepair. Regarding the latter, I draw on the work of AbdouMaliq Simone who argues that infrastructures are not merely built environments, but also human activities and forms of social organization.[61] My account of how infrastructural techniques diffuse social expressions of resistance and collective mobilizations sheds light on the limits of counter-conduct under an authoritarian regime.

In these ways, forms of counter-conduct are not outside of or external to ecological expressions and constitutions of power. Rather, state techniques delimit how society exercises power. As everyday citizens navigate ecological expressions and constitutions of state power, they actively reshape their own social trajectories.

While undoubtedly important to people in China, these relationships increasingly bear on life everywhere else. How the Chinese state approaches environmental governance is poised to shape the future of global sustainability and geopolitics. The epilogue considers China's environmental governance in global contexts. The task between now and then is to chart the role of ecology in consolidating state power and shaping citizens' uneven social trajectories.

Part I
ECOLOGY AND STATE POWER

1

MAKING ECOLOGY DEVELOPMENTAL

Chen Xueming, professor of ecology at Yunnan University and a leading scientific assessor of ecological protection areas, welcomed me into his office. He pushed aside a stack of books on a wooden desk to make room for two teacups. Taking on a professorial air of someone who has lectured on the subject for decades, he began talking about ecology by situating it in relation to place, people, and global exchanges. Through interviews with ecologists, such as Chen, as well as archival research, I learned about key natural and social scientists and a palimpsest of global influences, travels, and trainings that shaped ecology in China.

Meanings surrounding ecology shifted alongside transformations in the Chinese state and society. In different eras, ecological thought became central to state governance, unevenly categorizing the citizenry, and to notions of historical transformation. Ecology represented, at times, the borderlands of national territory, surplus energies embodied in the citizenry, nature aesthetics, and scientific techniques to optimize socio-environmental relations. Over a century of scientific articulations, ecology came to figure centrally in logics of state governance and stage-oriented developmental progress toward a sustainable future.

Within China's party-state, ecology is inseparable from articulations of sustainable development and totalizing socio-environmental management—commonly discussed as "ecological civilization building" (*shengtai wenming jianshe*). China's Constitutional Amendment during the Eighteenth CCP Plenary of

2012 reads: "The Development of Ecological Civilization should be integrated into all aspects and the whole process of economic development, political development, cultural development, and social development."[1] Such broad statements, signal the cornucopian scope of what President Xi Jinping frequently refers to as a "new human relationship with nature." The Chinese Academy of Sciences has officially labeled the process of creating ecological civilization as the "second modernization." According to the Chinese Academy of Sciences' *Ecological Modernization Report*, Chinese society has moved through primitive and industrial civilization toward ecological civilization. Notably, the Chinese Academy of Sciences' officially claims ecological civilization to be the *highest level* of developmental attainment.[2]

This unitary scientific and political logic permeates popular media, green policy prescriptions, and the work of mainstream scientists.[3] Media accounts surrounding ecological civilization building suggest that the concept emerged in 2007 during a famous speech by Hu Jintao at the Seventeenth National Party Congress.[4] In the speech, Hu proclaimed the importance of "building an ecological civilization" by modeling economic growth and consumption, as well as protecting the environment.[5] Scholars of China's green modernization echo this narrative by framing ecological civilization building as a green alternative to "industrial civilizations" of the West.[6] Scholarship in this mode holds the pursuit of ecological civilization to be the "result of the constant progress of human civilization, and a higher stage in the evolution of human civilization than industrial civilization."[7]

In this chapter, I depart from this naturalizing mode of scholarship by delineating a genealogy of how ecology became developmental. I do so by detailing the historical production of what I call eco-developmental logics. By logics I mean ways of knowing nature that order how nature is to be properly acted on. Drawing on a genealogical method,[8] I situate ecology as a form of knowledge that takes on meaning through global exchanges—a situated universal that has become mobilized in the service of state power. Donna Haraway argues that knowledge formations are relational, and that knowledge is conditioned by the context in which it emerges.[9] Drawing on this insight, I contend that ecology, like any science, is a situated way of knowing that comes into being through social and political practices of exchange, writing, collective experimentation, interpretation, and claims making. Ecology emerged in the United States, for instance, as a science of complexity often deployed to undermine modernist claims about environmental controllability.[10] As such, environmental historians have tended to frame ecology in the West as posing a challenge to modernist thought.[11] In what follows, I focus on a lineage of ecological thought central to modernist narratives of civilizational attainment and sustainable development, which underlie expressions and constitutions of state power. In the vein of Raymond Williams, who argues that forms of nature are always the product of social and historical context,[12] I illustrate how ecological sciences in China have their own history and politics steeped in global exchanges.[13]

Scholars have demonstrated how scientific knowledge, often considered to be universal and emanating from Global North to Global South or West to East, is produced through global exchanges and localized meaning-making practices. Michael Hathaway, for instance, argues that knowledge circulates globally in contingent and multidirectional ways. For Hathaway, when ideas enter new geographic spheres, they take on meanings contingent on local contexts. New meanings generate novel scientific innovations, practices, and knowledge. Hathaway's key insight is that there is continual movement between the localization and universalizability of knowledge.[14] Hathaway conceptualizes the content and meanings of scientific knowledge, however, as coterminous across geographical spaces. In contrast, I contend that a plurality of meanings exists under a given scientific knowledge signifier.[15] Moreover, politics and power relations permeate the process of knowledge production. Ecology emerges from a multiplicity of actions, actors, places, and claims within localized contexts.

My conceptualization of ecological knowledge formation more closely aligns with Michael Lewis and Celia Lowe who emphasize that processes of knowledge formation are inseparable from power relations. For Lewis, what constitutes "ecology" is not merely a local instantiation of a global idea or process, but assemblages of powers mediated by cross-cultural exchanges, scientific practices, research agendas, and flows of ideas.[16] Analogously, Lowe illustrates how ideas of ecology emerge through interactions between local people, scientists, and development institutions—stratified through colonial legacies.[17] The global exchanges these scholars highlight shed light on how scientific knowledge and attendant meanings shift over time. Shifting meanings surrounding ecology, as I show in this chapter, shape the subjects of knowledge, as well as the techniques of science in relation to state power.

In this chapter, I illustrate the articulation of ecology and state power through the work of prominent scientists in China and their global exchanges spanning the early twentieth century up to the present, across botany, political economy, systems science, urban ecology, and ecological economics. Historically situating the confluence of ecology, sustainability, and state power reveals how forms of science take on meaning in localized social and political context. In doing so, I call into question how ecology and sustainability are conceptualized, how they function, and whom they serve.[18] I argue that ecology is a situated form of knowledge, wielded to define roles for the state, scientists, and the citizenry.

Scientists are crucial actors in making ecology developmental. They produce eco-developmental logics—knowledge that defines nature and how it is to be acted on, which undergird state power.

Ecological Formations

Before ecology connoted sustainable development and civilizational attainment, it was an emergent field of inquiry taking shape via global exchanges. Indeed, the Chinese term for *ecology* is a neologism that traveled from Japan to China through the work of late nineteenth- and early twentieth-century botanist Miyoshi Manabu. Miyoshi was born in 1861 to a Samurai family. From an early age, he was fascinated with plants, in particular cherry blossoms and irises, which were to become the focus of his life's work. After studying at the Imperial University of Tokyo, he traveled to Germany to attend the University of Leipzig. From 1891 to 1895 he studied under the guidance of German botanist and ecologist Wilhelm Friedrich Phillip Pfeffer. As he trained, he became deeply interested in the emerging field of ecology (*oekologie*) in Germany. Miyoshi earned a doctorate from Leipzig in 1895 and returned to Japan to become a professor of botany at Tokyo University and director of the botanical gardens from 1922 to 1924.[19]

Upon returning to Japan, Miyoshi coined the Japanese term for ecology (*seitaigaku*). The neologism came to China through Meiji-era texts created by Miyoshi and his students. Ecology came to be expressed in the Chinese language in two ways. Ecology expressed as *shengtai huanjing* connotes ecology and environment. This is analogous to the Japanese term *seitai-kankyo*.[20] The other is *shengtai*. Both mean "ecology," but the former connotes ecological conditions and environments interdependent with human activities. The latter connotes the science of ecology (*shengtaixue*) and relations between biotic and abiotic entities. Early ecologists in Japan, China, and the rest of the world, focused largely on the study of plant life.[21]

Miyoshi focused primarily on Japanese botanical specimens, including Japanese cherry blossoms (*prunus serrulata*), plum trees (*prunus*) and Japanese irises (*iris ensata*). In 1905, he began publishing what was to become the world's largest multilingual compendium on Japanese vegetation.[22] He produced fifteen sets within the compendium, the last of which was published in 1914. In addition, he published widely across scientific journals and magazines. Like other natural scientists of the day, his work entailed the aestheticization of natural objects of science.[23] In an 1890 publication in *The Botanical Magazine*, Miyoshi portrayed botanical samples alongside poetic descriptions of landscape. He wrote, "On the 9th of August, 1890 I found a species of *Pinguicula* on Mount Koshin in the province of Shimotsuke. It grows in great numbers on the moist exposed surface of the huge rocks which constitute the rugged outline of the peak."[24] Miyoshi proceeded to detail the roots, leaves, seeds fruits, calyx, and flowers. He also produced a stylized plate of the botanical sample.[25] This example highlights how Miyoshi's scientific work aestheticized nature—a phenomenon that remains central to ecology in China, albeit through different mediums.

With the advent of photography, scientists began using photos to capture and communicate biophysical features of their subject matter. Photography proved particularly useful in identifying species. For example, Miyoshi's photographic depiction of a cherry blossom in the 1921 publication *On the Conservation of Natural Monuments and Historic Sites: Plant Department* (figure 2), displays cherry blossoms in bloom and as buds. The darkened background and chiaroscuro lighting highlights a range of angles. Representational techniques of capturing and communicating features of scientific subject matter, such as photography and descriptive writing, were mediums through which botanists and early ecologists, like Miyoshi, aestheticized the natural world.

The neologism *ecology*, and the aestheticizing mediums that accompanied it, took root in mainland China during the Republican period. The Qing dynasty, the last of imperial China, fell in 1911. In the wake of empire came a period of cultural and scientific flourishing in which many young elites, in particular, went abroad to learn "modern" forms of science. During the Republican period, social movements called for adopting scientific worldviews to improve the country.[26] The New Culture Movement (1910s–20s), a youth movement aimed at reorganizing Chinese culture and society according to global norms of science, spurred an interest in so-called new sciences. The movement advocated that Chinese people familiarize themselves with "Mr. Science" (*sai xiansheng*) to replace traditional Confucian pedagogy. The global engagements of those who went abroad generated hybrid forms of scientific inquiry and practice. Early botanists, such as Hu Xiansu, exemplified, much like Miyoshi, the aestheticization of scientific subject matter in the process of producing knowledge.

Hu trained in classical poetry and literature at the Imperial University of Peking. Matriculating in 1909, he moved to the United States to study botany. After studying at the University of California, Berkeley, he obtained a doctorate from Harvard University in 1925. He returned to China and founded the Lushan Botanical Gardens in Yunnan Province in 1934, which was renamed the Kunming Institute of Botany in 1938. Exemplary botanists, such as Hu, laid foundations for plant ecology in China.

Through his fieldwork and writing, Hu defined the natural world in ways that melded Chinese science and aesthetics with Western scientific taxonomy. Following the eighteenth-century Chinese scientific tradition of evidential research (*kaozheng*),[27] Hu endeavored to match classical plant descriptions with his botanical observations to corroborate and therefore validate his finding in relation to the Linnaean classification system. This approach is evident in a series of articles

福 祿 壽

Prunus serrulata Lindl. f. contorta Miyos.

FIGURE 2. Miyoshi Manabu's cherry blossom photograph from a 1921 publication on plant ecology (Miyoshi 1921).

published in the popular Chinese-language journal "Science" (*kexue*) in which Hu matched Latin names for plants with names compiled in a botanical diction-ary from the Eastern Han period (ca. 100 CE). Discussing this process, natural historian Lijing Jiang argues that "it was through experiencing fieldwork that Hu found a consistent use of classical style for communicating botanical work."[28]

The fusing of Linnaean classification and Chinese poetic and classical lit-erary styles is further evinced by works produced during Hu's 1920 fieldwork expedition to Zhejiang Province, in which he conveyed scientific subject matter through classical literary styles. Hu published a series of poems, essays, and diary entries in the popular journal *Xuecheng*, in which he painted a literary portrait of the subject matter and surrounding landscape. He described steep precipices of Zhejiang's mountains, verdant pines, cypress, and bamboo, as well as the colors and scents of flowers.[29] His poetic landscape descriptions mirror classical land-scape poetry and travel literature, exemplifying the nexus of nature aesthetics and science in the early modern period.

Aestheticizing scientific subject matter and landscape occurred not only through written descriptions of plants' biophysical qualities, but also through oral depictions of botanical expeditions. Hu recounted his 1920 botanical sur-vey to Zhejiang during a 1927 address to the Science Society of Canton describing how, "sitting in a sedan chair, at three o'clock in the morning [I] was carried in half awakened dreams toward the heavily forest-clad sacred mountain only to find the towering forest giants of *Cryptomeria japonica*, mixed with *Cunning-hamia lanceolata* and the broad-canopied weeping *Cupresus fuenbris*."[30]

In this excerpt, Hu aestheticized subject matter and landscape through a writ-ing style that melds Chinese literary aesthetics with the Linnaean classification system.[31] This melding of aesthetics and science laid foundations for associating ecology with pristine natural landscapes, an aesthetic association that remains today. In contemporary China, ecology is widely associated with beauty and pro-cesses of landscape beautification.

In 2017, during the Nineteenth Central Party Congress, Xi Jinping articu-lated sustainable development as a process of building a "beautiful China." In the present, the association between ecology and beauty underlie state aesthetics and logics associated with building ecological civilization.[32] A shared aesthetic sense rooted in ecology as pristine nature is embedded in contemporary eco-developmental logics. In the introduction of this book, I discussed this aesthetic as an "eco-developmental sublime"—a shared aesthetic sensibility underlying the operation of state power. It operates through two aesthetic modes. The first is ecology as pristine natural object. This aesthetic sensibility, as I illustrated above, has roots in the early scientific practices of botany and the dawn of ecol-ogy in East Asia. The second mode is ecology as technically enhanced natural object. The second aesthetic register is interwoven, though contradictory, with the first. It has roots in early twentieth-century socialist thought in China.

As he poured a second cup of tea, I asked Chen to reflect on influential people in his training. I was surprised when, without hesitation, Chen began to talk about Mao Zedong. "Mao Zedong," he said, "did a lot to improve and modernize China. The time I spent struggling (*chiku*) in the countryside and learning about biology through tending plants and animals strengthened my resolve to become an ecologist." I listened to Chen talk about his life as a sent-down youth and the influence of ecological thought on Maoist thought. Mao's ideas surrounding historical transformation, political mobilization, and social improvement were shaped by an ecological rendering of Marxian political economy.

While many remember Mao as the historical figure who advocated for peasant-led revolution in China, the role of political economist Li Dazhao as a thinker of "Marxian science" and one of Mao's early influencers is often forgotten. Also overlooked are the politics of nature—ideas of human nature and natural cycles—embedded in their shared conception of sociohistorical change. Li, who on July 1, 1921, cofounded the Communist Party of China with Chen Duxiu, laid foundations for Marxian political economy in China and stage-oriented theories of historical change.

Li was born into a peasant family in Hebei province. From 1914 to 1916, he studied political economy at Waseda University in Tokyo, Japan. He returned to China to become one of the leading intellectuals of the New Culture Movement and the May Fourth Movement.[33] Li's political-economic work remade Marxian notions of class struggle, which, in the classical formulation, held the urban proletariat to be the key motor of revolutionary change. Li argued, instead, that China's peasantry would be the key class-leveling force and, therefore, the political source of revolution. For Li, and subsequently for Mao, political revolution could be brought about by harnessing social *forces* or *energies* latent within "backward" social groups at the right moment in a socio-natural cycle. These logics of historical change, social improvement, and projecting the future became central to Mao's efforts to lead the Chinese Communist Party to power and the formation of the People's Republic of China (PRC).

As an early interpreter of political economy and visionary for the Chinese Communist Party, Li considered the aim of writing and theory to be the transformation of social conditions. In his essays *My Marxist Views* (1919) and *The Essentials of Historical Study* (1924), Li argued that each generation makes their own futures through harnessing "social energies." Li developed his perspectives on historical revolution through engagements with the writings of Karl Marx, Leon Trotsky, and myriad enlightenment thinkers. Li read universalist historians, such as Nicolas de Condorcet, Henri de Saint-Simon, and Auguste Comte,[34] who Li argued were foundational to Marxist philosophy and the scientific basis of socialism.[35] His interpretation of Marxist historiography echoed the enlightenment principle that human interactions with the material environment drive historical transformation. Li conceived of historical change through linear evolutionary stage-oriented progressions of civilizational improvement directed by human action.[36] This position countered social Darwinist ideas that had gained popularity in the late Qing dynasty but waned during the Republican period. For Li, natural forces of historical change operate through the operationalization of surplus *social energies*.

Inspired by enlightenment historiography and Trotsky's ideas on permanent revolution,[37] Li viewed backwardness as a harbinger of potential for political change and that reaching a high level of developmental maturity would result in national stagnation. Given this, Li considered China's revolutionary potential to be lodged within the body politic of the peasantry. This position contrasted with Marx's writings that suggest an urban proletariat to be the wellspring of political transformation.[38] In the 1917, *A Comparison of the French and Russian Revolutions*, Li wrote:

> From the point of view of the history of civilizations. Any particular national civilization has its period of flourishing and its period of decline. The countries of Europe, like France and England, have reached a period of maturity in civilization. They no longer have the strength to advance any further. . . . Because of isolation, Russia's progress in civilization was comparatively slow with respect to the other nations of Europe, and just because of its comparative slowness, in the evolution of civilization, there existed surplus energy [*yuli*] for development [*suoyi shangyou xiangshang fazhan zhi yuli*].[39]

This excerpt indicates that Li understood latent potential for historical transformation to derive from socioeconomic backwardness. It also demonstrates that his ideas of historical change are linear and progressive. When Li became professor of economy and head librarian at Peking University in 1920, he employed a penniless peasant named Mao Zedong as a library clerk.

Mao formulated his ideas on socialism, historical change, political mobilization, and the nature of the peasantry through Li's reading groups. Mao internalized Li's ecological view on energies latent in human populations as natural drivers of historical and political change. Not only did Mao internalize them, but he militarized them. Mao's revolutionary class-leveling project was led by the peasantry—a social group filled with the "surplus energies" capable of forging a new nation.[40] Mobilizing the peasantry as a militarized revolutionary vanguard became central to Mao's, ultimately successful, efforts to form the PRC in 1949.[41] China's modern state formation marked the end of internal warfare between the Chinese Communist Party and the US-backed Guomindang.

The logic that backward social energies, lodged in human populations, can be improved through state intervention remains prominent today. Mobilizing social energies in rural populations to bring about revolutionary transformation remains a crucial logic underlying ecological civilization building. Yet, as I discuss in the following section, after Mao's reign the logic of transformation has been reconfigured as one of technical optimization. The second mode of eco-developmental aesthetics—technically enhanced natural object—has roots in Li's notions of malleable social energies but was rearticulated by reform-era earth systems scientists who conceived of social, natural, and economic relations as an integrated whole controllable through systems science modeling. During Mao's tenure, however, ecology was eventually relegated to the peripheries of the new nation-state.

Mao's geographical placement of ecology research institutes reflected his imaginary of nature and national territory. According to Chen, Mao equated ecological sciences with the study of pristine nature. Mao, accordingly, moved departments of ecology closer to their subject matter. In the early 1950s, China's premier ecologists were sent to two universities on the borderlands, sites far removed from the seat of state power. One was Yunnan University near the southwest border, where Chen and I drank tea and discussed ecology. The other was Inner Mongolia University, along the northeastern border in the city of Hohhot. Chen described the movement of ecological research institutes to the peripheries as a political move that reflected Mao's imaginary of ecology as the study of pristine landscapes and untamed nature, the locations of which are far from the capital.[42] The role of ecologists during this period was to define nature and, in doing so, bring knowledge of what lies along the national hinterlands to the political center. Many of the early ecologists who took on this task were trained abroad. Chen highlighted several "fathers of ecology" who received training through what he referred to as the US-English school (*yingmei xuepai*) and the French-Swiss school (*farui xuepai*) of ecology.

Qu Zhongxiang (1905–90), Chen noted, was one of these fathers of ecology. The year prior to the founding of the PRC, Qu received an MA in plant ecology from the University of Minnesota under the guidance of ecologist William Skinner Cooper. He returned to China to contribute to the nation-building project. After teaching at Fudan University, Qu was promoted to the head of Yunnan University's ecology program as a part of Mao's effort to reorient ecology to the borderlands. This entailed moving from Fudan University to Yunnan—the southwestern edge of national territory. Qu's ecology program transferred along with him. He was joined by his Fudan University colleague and another father of ecology Zhu Yancheng, who was trained in the French-Swiss school of ecology.

When Mao assigned Qu and Zhu to Yunnan University, he also reassigned prominent ecologist Li Jitong to Inner Mongolia. Li was trained in plant ecology and botany at the Yale School of Forestry. He matriculated, first with an MA in

1923 and then a doctorate in 1925. In 1957, responding to Mao's decree, Li moved with his Peking University staff to Inner Mongolia University to head another ecology department relegated to the borderlands. In Inner Mongolia, he focused on forestry and vegetation surveys. From the late 1950s to the end of the Maoist period, Yunnan University and Inner Mongolia University became the nation's peripheral "centers" of ecology. Both departments focused on plant ecology.[43] An abrupt shift in the latter half of the Maoist period reflected the turbulent political times of the Cultural Revolution.

From the dawn of the Cultural Revolution in 1966 until Mao's death in 1976, ecology was not taught in China's universities. Ecology became framed as one of many "foreign" and "bourgeois" sciences. Many ecologists were sent down to the countryside (*xia xiang*) to labor in the fields as part of reeducation campaigns. Red guards orchestrated impromptu trials and violent struggles against class hierarchy and bourgeois ideas. Many ecologists, especially those educated abroad, were targeted as symbols of foreign bourgeois education. Some ecologists drew on their knowledge of medicinal plants to become "barefoot doctors." Barefoot doctors traversed villages to provide medical services with limited medical training. Other ecologists spent years laboring in the countryside.[44]

At the end of the Maoist regime and with the dawn of the reform era, there was a resurgence of the sciences under the "four modernizations." This modernization drive emphasized strengthening agriculture, industry, national defense, science, and technology. A renewed focus on science brought about a resurgence of university education, in which ecology came to figure centrally. The university entrance exam (*gao kao*) was reinstated thereby allowing people young and old to seek university education, after over a decade without the opportunity. Following the reinstatement of the college entrance exam, Yunnan University and Inner Mongolia University welcomed back their former faculty members. Chen was part of the first cohort to take the reinstated college entrance exam. He tested into Yunnan University where he studied botany before pursuing a doctorate in Beijing. Although Mao effectively halted university education during the latter portion of his reign, Chen felt like the lessons he learned as a sent-down youth working in the countryside gave him a strong background in biological processes, and the resolve to become an ecologist.

From the late 1980s to the present, the geographical locations of ecology research institutes shifted—once again—in ways that reflected evolving imaginaries of ecology. This time ecology research centers moved from the national periphery to the capital. This geographical shift not only reflected the increasingly prominent role of ecology in state-led development, but also economic and geopolitical shifts. The state instituted market reforms in the early 1980s, in which China welcomed foreign direct investment (FDI) and capitalist market forces. Over the first two decades of reform, FDI was largely concentrated in cities located in the southern and eastern seaboard, including Beijing. The Chinese Ecology Institute headquarters moved to Beijing in the 1990s, effectively centering ecology at the heart of national political leadership and urban culture. The reorientation of ecological research institutes from the hinterlands to the capital exemplified the growing importance of ecology in the eyes of the state and its changing meanings. Chen completed his systems ecology PhD in Beijing at a time when the field became central to defining notions of sustainable development in China.

During the early reform era, logics of social improvement, with roots in Marxian political economy, melded with earth systems science logics of socio-environmental controllability and technical optimization. These coalesced through the work of Beijing-based earth systems scientists who articulated systems science approaches to sustainable socialist development.[45]

Earth Systems Science Rationales for Sustainable Socialist Development

Reform-era systems scientists, like Ma Shijun, laid foundations for logics of sustainable development. Ma matriculated from the University of Minnesota in 1950 with a study on moth larvae control and returned to China in 1952 to become one of the nation's premier systems scientists. During the early reform era, he rose through the ranks to become a national-level leader and state representative on environmental affairs. The systems techniques he promoted, which are now ubiquitous in China, include socio-environmental modeling and functional land zoning.

Notions of ecological balance, rules by which ecosystems function, and what became known as sustainable development rose to prominence in part due to Ma's work. In the late 1970s, he began publishing on "sustainability" and "sustainable development." Ma first wrote about the former concept as "continual regeneration potential" (*chiyongxu de zaisheng chuanli*) and the latter as "continuous development" (*chixu fazhan* and *kechixu fazhan*). Ma served on the Brundtland Commission as a member of the United Nations World Commission on the Environment and was one of the principal authors of *Our Common Future* issued in 1987.[46] The work defined sustainability globally for decades. During the post-Brundtland era, when sustainability became a globally circulating term, kechixu fazhan came to be translated as sustainable development.

Ma's "social-economic-ecological systems theory" (*shehui jingji shengtai xitong*), published before the Brundtland Report, *Our Common Future*, provided direction for China's social and natural management from the 1980s to the present. In the 1981 article *The Function of Ecological Rules in Environmental Management,* for instance, Ma laid out a structure of ecosystem functioning as an integral whole that he refers to as the "social-economic-ecological system."[47] His theorization of systems science management revived logics of social evolution by conceiving of human progress and civilizational transformation through interactions within an integrated social-economic-ecological complex system. In his teleological narration, humans begin as "primitive" (*yuanshi*) beings that maintain their material lives through struggling with nature.[48] As humans develop scientific technologies, society progresses through stages of development tending toward modern (*jindai*) humanity in a linear stage-oriented fashion. But modern capitalist development, Ma suggests, has also brought about ecosystem disequilibrium. Disequilibrium, for Ma, emerges from monopoly capitalists' ignorance of human dependence on the natural environment and predatory approaches to natural resource use, which have brought about ecological crises.[49] Ma advocated for a new relationship with nature through socialist environmental planning based in earth systems science.

For Ma, modern socialism requires a merging of evolutionary ecology and ecological economics from which state scientists can restructure relationships between socioeconomic organization and the natural world. Bringing about this new stage of "scientifically based socialism," Ma argued, entails adopting systems science principles to manage natural resources and industrial production, which could maximize production and generate a harmonious relationship (*xietiao guanxi*) between humans and nature.[50] To do so, he advocated for mechanistic approaches to optimizing ecosystem functionality. One way to optimize functionality, for Ma, is through functional land zoning and subsystem modeling, which he claimed, can maximize the production and circulation efficiency of energy and material goods in industrial and agricultural production process.[51]

Ma held that a scientifically managed complex systems structure (*fuhe xitong jiegou*) could be achieved through coordinating industrial production and natural metabolic functions. He contended that systems scientists could manage a holistic network of circulation by optimizing the material metabolism of waste (*feiwu*) and energy (*nengliang*). This can be achieved by coordinating "open" natural systems (*ziran kaifangxi*) and human-made "closed" engineered systems (*rengong gongchengde bihuan xitong*) of industrial production.[52] Central to this schema, Ma argued, is creating coordinated functional zones with built environments for human habitation (*juminqu*) at the center. The functional zones he advocated include agricultural production areas (*nongye shengchanqu*), industrial production areas (*gongye shengchanqu*), water storage areas, and natural ecosystem areas (*shengtai xitongqu*) (figure 3). Each functional zone within the

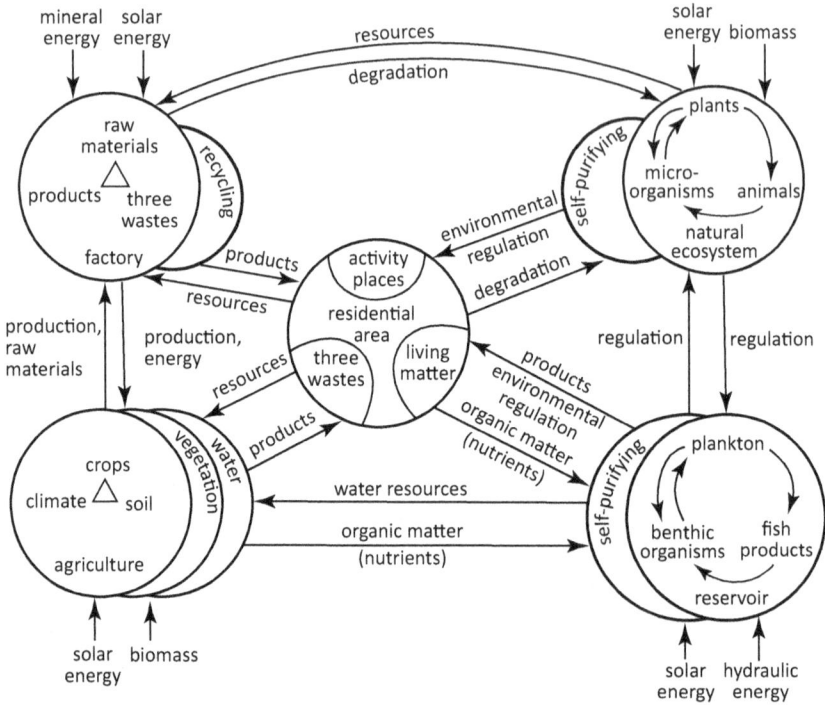

FIGURE 3.   A redrawing of Ma Shijun's 1981 complex systems model.

integrated whole has distinct, yet integrated, material metabolisms that supplement subsystem functionality (*buchong zuoyong*).[53] Importantly, Ma held that
systems modeling was necessary to manage the relationship between functional
zones.

Earth systems science logics proliferated in conjunction with Ma's positions as
a state adviser and leader of scientific organizations. In 1981 when *The Function
of Ecological Rules in Environmental Management* was published, Ma was a leading scientist in the Chinese Academy of Sciences. Several years later he became
chairman of the Chinese Ecological Society and then an adviser for the State
Council Environmental Protection Commission. He served on multiple national
and international environmental boards from the late 1970s up to his death in
1991. Ma's ideas remain central to socio-environmental management in China,
in part through the work of his students. While much of Ma's focus was on industrial and agricultural relations, his student, Wang Rusong, articulated systems
science logics in relation to urban systems.

Wang Rusong's scientific work brought systems science thinking to urban
planning. In 1984, Ma Shijun and Wang Rusong jointly published a research

article called *The Social-Economic-Natural Complex System*.[54] This article reiterated the social-economic-ecological system concept, discussed by Ma in 1981. But it situated the theory as crucial to sustainable *urban* development. In this work, the authors advocated for coordinated systems management of cities and urbanization processes. Ma and Wang described the social, economic, and in this iteration, "natural" (*ziran*) as part of an interlinked system, within which no parts are totally separate. Optimizing cities entailed managing the relations between spaces of human habitation and natural ecosystems that support them.

Ma and Wang argued that to optimally manage urbanization processes scientists must recognize the multiple relational feedbacks in complex systems. These feedbacks could be stabilized, they contended, through mechanistic managerial techniques, such as modeling and functional zoning to optimize socio-natural systems. They claimed that once scientists optimized relations and obtained functional equilibrium, development would be *sustainable*. The key contradiction within this logic is the assumption that mechanizing system functions can simultaneously achieve biophysical equilibrium and economic growth. In an ecological economic sense, when an economy is at equilibrium, or has achieved a steady state, it does not grow. Despite the contradiction, they claimed that scientists could orchestrate economic growth and biophysical equilibrium through systems science approaches to socio-environmental management.[55] In order to attain this contradictory symbiosis they advocated for functional land zoning, particularly within cities. Ma and Wang called for building satellite cities and "new areas" around larger cities to integrate economic and ecological functions.

Zoning cities into planned functional areas was a key legacy of these scientists. As a leading urban ecologist and public scholar in China, Wang Rusong promoted eco-city development from the 1990s through the early 2000s. He also served as the president of China's Ecological Society and director of the Department of Systems Ecology in the Chinese Academy of Sciences.[56] Functional land use modeling and urban regional zoning were actively experimented with from the late 1980s and fully embraced by the end of the Hu Jintao period (2002–12). These systems techniques were articulated as central to creating what President Hu Jintao called a "harmonious society"—the balancing of environmental protection with socioeconomic development. Environmental modeling, satellite cities, and functional zoning became key components of city management over the course of the 1990s and early 2000s. These techniques have since become a central feature of socio-environmental management and urban-rural comprehensive planning in the Xi Jinping era (2012-present). In the eyes of the state, these techniques are key to building an ecological civilization.

Ma and Wang's student Ouyang Zhiyun is currently directing the central state's project of nationwide functional land zoning. The project aims to totalize management of ecosystem services nationwide. Ouyang obtained his PhD from the Chinese Academy of Sciences in 1994 under the tutelage of Wang Rusong and Ma Shijun. As the director of the Research Center for Eco-Environmental Sciences in the Chinese Academy of Sciences and director of the State Key Laboratory of Urban and Regional Ecology (SKLURE), Ouyang is spearheading China's national ecosystem assessment programs and central government efforts to institute national functional zoning and ecological redlining programs across the country.[57]

Wang and Ouyang's 2012 article, titled *Social-Economic-Natural Complex Ecological Systems and Sustainable Development*, reprised systems science logics for totalizing "ecological management." Wang and Ouyang argued that systems science theories should be applied to urban and rural construction projects through techniques of "ecological planning, ecological engineering, and ecological management."[58] They emphasized improving the environment by using engineering technologies that model nature (*moni ziran de yi men gongcheng jishu*). By modeling nature, they suggested, scientists can cultivate moral character (*xiushenyangxing*) and create an ecology that is pleasing to the eye (*yishen yuemu*). An aesthetically pleasing ecology, Wang and Ouyang argue, would help society to realize the aesthetic beauty of nature (*ganwu tiangong de yimenziran meixue*). This exemplifies how scientists continue to advance an aestheticized conceptualization of ecology.

The work of reform era scientists, however, marks a shift toward the second mode of the eco-developmental sublime—ecology as technically enhanced natural object. Systems scientists advocated for mechanizing nature to improve moral quality, socio-natural relations, and landscape aesthetics. They posited that beauty can be introduced through scientific techniques. Landscapes engineered for ecological functionality, they claimed, can produce not only improved relations within a complex system, but also beauty. I turn to the materialization of this logic in the following chapter.

At this point it is important to emphasize that through such works a key temporal logic emerged, namely, that systems science techniques of mechanizing nature could bring about the condition of an ideal state of harmony between humans and nature.[59] This ideal state, according to logics put forward by systems scientists, is a state of totalized biophysical, social, economic, and aesthetic optimization. These leading advisers to the state expressed these logics through the Sinification of systems science.

Wang and Ouyang communicated systems science through the language and aesthetic symbolism of the five phases (*wuxing*). Five phases refer to the five core elements that comprise the ontological substratum and cycles of the earth in classical Chinese cosmology. Five-phase cosmology stems from the classic text *Yijing* (ca. 1000 BCE). The cosmology also correlates with Daoist writings that describe metaphysical relationships and cycles of change between a wide array of natural phenomena including cosmic cycles and the functioning of human internal organs. As a worldview, it undergirds classical logics regarding humanity's place in the universe, as well as expressions of power in the built environment.[60]

Wang and Ouyang reiterated their complex system theory through textual and visual representations of the interactions of subsystems couched in allusions to five-phase cosmology. They represented the functioning of natural subsystems through circulations of elements. These phases, they contended, are bound within an integrated system, consisting of social subsystems, scientific subsystems, and economic subsystems. They represented natural subsystems through a five-starred diagram consisting of air (*qi*), earth (*tu*), minerals (*kuang*), water (*shui*), and biological life (*sheng*). These elements intersect with dynamic economic, social, and scientific subsystems. They discuss the economic subsystem in relation to production, circulation, consumption, restoration (*huanyuan*), regulation, and control (*tiaokong*). Scientific subsystems, for them, involve the technical management of time (*shi*), space (*kong*), measurement (*liang*), structure (*gou*), and order (*xu*). At the center of the model is the social subsystem consisting of knowledge, culture, and system structure (*tizhi*) (figure 4).[61]

In communicating earth systems science through five-phase cosmology, Wang and Ouyang joined a long line of China's scientists in aestheticizing ecology. Through works such as this, systems science logics converged with materialist cosmologies of transformation. Their work frames modern techniques of functional land use zoning and socio-environmental modeling as aligned with classical Chinese philosophical precepts. This symbolic and material remaking of ecological thought holds earth systems science approaches to socio-natural management to be consistent with China's multimillennial history.[62] Much like their mentor Ma Shijun, Wang and Ouyang argued that socio-environmental modeling would bring about societal progress and environmental protection (*shehui jinbu he huanjing baohu*) ultimately culminating in an "ecological society."[63]

Teleological logics of progress are embedded within systems science logics for socio-natural management. Earth systems scientists, such as Wang Rusong, argued that ecological society is a higher stage of development than "traditional agricultural" society.[64] Figure 5 illustrates how Wang represented this teleological logic. A directional arrow indicates that sustainable development entails progressive steps to transform a traditional agricultural society into an ecological society.

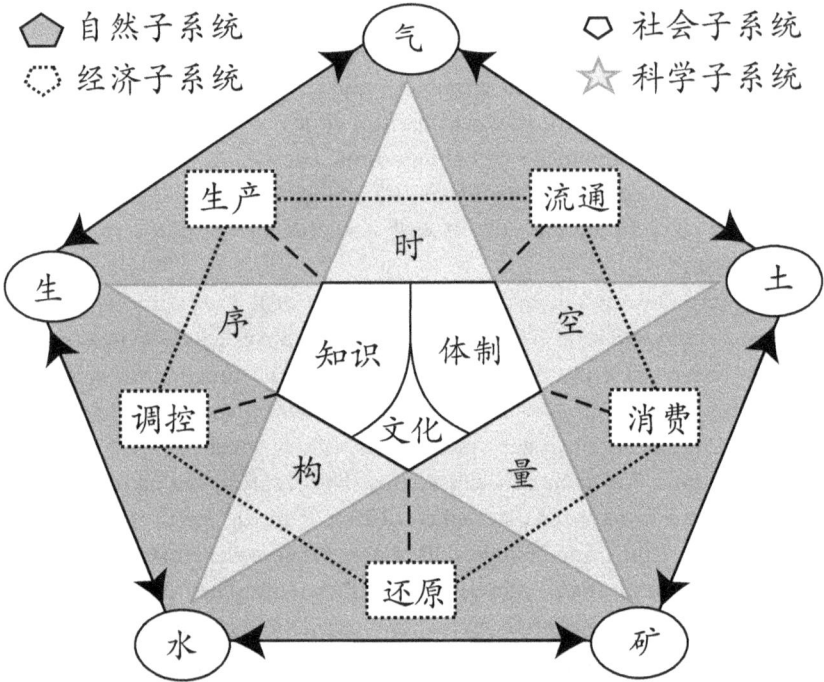

FIGURE 4. A redrawing of Wang Rusong and Ouyang Zhiyun's 2012 complex systems model. The diagram uses five-phase cosmology to communicate socio-environmental modeling approaches to sustainable city management. Natural subsystems in the larger upright pentagon include (clockwise from the top) air (*qi*), earth (*tu*), minerals (*kuang*), water (*shui*), and biological life (*sheng*). Economic subsystem in the upside-down dotted pentagon include (clockwise from the top) production, circulation, consumption, restoration (*huanyuan*), regulation and control (*tiaokong*). Scientific subsystems, in the star-shape, include (clockwise from the top) time (*shi*), space (*kong*), measurement (*liang*), structure (*gou*), and order (*xu*). The smaller upside-down pentagon includes social subsystems consisting of (clockwise from the top left) knowledge (*zhishi*), system structure (*tizhi*), and culture (*wenhua*).

Eco-developmental logics have come to inform state techniques of socio-natural management from the 1980s up to the present. Functional land zoning, for instance, has become a prominent land management technique nationally.[65] Similarly, ecological construction models were introduced at various government administrative levels in the 1980s and became ubiquitous from then on. Through the 1990s, ecosystem engineering principles coupled with administrative planning precipitated demarcations of "ecological villages," "ecological cities," "ecological provinces," and "ecological counties" as models of ecological construction

生态社会

生态产业

生态农业

石油农业

传统农业

可 持 续 发 展

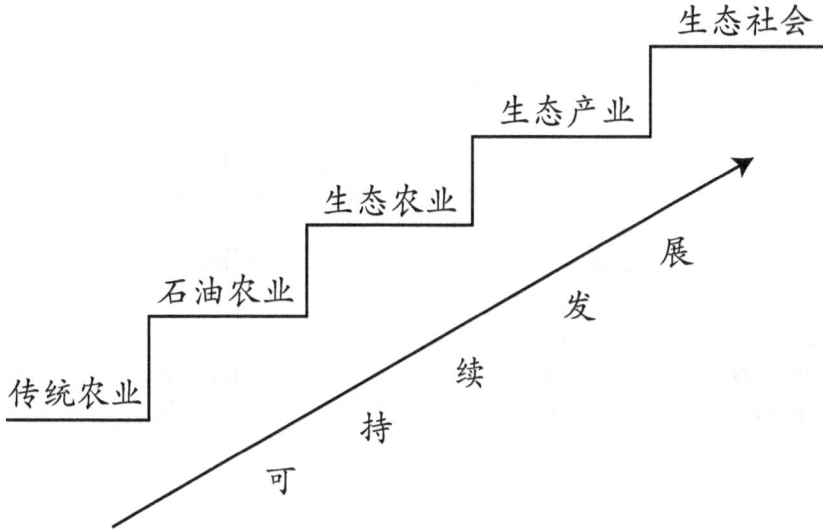

农村建设的几大台阶

FIGURE 5.   Wang Rusong's 1999 illustration titled, "Major Steps toward Building the Countryside." It indicates progress from "traditional agriculture" (bottom) to an "ecological society" (top). The line underneath reads "sustainable development." The intermediate steps include "petroleum agriculture," "ecological agriculture," and "ecological production."

(*shengtai jianshe moshi*) and symbols of progress.[66] During the 2000s, the already wide array of ecological land demarcations expanded to include national parks and ecological redlines.[67] I address these techniques and their effects in the following chapters.

At this point, I want to emphasize that systems scientists were instrumental in producing eco-developmental logics that undergird state techniques of socio-natural management. Earth systems science logics hold the human as part of nature, yet distinct from and in control of nature. They therefore justify technical control of socio-natural systems. This mechanistic approach requires continual state intervention. As such, ecology became a unitary scientific paradigm supporting state interventions in the name of socio-natural optimization. Through the work of systems scientists, ecology became associated not only with pristine natural beauty, as it has been since the Republican era, but also with an eco-developmental aesthetic introducible through human intervention.

Finally, systems scientists argued that an ecological society would be created through the mechanization of nature and optimization of socio-natural relations. These eco-developmental logics, which undergird ecological civilization building, hold that socio-environmental modeling and functional land zoning will transform agricultural society into an ecological society.[68] Underlying these logics is the unequal positioning of China's citizenry. Systems scientists not only imagined the technical management of urban and rural systems as central to sustainable development, but they also imagined traditional agricultural society as a primitive relic that state-led scientific management can transform. This logic, rooted in the scientific expressions of reform-era systems scientists and urban ecologists, continues to justify an array of techniques aimed at producing ecological balance and an ecological society.

Ecological Society as Urban Society

In 1989 Chen received a government grant to study urban ecology in Germany. This international exchange indexes a shift, noted above, toward systems science approaches to managing socio-natural relations and sustainable urbanization. While in Germany, Chen trained in indicator systems, ecological economics, and urban environmental land survey methods. Chen now oversees environmental monitoring and ecological protection assessment across levels of government. He is one of the principal consultants and assessors of ecological protection areas. His training abroad in urban ecology coincided with the party-state's advocation of urbanizing the rural population as a key part of building an ecological society and a beautiful China. The Eighteenth and Nineteenth National congresses of the Chinese Communist Party and the 2014–20 New-Type Urbanization Plan explicitly aim to increase the urban population from 50 percent to 60 percent, with a long-term plan of increasing the urban population to 70 percent by 2035.[69]

These plans indicate a substantive shift in the role of China's rural population within the eyes of the state. As discussed above, Mao came to power, in part, due to his mobilization of the peasantry, which he viewed as the source of revolutionary potential dialectically situated between class differences and material interests.[70] In contrast, the Xi regime believes that urbanizing the rural population is central to building an ecological civilization. In this section, I account for this shift in logic through the work of reform-era ecological Marxists and ecological economists. Scientists in these fields argued that the backward nature of rural people require state-led urbanization to ensure a sustainable socialist future.

Under Mao's reign, the peasantry continued, at least rhetorically, to hold an elevated position within official state ideology as the vanguard of the party.[71] The fact is, however, that China's socialist command economy pricing system deflated the value of agricultural products while artificially raising the value of industrially produced goods. This policy economically and materially repressed rural people.[72] As the Maoist period came to an end, Deng Xiaoping instituted postsocialist economic reforms. During the long 1980s (ca. 1978–92), as Chinese socialism began to integrate with global capitalism, the Maoist political narrative of suppressing capitalist tendencies in effort to create an egalitarian society through a peasant vanguard became untenable.

Theoretical repositioning of the role of the peasant emerged from two interrelated necessities. The first was the need to retheorize state-led socialism as it went through market reforms, within discourses of science and modernity. This was necessary for the party-state to portray political continuity with socialist predecessors. Secondly, postsocialist socioeconomic transitions, including the decollectivization of land, the introduction of a household responsibility system that individualized agrarian production, and massive infusions of state funding into the rural economy, created a new reality of the "peasant" as an entrepreneurial farmer. This reality was logically inconsistent with the notion of the peasantry as a source of revolutionary potential. In order to explain marketization processes and growing inequalities that emerged through integration with capitalist market forces, the figure of the peasant required new political-economic rationalization.

Through global engagements with ecological thought and environmentalism, reform-era economists reimagined the nature of China's peasantry, not as the key agent of revolution, but as a regressive social force holding China back from ecological civilization. A February 1985 article titled *The Way to Cultivate Individual Ecological Civilization Under Conditions of Mature Socialism*, published in the *Guangming Daily* newspaper, is among the earliest Chinese-language publications to discuss ecological civilization building.[73] This article summarized a conference on Scientific Marxism at Moscow University on the theme of remaking socialism in ecological terms. The article claimed that conjoining Marxist-Leninist science with ecological sciences would restore degraded relationship between humans and nature, thereby, cultivating an ecological civilization. This process involves transforming the "holistic makeup of all individuals to develop harmoniously" with the earth (*meige ren zhenzheng quanmian, xie de fazhan*). Subsequent work throughout the 1980s and 1990s detailed how ecological civilization could be cultivated through technocratically orchestrating industrial and agricultural production.[74]

The 1986 article *Ecological Marxism and Ecological Socialism*, written by Wang Jin, Renmin University professor of Marxist-Leninist thought, crystalized the new roles of the rural population and the state.[75] Wang elaborated a vision for China's ecological Marxism through references to two movements in the industrialized West. One is the scholarly work of North Atlantic political economists. The other is the establishment of Green parties in Western Europe. Wang suggested that China look to scholarly and political movements in the West to remake its socialist system as "ecological socialism." In laying foundations for ecological socialism in China, Wang discussed how an ecological consciousness (*shengtai yishi*) emerged in the West during the late 1960s. He historicized this environmental awareness and the emergence of ecological Marxism through Kenneth Boulding's *The Organizational Revolution*, Ben Agger's work on Western Marxism, William Leiss's critique of the commodity production glut in *The Limits of Satisfaction*, and E. F. Schumacher's economic argument that "small is beautiful."[76] Drawing on these works, he detailed an ecological Marxist vision for revolutionizing production. Remaking production and consumption within industrial capitalism, for Wang, entailed reorganizing labor through new technologies and state-directed socio-environmental management.[77]

In this revisioning of socialism as ecological socialism, Wang praised Green intellectuals as an emergent force of industrialized capitalist nations. In contrast with Li Dazhao and Mao Zedong, Wang argued that the source of social transformation lies not with the peasantry, but with scientists. He held that intellectuals (*zhishifenzi*) should direct technical solutions to socio-environmental management. He lauded the Green parties emerging in Germany, Finland, and Belgium during the 1980s. Wang attributed the popularizing of an ecological consciousness to these movements.[78] Yet in a departure from Marx, Wang portrayed ecological socialist movements in Malthusian terms advocating for strict population and resource control, most likely to align with population control policies introduced in 1979. The notion of creating equilibrium between population growth, economic growth, and environmental protection, discussed in Wang's article as "steady-state economics," aligned with earth systems science logics. The logic, however, suffers from the same contradiction. While steady-state economics are often discussed in terms of a national economy that does not fluctuate in size, Wang framed the steady-state economy as a national economy that cannot exceed the limits of natural resources.[79] He called this the "steady-state socialist economic model" (*wentai de shehui zhuyi jingji moshi*).

Although Wang's articulation of ecological Marxism drew on a host of North Atlantic political economists, he was critical of their weak accounting for the role of the state. Critiquing what he viewed as their shortcomings, Wang argued that strong state intervention was essential to bring about the socialist steady-state economy. Only with strong state intervention, he argued, would it be possible to reorganize society.[80] This vision materialized in state-led managerial techniques, such as socio-environmental modeling, functional land zoning, and measuring carrying capacity—coordinated by scientists and intellectual elites.

The work of ecological economists, such as Ye Qianji, produced socio-natural models for state intervention called for by systems scientists and ecological Marxists. Through exchanges with ecologists and economists across the globe, ecological economists in China, such as Ye, drew on industrial agricultural models to argue that the rural population was environmentally degrading.[81] To control this population, Ye promoted the quantification of material flows and production processes. Ecological economists, much like systems scientists discussed above, portrayed nature as a set of integrated material flows that can be measured, assigned values, and managed.[82] In their vision, the technical management of agriculture and the rural population are key to securing ecological balance. To support this managerial enterprise, they advocated for socio-natural systems models.

Ye was among the earliest agricultural economists to draw on ecological civilization building in his theorization of how to manage land, population, industry, and agriculture.[83] Ye's ideas surrounding the reorganization of agricultural production and transforming the rural population became popular during the reform era.[84] Drawing on his training in agricultural economics and a litany of Euro-American industrial ecologists, Ye promoted what he called "ecological agriculture" (shengtai nongye).

In his premier work Ecological Agriculture: The Future of Agriculture, Ye argued that engineering society and the environment to balance economic and ecological feedbacks would bring about a higher stage of development.[85] Ecological agriculture entailed the modernization of agriculture through "rationally" engineered industrialization, comprehensive design, and spatial management.[86] Ye argued that ecological agriculture required scientific regulation of feedbacks in the "population-land-commodity cycle" (renkou-tudi-shangpin liangxingxunhuan).[87] Ye expressed this argument through cyclical models, which detailed positive and negative feedbacks between population control and quality, commodity production and flows of capital, rational land use and ecological functions (figure 6).[88]

In discussing this model, Ye argued that "only when the population quality [suzhi] and numbers stabilize will humanity be able to rationally develop and use land to create a rational structure of industrial production."[89] This claim is directed toward the role of scientists in socio-environmental management, as well as the nature of the peasantry as a "low-quality" population that perpetuates

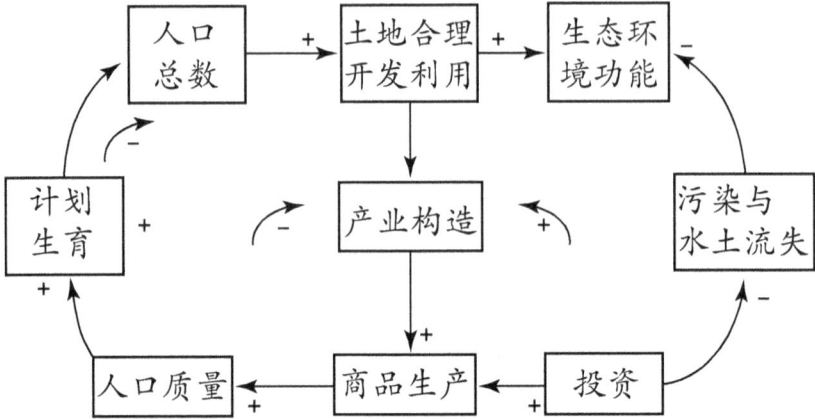

FIGURE 6. A redrawing of the Population-Land-Commodity Cycle Model, from Ye Qianji 1987. This model shows positive and negative feedbacks between "population control" (far left and moving clockwise), "total population, rational land use development, ecological functions, pollution and erosion, investment, commodity production, population quality, and [in the center] industrial structure."

inefficient agricultural production practices.[90] Ye described "rational management" as an intensification of efficiency in the use of energy, labor, capital, and technology, which will be mutually beneficial (*xiaoyi*) to ecology, economy, and society. Obtaining this level of efficiency, for Ye, entails dissolving the peasantry and instituting state-directed socio-environmental management. Ye's position as a state scientist helped popularize these ecological economic logics, which featured prominently in subsequent state plans.

There are, however, prominent Chinese thinkers who challenge such logics and advance alternative arguments. The work of agrarian economist Wen Tiejun is one example. During the 1990s and early 2000s, Wen critiqued the state's approach to rural marketization, the urban-rural binary system, and nationwide urbanization policies.[91] He became an outspoken critic of state-directed rural modernization, as well as the fetishization of technocratic modernization models—such as those popularized by systems scientists and ecological economists. In recent years, Wen began articulating his heterodox views for sustainable development by explicitly drawing on the language of ecological civilization.[92] Such efforts are aimed at reshaping state policies to foster greater attention to equity for rural people.[93] Wen's alternative formulation of ecological civilization building and sustainable development entails maintaining aspects of traditional rural lifeways, while supporting income parity, small-scale production, and social justice.[94] Alternative articulations such as this, however, remain on the fringe of state logics for socio-natural governance.

Eco-developmental logics that frame the rural population as a backward social force continue to be exemplified in the work of ecological economists who occupy high-level state advisory positions, such as Pan Jiahua. Pan is the director of the Institute for Urban and Environmental Studies in the Chinese Academy of Social Sciences. He is also the vice president of the Chinese Society of Ecological Economics. He advises the National Ministry of Environmental Protection, the National Panel on Climate Change, and was an author on the third IPCC working group assessment report on climate mitigation. I highlight Pan's work for two reasons. First, it typifies ecological economic logics that state-led urbanization is central to building ecological civilization. And second, Pan is among the most prominent figures in the new cohort of ecological economists with key leadership roles in the CCP. As an adviser to the central government and party-state, his work reflects state-sanctioned scientific logics for socio-natural management.

Much like earth systems scientists, discussed above, Pan draws on the social-economic-ecological complex systems triad. Embedded within systems logics is the notion that human behavior can be modeled within a complex system. As such, human behavior can be operationalized to specific ends through technical modeling and state control. Pan derived this mechanistic approach from notions of circular economy and ecological carrying capacity. The circular economy began to be widely discussed in the upper echelons of the CCP from 1992 onward, the same year Pan finished his doctorate in economics at the University of Cambridge.[95] Pan advocated for making the economy circular through ecological agriculture and measuring carrying capacities across administrative levels. These mechanistic approaches harbor key contradictions related to the governability of nature.

In his 2013 book titled, *China's Environmental Governing and Ecological Civilization*, Pan writes, "The principle of ecological civilization is that we should show respect for nature and live in accord with its laws [*sic*]. . . . To conform with nature, we need to observe the rigid constraints of ecological capacity."[96] "Nature" for Pan has rigid quantifiable properties and static features. Moreover, Pan suggests that defining and managing carrying capacities—the intrinsic limit or environmental threshold a given region can support—is a civilizational undertaking that contributes to modernization and national beautification. He writes, "To build a beautiful China, we should develop the economy and improve the environment under current technological and economic conditions in line with the carrying capacity of our ecosystems."[97] As geographer Nathan Sayre argues, measurements of carrying capacity tend toward idealized states that never exist. Numerical estimates are subject to discretionary errors and the problem of bounding patches within ecosystems.[98] Despite substantial critiques, coordinated planning through the measurement of ecological carrying capacity became a key feature of China's state planning since the early 2000s.[99] Such techniques bolster narratives about scientific land management as progressive and justify rural displacement from land.[100] Prescriptions for measuring ecological carrying capacity were written into the twelfth (2011–15) and thirteenth (2016–20) five-year plans as integral to national sustainable development.

For Pan, managing carrying capacity is not only crucial to protecting nature but also for "human development." Pan argues that humanity originated as a "primitive" civilization organized around hunting, fishing, and gathering followed by what he refers to as "agrarian civilization." He considers these earlier developmental stages, before the dawn of industrialization, to be marked by a harmonious relationship with nature. Pan writes that "ecological civilization is a *new development stage* of human society . . . after primitive civilization, agricultural civilization, and industrial civilization."[101] Echoing scientific logics of his predecessors, he contends that state interventions in socio-natural management are central to bringing about an ecological society.[102]

In this historical narrative of evolutionary social change over time, rural people inhabit a preindustrial mode of existence. They are, according to this logic, closer to a primitive form of human nature—a relic of "agrarian civilization" that can be transformed through eco-developmental techniques. Pan asserts this logic in claims such as, "Ecological civilization in the modern age is no longer the passive accommodation of nature . . . but harmony between human and nature based on modern science and technology."[103] In this quote, agrarian civilization is characterized as passive in contrast to an active ecological civilization. This dichotomous trope of active and passive natures reflects an othering of the rural citizenry within unitary scientific logics. The rural population, for Pan, is temporally out of sync with China's modernization drive. This logic subjectifies the rural population as deficient in comparison to their urban counterparts and, therefore, in need of improvement through urbanization. Geographer Tim Oakes argues that the "urban" in China is ideological. Imaginaries of the urban, Oakes suggests, shape how people consider both the past and the future.[104] Building on this assertion, I am highlighting the confluence of the urban and the ecological, which in tandem inform eco-developmental logics wherein urbanizing the rural population is the pathway to building an ecological civilization. These future-oriented logics entail urbanizing-cum-civilizing the rural population through state-directed socio-natural management.

Underlying this logic is the assumption that the rural population is incapable of rational land management. Statements by state scientists asserting this logic are common, though they are rarely supported. In discussing grazers in the Ningxia region, for instance, Pan suggests that no matter where they go "each locality's natural resources are inadequate to support its population; wherever these people go, extra capacity will be needed."[105] In addition to the notion of producing "extra capacity" being logically contradictory with carrying capacity as an intrinsic limit or threshold a given ecosystem can support, Pan assumes that rural people's agricultural and herding practices are monolithic across contexts. This rationale presumes rural people are static actors. As such they will act the same regardless of location. Wherever rural people are, according to this logic, the carrying capacity of the region will be violated causing systemic imbalance, and "more capacity" will be needed. According to Pan, rural people can be accordingly modeled like any natural feature. This techno-scientific logic supports totalizing claims that rural people's land use is essentially degrading or violates regional carrying capacity. Such claims are assumed rather than supported by place-based field research.[106] Nevertheless, logics of optimizing nature and society remain central to party-state ideology and state socio-natural management.

China's environmental planners, like Pan, frame urbanization as the pathway to achieve ecological balance and a new civilizational mode of being. In Pan's articulation of this logic, he contends that peasants have lost their connection to primitive ecology and have become an environmentally degrading social force. The "rational" state intervention is to urbanize rural people. In support of this intervention he writes, "Urbanization is both the carrier and driving force of China's economic development and social progress. Its benefits are significant and sustainable in the process of social and economic transformation and ecological civilization construction."[107] Constructing ecological society, for Pan, necessarily entails urbanization.

Eco-developmental logics, which took shape over a century of global scientific exchanges, frame state interventions as necessary to optimize socio-natural relations and bring a backward population in sync with modernity. Implicit within eco-developmental logics are ways of conceptualizing time, the role of the state, and the nature of China's citizenry. Even though divergent arguments emerged among China's reform-era intellectuals critical of orthodox Maoist views, the prevailing logic held the rural citizenry as a backward social group prone to populist politics emblematic of the failures of the socialist state.[108] These logics are apparent in central state development plans. For instance, the thirteenth five-year plan (2016–20), called for state intervention to "accelerate systems building to promote ecological progress . . . protect the ecological environment [*shengtai huanjing*] and promote modernization that features harmonious development between people and nature."[109] Substantial state intervention is critical to enact the totalizing scientific management of nature, society, and space.

* * *

As Chen and I neared the end of our last cup of tea, I asked him to summarize ecological civilization building in his own words. His response reprised stage-oriented progressive models of historical transformation toward a sustainable future, common among China's scientific communities. Chen reflected:

> What is ecological civilization? Previously there was agricultural society, then industrial society, now we are entering into ecological society. This cannot be totally human-centered but must consider other organisms and the environment in a totality. A simple way to communicate this is as "picturesque scenery" [*shanqingshuixiu*]. . . . Every place will have plant and animal diversity. Eventually Chinese history will bring the unity of humans and nature [*tianrenheyi*]. We will no longer struggle with the heavens and earth [*bu yao he tian dou, women ye bu he di dou*]. Instead, we will be in harmony [*hexie xiangchu*]. . . . The most important thing in ecology is ecological balance. We cannot cause disequilibrium. Humans are exploring how to do this. If we take the city as an example, how can we organize social structures? How can we organize labor? And how can we coordinate nature? If these are done well, then we will have an ecological society.

This response highlights how ecology and development have become deeply intertwined. Underlying Chen's reflection are eco-developmental logics that nature, society, and space can be optimized through socio-natural governance. These logics emerged through scientific claims and arguments that came to define ecology in relation to sustainable development and an unequal citizenry. Natural and social scientists produced logics of ecological civilization understood as the developmental outcome of progressive stages of state-directed socio-natural engineering. They portrayed building an ecological society as the natural end of this teleological process. As such, ecology came to be enrolled in a moral and temporal narrative of progress through which the rural population figures as the vanguard of transformation into modern *civilized* urban subjects and rational economic actors.[110]

Detailing the articulations of premier Chinese scientists and their global exchanges through which ecology took on developmental meaning decenters ecology as a singular form of science. This means we cannot assume the universal totality of bounded scientific disciplines. Nor can we assume that ecology in a particular locality is coequal with ecology elsewhere. Ecology, like all sciences, is contingent on the social, historical, and political conditions that shape it. It is a situated way of knowing that comes into being through practices of communicative exchange, writing, and claims making. In detailing how ecology took on developmental meanings in China, I illustrate ecology as a relationally situated form of knowledge emergent through global engagements. Underlying eco-developmental logics that define the role of the state, scientists, and China's citizenry is the inference that state-led scientific intervention will create the right relationships between society and nature to bring about a sustainable future. State interventions, scientists claim, will not only transform society but also the aesthetic character of national landscapes.

From Mao to Xi, ecological thought was central to consolidating state power and shaping myriad state interventions. In the present, eco-developmental logics justify governmental techniques, such as municipal conservation and functional land zoning, urban-rural comprehensive planning, and urbanizing the rural citizenry—techniques I explore in the following chapters.[111] The next chapter turns to how eco-developmental logics shape techniques of ecological restoration.

BOTANY, BEAUTY, PURIFICATION

Wang Liu, a high-level environmental planner for the city of Kunming, headed ecological restoration of the Lake Dian basin. During an interview in his office, Wang discussed his bureau's approach to ecological restoration planning, saying, "Since Xi Jinping came into power, there has been a major emphasis on building ecology [*shengtai jianshe*]. The central state and the whole country look highly on building an ecological civilization. In fact, all our work is aimed at building an ecological civilization." I asked Wang how his government bureau builds ecology.

Wang walked to a nearby cabinet, pulled out a map of the city several meters in diameter, and rolled it out across a table. Pointing to different shades of green on the map, Wang explained that they represent areas zoned (*quhua*) for ecological protection. The municipal government had created ecological protection areas across the municipal region as part of urban-rural comprehensive planning. These planning processes are techniques through which the government builds ecology, Wang continued. The central state requires 20 percent of land in municipal regions to be zoned for ecological protection.[1] Ecological protection sites in Kunming were designed to address local problems of pollution and environmental degradation in the Lake Dian basin.

Lake Dian, once known throughout China as the "pearl of the plateau" for its pristine beauty, has in recent decades become better known for blue-green algae blooms. In 2009, Kunming mayor Zhang Zhulin called the lake an eyesore that typifies one of the most challenging pollution problems in the country.[2] For decades, Lake Dian suffered from industrial effluent pollution, upstream agrichemical runoff, and insufficient wastewater infrastructure. During the reform era, untreated urban wastewater and industrial pollution were dumped directly into the lake. The municipal government has since bolstered the city's water treatment infrastructure and introduced multifaceted ecological restoration projects.[3] The municipal state, in conjunction with corporate partners, constructed surface-flow treatment wetlands around the banks of the lake to mitigate effluent pollutants from tributary rivers.

In Kunming alone, more than 2,500 square kilometers of the municipal region were zoned for ecological protection, displacing tens of thousands of peri-urban villagers in the process.[4] The ecological protection areas Wang spoke of featured nature aesthetics and served a bourgeoning leisure industry. These sites' aesthetics, however, differed from the Thoreauvian "wild" nature that may be familiar to Western readers and conservationists.[5] Many ecological protection areas, in contrast, appeared as modernist arrangements with carefully planned landscape features and tourist infrastructure. They exhibited a pristine-looking nature produced through substantial landscape interventions.

In discussing ecological restoration in the Lake Dian basin, Wang articulated an aesthetic rationale for displacing and resettling rural people grounded in eco-developmental logics. The rural citizenry, according to these logics, was a key source of environmental degradation and disorder. Socio-environmental engineering, he posited, would not only optimize biophysical and aesthetic conditions but also improve the rural citizenry. Resettling rural people into orderly high-rise apartments, he contended, would mitigate a key source of environmental degradation. Wang articulated these logics in relation to his bureau's ecological restoration techniques saying:

> Considering the problem of environmental restoration . . . there are two kinds. With one kind we hope to restore the landscape to an image of what it was once before. This is called restoration [*huifu*]. There is another kind of environmental improvement called reconstruction [*chongjian*] in which the ecology is already damaged. For example, if you consider the shores of Lake Dian over the last several decades, the area has become filled with farmers' fields, aquaculture fisheries, and houses—all of which now occupy [*zhan le*] these areas. . . . We remove the fisheries, remove the houses, remove the people, remove the agricultural fields. Then we bring back the wetlands, bring back the shores, bring back the land. This restores a previous state of time before degradation. Degradation was *caused by* the increase in the *rural population and their activities*.[6]

Such assertions typify a shared aesthetic sense among state environmental scientists and planners, echoed by popular media, which hold rural people and their activities as disorderly and environmentally degrading.[7] In order to protect nature and restore the lake to its former beauty, according to this way of seeing, rural people are to be removed from the landscape and resettled in spatially optimized housing.[8]

Pointing with two fingers to green representations of ecological protection areas covering one-fifth of the map, Wang asked rhetorically, "What is the relationship between the city of Kunming and Lake Dian? It is a relationship of planning restrictions. It is a problem of spatial and temporal arrangements. These green areas are zoned for ecological protection," he explained. "These ecological protection areas will help restore Lake Dian to the way it was before."[9]

When was the "before" Wang referred to? How did environmental scientists and planners determine ecological conditions of the past? Scientists and planners involved in ecological restoration ask and answer questions that delimit temporal, spatial, and place-based relationships. Debates in the field of restoration ecology abound regarding how to establish original ecological conditions and how the politics of establishing original conditions shape restoration techniques. Intervening in this debate, geographer Rebecca Lave illustrates how ecological restoration practices are steeped in local politics of environmental science. Ecological restoration, she argues, is undivorceable from the social worlds and political-economic contexts scientific communities inhabit. Scientific techniques take shape, in other words, within particular social and political milieus.[10]

In this chapter I bring critical attention to techniques of environmental science and power relations.[11] While my discussion in this chapter is organized around the case of the Lake Dian basin, it is important to note that ecological restoration techniques, across contexts, entail an amalgam of efforts to re-create a landscape based on socially produced and interpreted historical records.[12] A wide array of techniques can be used to form historical ecological baselines. The process of gathering and reading historical records is highly contingent on what counts within local scientific communities as an ecological record, the amounts of time and resources put toward collating records, and how records are read. In producing ecological baselines, scientists may consider historical documents, land use records, oral histories, maps, palaeoecological records, or archeological records.[13] Such broad historical cross-referencing requires significant time and resources. Not only were both in short supply in producing the Lake Dian basin's historical ecological record but obtaining a breadth of historical records mattered less to scientists than authoritative scientific works on botany and landscape beautification. The scientific community leading ecological restoration efforts perceived enhancing plant life and beauty as key to restoring ecological conditions.

In what follows, I discuss the aesthetic politics of seeing and sensing like a state environmental scientist.[14] I take an ethnographic approach grounded in scientific practices of ecological restoration and establishing the historical ecological record for the Lake Dian basin. Far from apolitical, the process of delimiting histories of ecology determines reference conditions for the past. Environmental scientists tasked with collating and reading the historical ecological record privileged works written by authoritative scientists—largely botanists and ecological engineers. Shared aesthetic senses shaped how state environmental scientists saw nature's past as they created an historical record, how they viewed restoration landscapes in the present, and how they planned ecological futures.

Drawing on insights from scholars of aesthetic politics, I argue that techniques of ecological restoration operate within and operationalize aesthetic regimes, thereby reinforcing state power. Jacques Rancière conceptualizes aesthetics as a shared distribution of the sensible. He defines an "aesthetic regime" as "a mode of articulation between ways of doing and making . . . corresponding forms of visibility, and possible ways of thinking about their relationships."[15] Aesthetics regimes, Rancière argues, shape how people come to know, see, and act in the world. Building on this concept, geographer D. Asher Ghertner demonstrates how a world-class city aesthetic regime became central to land governance in Delhi. Ghertner shows how governance regimes shifted from calculative statistics to judgments based on aesthetic appearance. Delhi's government officials draw on shared aesthetic senses of what appears "world-class" to render urban spaces governable, particularly those that appear unsightly. This normative aesthetic justifies widespread displacement of slum dwellers.[16] Analogously, techniques of ecological restoration in the Lake Dian basin reflect a shared aesthetic sense underlying expressions of state power and an unequal citizenry.

I discussed this aesthetic, in the introduction and previous chapter, as an eco-developmental sublime. The eco-developmental sublime functions via two interweaving aesthetic modes—ecology as pristine natural object and ecology as technically enhanced natural object. The latter finds expression within mechanistic models, and other means of optimizing and ordering socio-natural relations. The aesthetic character of technically enhanced ecology lies in ordered biophysical and socio-spatial outputs. This version of ecology, as technically enhanced object, exists alongside and in tension with ecology as pristine nature. Ecology as pristine natural object finds expression in landscapes designed to appear untouched by humans. This appearance, however, is the result of aesthetic conventions of landscape architecture and environmental engineering that stylistically mimic natural landscapes. These interdigitated aesthetic registers are expressions of an eco-developmental sublime.

State environmental scientists and planners' articulation of eco-developmental aesthetics is evident in the ways they see and sense rural deficiencies, civilizational backwardness, and out-of-placeness.[17] They see and sense the rural population as deficient, not just because scientific logics figure the peasantry to be environ-mentally degrading. Equally important, as this chapter attests, is the view that the rural population is unable to achieve the efficient aims of the state or the ordered sensorial semblance of state environmental control. Scientific interventions are seen as crucial to improving biophysical conditions, beautifying, and purifying the landscape. Even though there is a long history of agriculture in the Lake Dian basin, particularly on land undergoing restoration, scientists deemed agricultural land use extraneous to the historical ecological record. In their efforts to "build ecology," they first removed agriculture from ecological history and then rural people from the physical landscape. State environmental scientists and planners see planning ecological landscape functions (*shengtai jingguan gongneng*) for optimal efficiency and creating pristine-looking botanical features as means of building an ecological civilization and a beautiful China. Restoration efforts in the Lake Dian basin, therefore, exemplify state environmental scientists' shared ways of seeing and sensing, which align with an eco-developmental aesthetic regime.

Seeing Like a State Scientist

Wang Liu introduced me to the team of state environmental scientists who estab-lished the official historical record for the Lake Dian basin. I conducted indi-vidual and group interviews with these scientists, as well as joint field visits to restoration sites. In one of our early meetings, I sat with Zhang Xin, the ecologist who led efforts to produce the official ecological record. We were joined by his team of scientists. Zhang and his team shared with me the thirteen documents comprising the historical ecological record for the Lake Dian basin. All the items were scientific journal articles written by botanists, plant ecologists, or environ-mental engineers.

"This is the most important document in the ecological record," Zhang said, drawing my attention to an article titled *Dianchi Plant Groups and Pollution*.[18] The article was published in 1983 by plant ecologists Qu Zhongxiang (see chapter 1) and Li Heng. At the time of publication Qu and Li were affiliated with Yunnan University and Kunming Institute of Botany respectively. Zhang asserted that historical materials as comprehensive as this article were rare. Zhang's team of ecologists, seated at the table, nodded in agreement. For the team that collated the historical ecological record, this article was their most valued source.

The article identifies the loss of botanical life in Lake Dian through a com-parative longitudinal analysis. Qu and Li compared "visual observations" they made in 1975 with a study by Yunnan University ecologists in 1960. The authors claimed that, in 1960, submerged and emergent macrophytes covered 90 percent of the surface area of the lake. Submerged macrophytes constituted the majority. From their visual assessment, Qu and Li deduced that during the fifteen-year period the number of macrophytes decreased by 70 percent to cover 20 percent of the lake surface.

There are several valences, related to this key source, through which aesthetic politics operate. The first is in the article's methodology. The findings were deduced through scientists' visual accounting of botanical change. Qu and Li compared a 1960 report with their own visual assessment of the botanical composition of Lake Dian in 1975. The second valence relates to how contemporary ecologists read and valued the work of their predecessors. State scientists viewed Qu and Li's visual observations as reflections of past botanical realties, and to a lesser degree as part of a larger tapestry of sources. Third, scientists involved in determining Lake Dian's historical ecological record read this article selectively for evidence of rural people's culpability in environmental degradation.

In the article, Qu and Li attributed the decrease in aquatic plants to the rise of industrial and agricultural pollutants they refer to as the "three wastes" (*sanfei*). These include gaseous, liquid, and solid wastes.[19] As we discussed the article, I pointed to a section that read "industrial wastes, pesticides, and urban waste caused the pollution of Lake Dian's waters with easily visible (*xianeryijian*) changes to the aquatic plant species."[20] Zhang surveyed the section, paused, and redirected the groups' attention to another section in which Qu and Li claimed that pesticide use negatively affected the lake's water quality. Even though the article stated that urban and industrial waste caused pollution in Lake Dian and provided reference to studies that supported the claim, Zhang focused on the section of the article that emphasized environmental damage caused by agricultural practices.

Qu and Li drew on longitudinal measures of industrial and urban pollutants to estimate that the daily urban and industrial waste discharged into the lake, at the time of publication, was 682,000 cubic meters.[21] The authors suggested this number would soon dissipate since the city of Kunming was planning to install water treatment facilities to curb pollution. Urban wastewater treatment facilities, however, were not built in Kunming until the late 1980s and early 1990s. The majority were not built until the 2000s. Qu and Li provided specific measures of urban effluent pollution. But they did not measure, estimate, or reference sources to support their claims regarding agricultural pollutants. Instead of assessing agricultural effluent pollution, Qu and Li assumed that agriculture was a significant source of pollution. They made this explicit writing, "It goes without saying [*buyaneryu*] that agricultural pesticides harm aquatic plants, although it is a pity that we still have not done studies into the levels of pesticides in the waters of

Lake Dian."[22] Despite this admission, the authors claimed that agricultural practices surrounding the lake are having a negative influence on aquatic plant species.[23] In claiming this article as a key source for the historical ecological record
and selectively reading it, environmental scientists operationalized logics of rural
deficiency within their scientific practice.

In addition to selecting works composed solely by authoritative scientists,
the official historical record was constructed from a relatively small number of
sources with limited temporal range. When I first met with the team of scientists,
the historical ecological record consisted of thirteen scientific texts that were
published from 1963 to the early 2010s. Two texts were from the 1960s, four from
the 1980s, one from the 1990s, and six from the 2010s. The texts published in the
2010s advocated for ecological engineering approaches to restoration. Although
the works included in the official record are written by botanists, plant ecologists,
and environmental engineers, some of the materials detail extensive histories of
agricultural production and landscape transformation.

The Lake Dian basin has a long history of agriculture and environmental engineering. Land use maps in *Acta Geographica Sinica*, for example, illustrate how
the lake basin supported a wide array of agricultural types. One map from 1947
displays the basin as permeated with "alluvial plain fields, rainwater fields, dry
fields, and orchards" (figure 7).[24] Tellingly, however, the map does not demarcate
wetlands in areas that are now being restored through state efforts to construct
treatment wetlands. In recent years, these constructed wetlands have come to
encompass the banks of Lake Dian. Reading the 1947 land utilization map as an
historical referent suggests that the areas now being restored as wetlands were,
in the 1940s, agricultural land or lacustrine deposits.[25] In addition to agriculture,
environmental engineering and landscape morphology were notably absent from
the historical ecological record.

The lake basin is, in part, the product of ecological engineers who, during
the Yuan dynasty (1278–1368 CE), transformed the physical geography of the
lake. When the Mongol empire territorialized what is now southwest China in
the late 1200s, they instituted a multicentury effort of building dams, water
diversions, and irrigation channels around Lake Dian. Transforming the lake
basin involved the labor of hundreds of thousands of people. Water diversions,
damming, and irrigation projects continued to be built and maintained under
the Ming (1368–1644) and Qing (1644–1911) dynasties up to the present day.
Environmental engineering processes involved dredging waterways, building
irrigation channels, and constructing reservoirs. These multicentury projects
drastically transformed water levels, morphological contours, and the spatial
extent of Lake Dian.[26] The lake's current biophysical and morphological conditions are the products of hundreds of years of ecological engineering, which

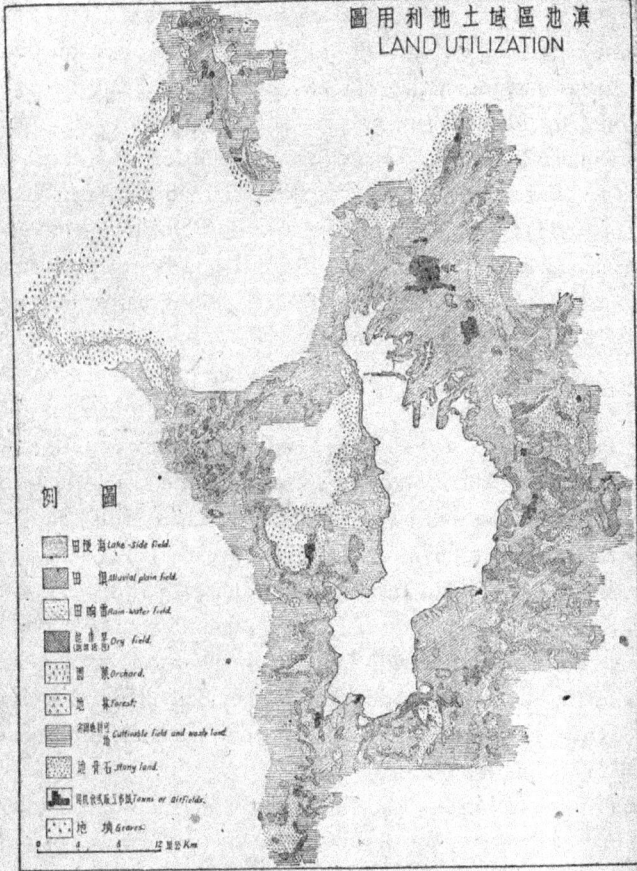

圖用利地土域區池滇
LAND UTILIZATION

例 圖

田壩 Lake-Side field.
田 Alluvial plain field.
田 Rain-water field.
旱 Dry field.
果 Orchard.
林 Forest.
荒地 Cultivable field and waste land.
貧瘠石 Stony land.
城鎮村鎮工事區 Towns or airfields.
地墳 Graves.

0　4　8　12 里公 Km

Fig. 3.　　圖　三

速整治，實為目前急圖。

本區聚落、墳地、交通道路諸類不生產用地，面積不大，且均盡量避免佔據生產力較高之處，縣、工廠、兵營、學校相繼建立，機場、鐵路、公路，不斷興修，耕地被佔用者，頗不乏少。

組成樹木，以松、栗、柏、杉居多。螺川河谷自安寧逆龍甸，以迄富民縣城，林木較易保存，河谷兩岸，幾盡為松杉與栗樹、青杠之混合林，故在谷區之中，林地面積，所佔百分比甚高。本區荒地所佔面積，梅為廣大。盆地之中，除以水田為主外，邊緣山坡，幾盡保荒地。此類荒地，除一部係石骨地，非人力所能利用外，大部實因強行耕墾，濫毀森林，以致侵蝕劇烈，成滿狀劣地，荒廢隨之。此類荒地，在盆地邊緣，分佈尤廣，且不斷擴張，破壞其鄰近之耕地，從

FIGURE 7. A 1947 Land Utilization map of Kunming's Lake Dian basin. The map details types of agricultural fields. Reproduced with permission from *Acta Geographica Sinica*.

reduced the surface area of the lake by half—from approximately 600 square kilometers to 300 square kilometers.[27] The decrease in water surface area and the creation of sophisticated irrigation channels exposed soils enriched with sediment deposits and nutrients.

The reduction of the lake's surface area laid bare highly fertile land, which became renowned for agriculture. Agricultural production flourished in soils enriched with alluvium deposits accumulated over centuries. Yet, this history of environmental engineering and landscape morphology did not count for state environmental scientists. At least not enough to be considered part of the official ecological record. Ecological restoration efforts in the basin have displaced tens of thousands of rural people from land which, for the greater part of a millennium, supported agriculture. State scientists and planners consider rural resettlement necessary to restore biophysical conditions, particularly aquatic plant life recorded in scientific documents.

In subsequent meetings, Zhang explained how his research team had come across a reference to an English-language source on botany they had yet to acquire. The source was a collated series of taxonomies and descriptions published in the *Journal of Botany* between 1934 and 1935. The texts were collated from the late 1800s and early 1900s, a time when British and French botanists frequented Yunnan Province.[28] They included journal entries, ranging from 1887 to 1920 collected by botanist James Edgar Dandy of the Linnaean Society and the British Museum of Natural History. When I obtained copies through digital archives and shared them with the team of scientists, they exclaimed that the texts were further proof of a botanical past they had already begun to re-create. In 2016, Zhang and his team began experimenting with reintroducing aquatic plant species noted in these records.

State scientists aimed to restore biophysical conditions that could host emergent macrophytes, such as those described in the *Journal of Botany*. Zhang's team considered these anglophone writings to be among the earliest Western botanical records of the Lake Dian basin.

Entries described plant taxonomies of Yunnan Province's large freshwater lakes and highlighted locations, elevation, and dates of botanical observations. They drew on Linnaean classification to identify the aquatic plant *Ottellia* (*haicaihua*) as indigenous to the region. *Ottellia* is a genus of aquatic plant and part of the *Hydrocharitaceae* family. The texts identify the following species: *Ottellia acuminate, Ottellia yunnanensis, Ottellia polygonifofia, Ottellia cavaleriei. Ottellia yunnanensis* was named after Yunnan Province where it is endemic. The journal entries also identified several native varieties of *Ottellia* in Lake Dian, Lake Erhai, and Fuxian Lake. Other, more recent, sources note *Ottellia acuminate* and *Ottellia yunnanensis* as common to the region.[29] When *Ottellia* were abundant, they were harvested for their roots, much like lotus, which were used as a source of sustenance.[30] Presently, due to high levels of chemical pollutants in Lake Dian, *Ottellia* can hardly grow. State scientists were keen to include these writings in the historical record because they provided historical precedence from turn-of-the-century botanists for efforts to reintroduce plant varietals already underway. The documents that I shared provided additional authoritative scientific voices to support their restoration efforts.

Ecological restoration scholar Eric Higgs argues that "restoration ecology version 1.0" entails practices of seeing a limited set of records as sufficient reference to a past reality.[31] Reading limited historical records in this way ignores social and cultural connections to land and histories of place. Moreover, ecological restoration 1.0 realities are informed by renditions of the past that appear significantly different when a wider scope of sources are considered. Historians of science lodge similar critiques. They are critical of considering fragmentary historical accounts as a set of facts to guide ecological restoration.[32] Analogously, scholars of restoration ecology have been critical of restoration projects that neglect lived experiences and oral historical records.[33]

Historical records are always partial. Techniques of reading and collating partial historical records reflect aesthetic milieus within which scientific communities operate. In the case of ecological restoration in Lake Dian, state environmental scientists hoped to restore Lake Dian in ways that reflected its storied past as one of China's most beautiful lakes. State scientists, operating within this aesthetic milieu, selectively constructed authoritative sources on botany and ecological engineering as references to past ecological realities. In their role as definers of nature, scientists prescribed what counts as nature and how nature is to be acted on.

In curating an historical record that focused on botanical features, but excluded histories of human habitation and agricultural production, state scientists effectively erased the rural population from the official history of the Lake Dian basin. Additionally, scientists' historical selection of records and their selective reading overlooked the *longue durée* of environmental engineering from the Yuan dynasty to the present, including the Maoist era campaign to "fill in the lake" (see the introduction). The histories they occlude are suffused with efforts to create agriculturally productive landscapes—inherently botanical interventions. The state directed many of these efforts. In the Maoist era, for instance, the campaign to fill in the lake with earth to increase the amount of arable land (*weihai zaotian*) mobilized thousands around a central task.[34] The campaign, however, disrupted Lake Dian's biophysical and chemical composition, which was further altered by decades of urban industrial pollution.[35] Yet, state scientists tasked with reconstructing the historical ecological record readily ascribe blame for ecosystem disruption to the rural populations' agricultural practices.

As one environmental scientist put it:

> If we want to restore a lake to a time before it was disturbed, how do we do it? Why do we have to do it? Because it has been damaged [*pohuai*] by peasants. . . . For instance, large parts of the lake area had fishponds dug for rearing fish. But now that life is better, we don't need aquaculture to raise fish. First, we restore the area's natural features by planting appropriate vegetation and intervening in the landscape. We introduce plant varietals based on the record of aquatic vegetation in Lake Dian. This aids the process of restoration.[36]

In this quote, aquaculture projects near the banks of the lake are held up as examples of environmentally damaging agrarian practices causing ecosystem disequilibrium. This scientist sees the reintroduction of botanical life as means to restore the past. State environmental scientists' efforts to optimize purification functions (*jinghuade gongneng*), landscape functions (*jingguan gongneng*), ecological landscape functions (*shengtai jingguan gongneng*), and aesthetic functions (*shenmei gongneng*) produce ecological restoration landscapes that reflect an eco-developmental sublime.[37] Ecological restoration, therefore, is shaped by aesthetic senses of what looks beautiful and natural, yet scientifically ordered.

After interviewing and exchanging materials with state environmental scientists, I was struck by how closely ecological restoration in the Lake Dian basin resembled what Wang Liu described as "building ecology." State scientists and planners produced an ecological record that reflected their shared aesthetic sense that botanical features enhance the beauty of the landscape—an expression of ecology as pristine nature. This shared aesthetic shaped what counted as a record of ecology, how that record was read, what belonged within a restoration landscape, and what did not. The presence of rural life appeared disorderly vis-à-vis scientifically ordered ecological restoration landscapes. Resettling rural people, reintroducing botanical features, and aestheticizing the landscape were seen as means of scientifically optimizing socio-natural relationships.[38]

As ecological restoration scholar Robert Elliot argues, establishing a record, from which to design biophysical relations, provides a platform for powerful actors who promise a return, often nostalgically tinged, to a site's former conditions.[39] Ecological restoration, as the case of Lake Dian reveals, has as much to do with imaginaries of a past, when nature was pristine, as it does with imaginaries of an improved future. Scientists looked back to a history of botany and beauty to justify displacing and resetting rural people, as well as constructing novel landscapes. The ecological restoration landscapes that emerged function as sensorial proof of the state's power to operationalize ecology for governmental ends. They appear not only as material instantiations of beauty and ecological optimization but also as symbolic markers of purification.

Sensing Beauty and Purification

Kunming Waterfall Park was constructed as part of ecological restoration efforts in the Lake Dian basin. It serves as a grand spectacle of landscape optimization (figure 8). The park, at the northern edge of the city, boasts the largest human-made waterfall in Asia. Water cascades down nine separate falls. The main falls is four hundred meters wide and drops roughly thirteen meters. Landscaped vegetation punctuates the falls. Walking trails surround the rim. The site is emblematic of an eco-developmental sublime, reflecting both aesthetic registers: ecology as technically enhanced object and pristine natural object. This aesthetic conveys the power of the state to mechanize nature and beautify landscape. I visited this site often and observed people taking pictures with the falls and marveling aloud to one another about the site's "beautiful ecology."

FIGURE 8. Kunming Waterfall Park. Photo by author.

The water flowing through the constructed waterfalls comes from the state-engineered redirection of the Niulan River and the headwaters of the three parallel rivers in northwest Yunnan. As of 2013, ecological engineering projects to restore the Lake Dian basin had over US$21 billion in state investment.[40] The Niulan River-Dianchi Water Project, included in these efforts, diverts 566 million cubic meters of water per year through the waterfall park into Lake Dian. Environmental planner Yang Bin claimed that "there are 1.8 billion cubic meters of water in Lake Dian, but the water basin can't support four million people. . . . The Niulan River diversion project increases the water supply and the speed of nutrient cycling."[41] Yang described how the water is "purified" by aerating as it flows down the waterfall. State scientists claimed that redirecting the river to flow down the waterfall, accelerates the speed at which effluent pollutants cycle through the lake. Increasing fluvial speed, thereby, decreases the time chemical pollutants, excess nitrogen, and blue-green algae remain in the lake.

Three villages were demolished to make the Kunming Waterfall Park. Villagers displaced from the site were moved into nearby high-rise resettlement housing. High-rise commercial apartments and villa-style housing were still being constructed adjacent to the park. Villagers north of the waterfall park readied themselves for the next wave of resettlement.

I entered the sales office for the new apartment complex bordering Kunming Waterfall Park in the fall of 2016. Salesmen, smartly dressed in black suits, walked around models of the park and new apartment complexes. The contrast between the models and our surroundings was striking. In the surrounding area, scattered demolitions were underway leaving mounds of housing scrap and appliance parts. These scattered parts were periodically gathered by informal collectors for sale on the secondhand market. In contrast to the reality outside, the models in the sales office displayed sleek apartment complexes next to a school and hospital. Single-family villa housing, glowing from the tiny lights inlaid within the model, were surrounded by green velvet and mini-palm trees (figure 9).

A salesman approached me in a black suit smiling. "This area is surrounded by green space to the East and to the West. These are ecological protection areas [*shengtai baohuqu*], so you are guaranteed to have green space here, which will give you an escape from the noise of urban life," he said to me as he pointed to different green patches on the model. "Each set of apartments [*xiaoqu*]," he continued, "will have a surveillance system and a new school. Some of the local farmlands nearby will be made available to residents of the apartment to rent. You can even have a peasant farm for you. The produce will be delivered to a locker

FIGURE 9. Model of apartments and housing developments surrounding Kunming Waterfall Park. Photo by author.

box on the first-floor service center of every apartment." The salesman assured me that, since there is a state-owned enterprise backing this construction project, it is a reliable investment. "The government has money" he said, "as opposed to developers [*kaifashang*] who are known to go bankrupt mid-project."

After touring the dusty concrete trappings of what was to become a new apartment complex, I was offered the option to buy one of the available units. According to the salesperson, given the popularity of the new complex only a third of the units were still available. Clearly real estate companies were capitalizing on proximity to land demarcated for ecological protection. Urban housing surrounded by state-guaranteed greenspaces is valued highly. Their proximity pointed to the confluence of economic opportunism and restoration efforts. Producing an eco-developmental aesthetic heightens the value of nearby land and real estate. Its production, however, is contingent on displacement.

In discussing restoration efforts, environmental scientists and planners routinely described rural infrastructures and activities as unsightly and environmentally degrading. The role of rural people in this aesthetic regime is to adopt urban modes of life. Bing Zhou, an environmental scientist working in a branch of Kunming's urban planning bureau, remarked on the relationship between aesthetics, rural displacement, and ecological restoration saying:

> We hope we can restore sites to the way they were before degradation. What was it like before? . . . Lake Dian, in the past was very beautiful [*hen mei*], but now so many rural people have come to occupy the banks. We are slowly restoring them. We have removed over 50,000 mu [about 8,240 acres] of agricultural fields. We have removed more than 200,000 rural people, many homes, and fisheries. We have made these into wetlands. We pushed [*tuichu*] farmers off the lands where they used to grow vegetables. So now they don't grow anymore . . . we plant botanical species in the lower areas where we built wetlands. This is, as much as possible, how we can restore the past.[42]

This quote illustrates the scale of state intervention in the Lake Dian basin and how Bing views rural displacement as imperative to restoration. His statement reflects how rural people and their practices are coded as unsightly and out of place.

Yang Liu, vice deputy of an environmental planning bureau, emphasized the importance of making the public aware of ecological purification and aesthetic functions within ecological restoration planning. He said:

> The main component of planning ecological functions [*shengtai gongneng*] is to emphasize the appropriateness of the plants and species selection. We want to maximize biological diversity and plant diversity. This is one kind of function. The purification function focuses on the water in the fluvial system and the water distribution systems including wastes from farmland. The landscape function [*jingguan gongneng*] is basically contingent on the locality. If the site is close to the city, the municipal government can suitably remake it. We choose the appropriate botanical system. And we create landscapes. Lake Dian's new treatment wetlands have been called the most beautiful in the country. . . . One aspect is to make sites of ecological construction really beautiful. Another is to let other people know and recognize this beauty.[43]

Yang's statement provides a lens into how environmental planners understand fostering a shared aesthetic sense to be part of ecological restoration efforts. Through their practices, state scientists and planners aim to broaden eco-developmental aesthetic awareness within the wider public.

Yan Hong, vice director of an urban waste water treatment plant, spoke at length about aesthetics in relation to the wastewater system she manages. The fluvial treatment system releases treated wastewater into recently built surface-flow construction wetlands as part of a secondary wastewater purification process. During our interview, Yan invited me to see the process for myself. We walked up to the balcony to view the water treatment infrastructure. She pointed across the road to the artificial treatment wetlands that stretched as far north and south as we could see from that vantage point. Yan insisted that the few village houses inside the wetlands were nail households [*dingzihu*]—referring to those who resist government-ordered relocation.[44] She also stated that agricultural production in this area had been polluting the lake for decades. When I asked how her team came to this finding, Yan first noted that she wasn't aware of a particular study that measured agricultural pollution, then provided her own visual assessment of how rural resettlement beautified the landscape. She said:

> Take a look at how beautiful [*piaoliang*] these wetlands are. Take a look! Before this ecological protection area [*shengtai baohuqu*] was formed, all this land was covered with vegetables. It was full of plastic greenhouses. We have moved them off this site. When we first set up this water treatment plant this whole area was full of greenhouses. Now look, the whole area has been restored. We pushed them out [*tuidiaole*] and made the site into wetlands. And the wetlands are so beautiful [*hen mei*]. . . . One component of ecological restoration is making the area beautiful [*piaoliang*], another is protecting the lake. This site won't have agricultural fields again. With all those greenhouses and vegetables, of course there are going to be pesticides and herbicides to get rid of insects. After it goes on the plants and it rains, of course chemicals will run off into the lake. So now you can see the effects. This is what removal [*tui*] looks like. We built them apartments and relocated [*banqian*] these villages.[45]

This quote illustrates multiple facets of how Yan senses beauty and purification. In this example, plastic greenhouses represent a polluting agricultural activity. Yan sees removing greenhouses and building treatment wetlands as ways to beautify and purify the landscape. Aesthetic senses that Yan shares with her environmental scientist colleagues informed how she saw the constructed treatment wetland, as well as the village houses that remained. As Yan looked across the few remaining village houses, she saw a landscape degraded by rural activities. Measuring the effects of local agricultural practices on the water quality was unnecessary. For Yan, evidence was visible on the landscape.

The aesthetic regime underlying how state environmental scientists and planners, such as Yan, Yang, and Bing, sense beauty and purification correlates the visual presence of rural people with environmental degradation. Shared senses of beauty are not merely inherent to technical processes of optimization but visible in physical landscapes. This is significant because logics of deficiency are used to justify rural displacement. When notions of deficient rural natures inform environmental planning practices, they reproduce the inferior positionality of rural people within the citizenry. An eco-developmental sublime materializes through scientific techniques that target rural populations and biophysical relations.

Extant studies, however, suggest that local agricultural production is not the main contributor to Lake Dian's pollution problems. The majority of nitrates and agricultural runoff flowing into Lake Dian come from far upstream, not from areas where extensive displacement is underway—where Yan and I overlooked the treatment wetlands. Contrary to the way state environmental scientists saw the landscape, greenhouses tend to reduce pesticide runoff in comparison with open-air farming.[46] Yet, the sense that local agricultural production is environmentally degrading was reiterated throughout my interviews. For scientists and planners purifying the landscape was undivorceable from this shared aesthetic sense.

Aesthetic senses of rural deficiency and modernist improvement also manifest in state techniques of classifying slums. Across municipalities, government bureaus draw on policies of "slum reform" (*penghuqu gaizao*) to consolidate control over space.[47] In 2014, the same year that the New-Type Urbanization Plan was announced, the central government released *Notification Number 535 of the General Office of the Ministry of Housing and Urban-rural Development on Issues Concerning the Defining Standards of Slums*.[48] The document stipulates that each level of government can make their own definition of what constitutes a "slum." Slums, in other words, can be defined and demarcated across levels of government. Definitions, therefore, differ across administrative units and jurisdictions. The Kunming municipal government, for example, defined slums as areas within the municipal jurisdiction that have simple structures (*jianyi jiegou*), poor housing quality, safety hazards, or inadequate facilities. Inadequate facilities can connote both "housing settlements that are too concentrated or too dispersed," as well as areas with "incomplete use functions" (*shiyonggongneng bu wanquan*).[49] Definitions as broad as this reflect the scope of local governmental discretion in how and where to demarcate slums. Many slums are classified in areas newly demarcated for ecological protection. The spatial relation between slums and spaces zoned for ecological protection is explicit in the Chengdu municipal government definition of slums.

Chengdu has a four-part classification system for slums.[50] "Type-one slums" can be demarcated on any site, which has infrastructure overlapping with urban greenspaces. Similarly, "type-four slums" can be classified in any area that the Chengdu municipal government changes to a different land use type. By simply classifying a space for ecological protection or by changing a land use type, the municipal government can classify any area as a slum. These discursive definitional and classificatory techniques have significant material effects.

Following slum classification, infrastructure can be demolished by municipal governments in the name of "slum reform." As is the case across contexts, slum demarcations facilitate displacement as a form of environmental improvement. In addition to justifying spatial control over land, classifying a rural area a slum discursively frames rural spaces as low-quality, disorderly, and infrastructurally unsound, thereby reifying logics of rural deficiency. These techniques are material expressions of a shared aesthetic sense wherein disorderly landscapes and people are provided with ordered resettlement housing from the state. Scientifically optimized landscapes, such as Kunming Waterfall Park and Lake Dian's treatment wetlands, are emblematic of this aesthetic.

Each landscape, rural and eco-developmental, is imbued with a sense of time and place—a sense of meaning and developmental directionality. Zhang Jielin, the deputy director of an institute involved in urban ecological protection planning, portrayed rural developmental deficiency as follows:

> The village and the city are not the same. The city is compact like this, but villages are really dispersed [fensan]. Their surface area is really wide. So up until now, they have not matured [chengshu]. This form of governance is not only a plan, but it is also a structure of the city and countryside in which we take the dispersed and concentrate it vertically. When the scale is very large it is much easier to deal with. If you deal individually with every single [village] household, then it becomes increasingly difficult. . . . We have tried to move villages to a point [qiancunbingdian], which involves concentrating many villages together. That is, we concentrate dispersed built areas to deal with them [lai chuli].[51]

This quote indicates how state environmental planners, like Zhang, perceive the relationship between the city and the countryside, developmental differences between the urban and the rural, and their own role in socio-environmental management. In discussing the process of concentrating rural people into resettlement complexes, government officials repeatedly framed villages as *lagging behind* cities. Zhang referred to rural built environments as immature, suggesting they exhibit an earlier stage of development compared with urban built environments that have been rationally planned. In this, Zhang articulated a shared aesthetic sense that vertically concentrating villagers is integral to socio-spatial optimization and bringing about a higher developmental stage.

FIGURE 10.   A peri-urban village undergoing demolition. Resettlement housing is visible in the background. Photo by author.

Greening slums, for state planners, entails relocating rural people into resettlement housing, what planners commonly referred to as "moving villages to a point" or "concentrating villages" (*qiancunbingdian*) (figure 10). Zhang continued:

> "Moving villages to a point" [*qiancunbingdian*] is one way we transform villages. The second way is to export labor. We take those animal rearing industries, pig husbandry, cow husbandry, sheep husbandry, chicken husbandry, duck husbandry, all animal husbandry as well as those in the flower industry and move them out of the Lake Dian area. . . . They are just polluting this area.[52]

In addition to socio-spatial optimization, many environmental scientists and planners saw resettling rural people as one of the many economic benefits they receive through restoration efforts. Ze Jian, a mid-level government official, claimed that building constructed wetlands was not only necessary for environmental protection but was also economically beneficial to those relocated.

> The government made wetlands and pushed out rural people in these areas, but they participate in economic processes involved. For instance,

many sell things outside of the wetlands or rent kiosks. So, this is a really a good reciprocal interaction for them. We are encouraging them to pro-tect the wetlands. If they protect the wetlands, then they will benefit as well, directly and indirectly. Rural people really don't take care of land. They destroy it, especially if they don't get a subsidy or some financial support.[53]

Claims such as these reflect a shared sense among state scientists and planners regarding the rural citizenry, as well as the role of science and planning in reorder-ing nature and purifying the landscape. Many planners, however, have a limited understanding of how displacement processes affect villagers in socioeconomic or experiential terms. Because state conservation efforts have displaced millions of peri-urban villagers across China, it is not surprising that rural people facing resettlement view the prospect of becoming part of the "urban" citizenry quite differently.

* * *

Villagers, whose land and housing are unevenly incorporated into ecological protection areas, see ecological restoration efforts through alternative aesthetic lenses. Wang Jie, a peri-urban villager, participated in my photovoice research during which he and other participants photographed changes brought on through the process of ecological protection zoning (see the appendix).[54] The photos became material for interviews and focus group discussions on transi-tions in village life, livelihoods, and shared experiences.

Wang held up photos of newly built restaurants within an ecological protec-tion area on his village's former agricultural land. He placed the photos next to others he took of constructed treatment wetlands, village houses, and a kiosk. He said:

> This kiosk and the restaurants here are run by a national investment corporation, which is claiming to protect Lake Dian by removing us. But they came and built these structures and then rented them out. Then they opened these big restaurants. It's totally irrational. We [villagers] are not allowed to do this within the ecological protection area.[55]

Wang suggested that companies involved in environmental management were profiting in ways that excluded villagers. From the throngs of tourists coming to sites like the Kunming Waterfall Park and treatment wetlands surrounding Lake Dian, it was evident that they have substantial economic potential. Wang felt that he and his fellow villagers were excluded from economic opportunities associ-ated with ecological restoration efforts on the land they had farmed throughout their lives.

Upset by the transitions underway, Wang countered state environmental scientists and planners' ways of seeing and sensing. He offered an alternative aesthetic in which rural infrastructure signified beauty and belonging. Pointing to pictures he took of houses in his village he said:

> Now look at these village houses. *Look how beautiful they are.* These three pictures, these are really important. You have to remember these. In our area, they are building resettlement housing. . . . When it is built, they will move us out of here. This transformation will take place in two or three years. Now on their exhibition boards of this project, our village is marked a slum area reform project [*penghuqu gaizao*]. A slum area reform project! This means that they would call a village as *beautiful* as this one, with *beautiful* homes, a slum. What is a slum? Real slums are crowded areas. They have houses made of temporary materials that are not good to live in. They are dirty with poor traffic conditions. They are in danger of fires. That is what a slum is. The government spends lots of money to help those people who live in poor houses to move into better houses. And this is supported by the central government. But now our village flies under this flag as well—a slum—a slum area reform project! Look at these good houses here in this photo. We are not a slum. Calling this village a slum is just an excuse to make us move.

In this, Wang articulated an alternative sense of place-based belonging that contrasts with an eco-developmental sublime. He also pointed to a contradiction within state policy wherein any site—no matter how infrastructurally sound— could be labeled a slum through simple classificatory techniques.

In the case of restoring the Lake Dian basin, state environmental scientists and planners' aesthetic senses shaped their techniques of delineating and reading historical records, creating novel landscapes, and displacing villagers. Their techniques of optimization and beautification flex state capacities to order nature, society, and space.[56] Yet, even though an eco-developmental sublime has strong powers of signification within state circles, there are limits to its aesthetic resonance. As Wang Jie's photovoice commentary suggests, those most affected by the state-directed conservation efforts often express alternative ways of seeing and sensing. I explore these alternative aesthetics in chapter 5 through examples of what I call a "rural-ecological sublime." Despite limitations to eco-developmental significatory power, this chapter shows how an aesthetic regime shapes state scientists and planners' techniques of ecological restoration and contributes to reproducing an unequal citizenry. Their techniques not only operationalize power symbolically but are also crucial to municipal state territorialization of rural spaces.

In the following chapter, I detail how ecological protection zoning and urban-rural planning processes facilitate the extension of municipal state power over rural land. The chapter also discusses political-economic dimensions of developing land demarcated for ecological protection. Constructing novel landscapes and resettlement housing are costly endeavors. Infrastructural construction, as well as ongoing conservation-oriented land management, exceed the financial and managerial capacities of municipal governments. Yet municipal governments are beholden to provincial and central state authorities to carry out ecological protection zoning and comprehensive urban-rural planning.[57] How do municipal governments, with limited institutional and economic capacity, plan, construct, and manage ecological protection areas? The following chapter analyzes how opportunistic municipal government bureaucrats turn this problem into an opportunity to extend their administrative reach over rural land through new political, economic, and governmental alliances.

ECOLOGICAL TERRITORIALIZATION

During the urban-rural comprehensive planning process, peri-urban villager Zhang Jian's agricultural land was zoned for ecological protection. Afterward, a private corporation constructed a treatment wetland and extensive tourist infrastructure. Although Kunming's municipal planners claimed that ecological protection areas prohibited development, the site was inundated with tourists, rural-themed restaurants, retail shops, and meticulously landscaped flowers arranged by color. Villa-style commercial housing filled adjacent lots. Signs directed tourists to a line of people donning orange life preservers to ride boats on Lake Dian. A rural-themed museum with sheer glass exterior sold admission tickets to view displays of agricultural produce and bronze statues of rural laborers. Bike rental stations offered short-term use. Scannable QR codes next to model camp sites allowed tourists to book camping ventures in the ecological protection area. This site resembled an amusement park featuring opportunities to experience nature. These forms of infrastructural development appeared to violate the ecological protection mandates that barred development. As Zhang waited for the company to complete resettlement housing, he remained in his village home, unclear about how he would be compensated for his home and what his future held. After resettlement housing was complete, Zhang expected to undergo a process that municipal government officials referred to as "ecological migration." Ecological migration is the involuntary resettlement of people, almost exclusively rural people and ethnic minorities, as part of state-directed efforts to conserve or restore land.

What did the contradictions between state plans for conservation and commercial developments in ecological protection areas indicate about how policies were being implemented in municipal regions? What roles did ecological migration and urban-rural comprehensive planning processes play in peri-urban ecological protection zoning and conservation-oriented development? What organizations were involved in constructing peri-urban ecological protection area infrastructures and how were these sites governed? I carried these questions with me as I interviewed municipal planners, government officials, and members of organizations involved in peri-urban ecological protection area planning, construction, and management.[1]

In this chapter, I analyze the conservation and urban-rural planning processes, state-corporate relationships, and forms of displacement that facilitate municipal state territorialization of rural land. The confluence of these processes and governance relations result in ecological territorialization. In a broad sense, ecological territorialization can be thought of as an ensemble of spatial techniques and governance mechanisms through which power over natural resources is exercised in the name of environmental protection or socio-natural optimization. The specific form of ecological territorialization detailed in this chapter entails dynamic planning processes and tense mutualisms between municipal governments and organizations through which municipal states consolidate control over rural spaces. Each organization involved, whether state, semi-state, or private, operates under structural constraints surrounding land-based markets and political-economic opportunities to profit from land rents.

Land, as geographer Stuart Elden discusses, is a finite allocatable-resource over which there is always competition.[2] As such, controlling land is a political and economic enterprise entailing techniques that target socio-spatial relations. In accordance with the 2014 central state policy mandates outlined in the National New-Type Urbanization Plan, each municipality is required to zone 20 percent of land in municipal regions as ecological protection areas. The demarcation of ecological land can include ecological protection areas (*shengtai baohuquyu*) and ecological redlines (*shengtai hongxian*). Both are land classifications, not legal demarcations. Although there is much scholarly attention to delineating differences between these forms of ecological protection zones,[3] one of my key findings is that in the urban-rural comprehensive planning process municipal bureaucrats treat ecological protection areas and ecological redlines as coequal. The Ministry of Land and Resources put forth general guidelines for ecological protection planning and ecological construction. These include developing ecological principles and education, strengthening national resource surveillance, strengthening land use and comprehensive planning through the implementation of functional and scientific zoning, building ecological service systems, and land conservation.[4] But there are no central state specifications for implementation. The ambiguity of how land is to be made ecological conditions the political possibility for planning practices and state-corporate alliances that facilitate local state territorialization of rural land within municipal regions. Opportunistic bureaucratic implementation of state policies for ecological protection and new state-corporate alliances surrounding conditional responsibilities for constructing and managing peri-urban ecological protection land are crucial to consolidating land control within the municipal state hierarchy.

It is important, at the onset, to distinguish a "municipal region" (*shiqu*) from a "city" (*chengshi*) and provide a sense of the positionality of municipal states within China's hierarchical structure of authoritarian governance. When I use the word *city*, I am referring to built environments that exhibit a spatial density commonly associated with urban spaces. A municipal region, in contrast, is an areal unit containing multiple subdivisions, including urban districts and extensive rural areas. Municipal regions are a subunit of provinces. Municipal governments are not singular entities. Nor do the bureaus that constitute municipal states have a single agenda. Municipal states are hierarchies of interdependent bureaus orchestrated through various practices of governance and planning. Each bureau within a given municipal region has its own interests. And each operates within authoritarian governmental hierarchies. An enduring explanatory framework for China's hierarchical governmental organization is fragmented authoritarianism.[5]

The fragmented authoritarianism framework holds that policies emanating from the central state become increasingly malleable as they move down a vertical hierarchy to organizations with administrative control over a region.[6] China's fragmented authoritarian governance structure is often described as a *tiao-kuai* power matrix—translated descriptively as a "power-block" system, "vertical-horizontal" system, or "functional-territorial" system, to highlight a few.[7] The tiao-kuai power matrix refers to a vertically organized state hierarchy (*tiao*), each unit of which has specific governmental functions. Each government unit operates within a territorial system of distributed spatial control over administrative areas (*kuai*). There is considerable tension between the vertical organization of state power and the exercise of state power over space.

Geographer You-tien Hsing describes this tension in municipal regions as a territorial dynamism through which administrative orderings restructure local state power.[8] Local state power in municipal regions, therefore, is constituted through dynamic territorializing processes and governmental relationships. Territorializing processes and intergovernmental relationships are always in flux due to localized and strategic policy implementation. Hence, the Chinese state is Janus-faced. It is centrally coordinated, yet locally adaptive and self-interested.

Local states strive to follow mandates, while simultaneously generating opportunities for accumulating territorial power through creative policy implementation.

This chapter demonstrates how municipal states territorialize space by strategically implementing central state policies for ecological protection in the context of legally and constitutionally underdefined land use rights. Municipal governments wield ecology to *consolidate* power over rural land and housing. They then *disperse* land use rights and responsibilities for ecological protection land to organizations. Techniques of consolidating land control include multifunctional land zoning, urban-rural comprehensive planning, and ecological migration. Techniques of dispersing land control include what government officials refer to as assigning responsibility to organizations (*fuze jigou*) for ecological construction, financing, and managing ecological protection areas. Assigning responsibility entails granting or allocating ecological protection land to organizations—a process through which municipal governments can generate revenues.

Assigning responsibility to organizations not only forges new governmental alliances but also incentivizes organizations to capitalize on land designated for ecological protection. This process differs from other contexts, such as the United States, where both state and national parks fulfill recreational mandates through contracting construction and tourism to private firms, while states continue to invest in parks and run them. In contrast, China's ecological protection areas in municipal regions entail variegated political-economic relationships and regulatory techniques orchestrated by municipal state bureaucrats.

In this postsocialist moment of urban greening, ecological territorialization extends local state power across the peri-urban fringe and produces frontiers of conservation-oriented development. This form of local state territorialization, however, emerged from decades of postsocialist transitions within which municipal governments employed a variety of techniques to expand their regulatory reach over the surrounding countryside.[9] Ecological territorialization, therefore, is among the latest modes of postsocialist municipal state territoriality. The following section situates this new form of territorialization within the broader history of reform-era political-economic transformations. The remainder of the chapter illustrates ecological territorialization through an exemplary site and discusses it as a generalizable process.

Municipal States Surround the Countryside

Moving chronologically through the postsocialist period, this section illustrates how municipal states have territorialized the countryside and the new role of ecological protection zoning in municipal state territorialization. Land in China remains a state asset, within an otherwise globally integrated capitalist political-economic system. The Chinese Communist Party constitution differentiates between collective land ownership in villages and state ownership in cities. But this distinction remains vaguely defined, both within the constitution and in law. Neither articulates which state actors or branches of the state have regulatory control over land.[10] This ambiguity surrounding who can control land is continuously negotiated between various actors deploying a variety of techniques. Historically this negotiation resulted in economic ebbs from rural areas and flows toward urban areas and municipal state bureaucracies.

During the socialist period, centralized economic planning, which controlled pricing and allocation of resources, siphoned off enormous profits from rural areas and redistributed them to urban areas. The planned economy had no explicit tax system, but taxing was inherent in the socialist pricing system. Government financing from the early 1950s relied on state-owned industries.[11] The state allocated low prices for agricultural and mining products and higher prices for manufactured goods. This uneven price allocation privileged urban-based production units.[12] Urban built environments, during the 1960s through the 1970s, did not sprawl into the countryside in the same ways we see today across China's cities. Instead, growth was limited, dense, and compact. The central planning apparatus diverted profits from rural areas to cities, particularly to support urban state institutions and manufacturing. Through urban factory production, cities became important nodes for generating government revenues.

Beginning in 1978, the central state gradually reorganized the command economy. Regulatory and institutional reforms facilitated new land-control power vacuums. Land was decollectivized and the introduction of a household responsibility system individualized land-based production. Early in the postsocialist economic reform period, despite laws prohibiting formal marketization, rural land began to be informally marketized. Agricultural products were legally marketized, while household management rights for land contracts (*chengbao*) were not. In places where early rental markets for rural land emerged, they were often between kin or close friends. But in peri-urban land abutting cities, decommodifying rules were often broken, resulting in the sale and trade of rural land. Additionally, during the early years of reform there was a backlash against the uneven distributional politics of the command economy, which had predominantly favored urban areas. The early 1980s saw new agricultural subsidies and township-village enterprise (TVE) rural industrialization projects. These programs contributed to raising rural incomes and consumption patterns. Many administrative structural changes followed: the township (*xiangzhen*) replaced the commune, the administrative village (*xiangzhengcun*) replaced the brigade, the natural village (*zirancun*) or villager's group (*cunmin xiaozu*) replaced the production team.[13] Land remained under the ownership of the state. Although in rural areas, at this time, "villager groups" most often controlled rural land.

The reforms of the 1980s brought new economic opportunities for rural people, often through relations of production with urban areas. The growth of rural industry contributed to the expansion of cities, in part, because the bulk of rural industrialization catalyzed suburban industrialization.[14] Large cities provided market access, managerial expertise, and skilled technical labor such that, during the 1980s, there was an outflow of urban workers to TVEs in near-urban areas. As municipal governments started to keep a larger share of locally generated revenues, they gained more fiscal autonomy. Fewer taxes went to the central state. Restrictions on mobility between rural and urban areas through hukou regulation decreased. These reforms contributed to the expansion of cities and the interdigitation of urban and rural areas. Desakota landscapes formed.[15] Since land marketization of the late 1980s, actors within the local state began to find ways to capitalize on land's newly legalized market value.

The 1988 law legitimizing the land rent and transfer system (i.e., the valued use system *youshang shiyong zhidu*) introduced new land taxes and legally allowed for the generation of land rents. This attracted investment for land and real estate.[16] The law incentivized local state authorities to strengthen their regulatory power over newly commoditized land to generate tax revenues. After this law passed, municipal states began consolidating land control to generate profits.[17]

Through the late 1980s and into the 1990s there was a veritable explosion of municipal state regulatory apparatuses. State mechanisms increasingly infiltrated everyday social life, strengthening the regulatory power of municipal governments. During this time, municipal states "sprawled," to use the language of Vivienne Shue, into new administrative roles across peri-urban areas.[18] Municipal officers began to regulate economic activity that fell outside of the economic plan outlined by the central state. Municipal governments also began to regulate construction not only in cities, but also in peri-urban rural areas. Additionally, municipal states began to regulate business licenses, health permits, legal and illegal market activities. Some even established individual household laborers associations to disseminate market information. During the late 1980s and early 1990s, the local state retained roughly 50 percent of locally generated taxes. This figure contrasts with the late command economy and early reform era during which roughly 80 percent of local taxes went to the central state. The scope of municipal bureaucratic apparatuses transformed over decades of reform into routine administration of towns and villages beyond cities. The local state operated through forms of corporatist organizing and regulations.[19] The shift of power from rural-to-urban governments continued during the 1990s and 2000s.

From the mid-1990s onward, municipalities ballooned in size and administrative reach, in part fueled by fiscal reforms of 1994 wherein the central state expected local states to generate "nontax" revenues in the form of transaction fees on entrepreneurs and land developers. As administrative entities, municipal states began to span multiple spatial dimensions.[20] Some municipalities became large administrative zones. Others took on prefecture-level status. Still others engulfed numerous counties. Geographer Laurence Ma describes this spatial extension as the urbanization of governance. Ma detailed the urbanization of governance through three administrative restructuring processes: cities administering counties (*shi guan xian*), counties being converted into cities (*xian gai shi*), and cities annexing suburban counties.[21] Jae Ho Chung and Tao-Chiu Lam additionally detail the practices of turning cities and counties into urban districts (*xian shi gai qu*).[22] These territorial acts increased the scalar extension of municipal governments.

Accompanying the administrative urbanization of the 1990s and 2000s, was a movement of regional governments to vie for obtaining municipal administrative status. In doing so, regional governments could potentially rise within the hierarchy of decision-making and regulation. These administrative leaps of becoming a "municipality" did not necessarily require population growth or increases in the built environment. Instead, municipal territorial expansion occurred through redrawing administrative lines and expanding the reach of regulatory bodies. Municipal states were allocated de jure power to develop and profit from land under their control. In the midst of these administrative changes, municipal governments competed for land-based profits with what Hsing calls "socialist land masters"—state and nonstate institutions that held control over land during the socialist period.[23] Hsing details how municipal governments in the early 2000s also competed with township governments for land control from which they could derive revenues. As land is transferred to the secondary market for lease, municipal governments reap profits from land transfer fees.[24] Increasing the number of land transfers within municipal regions increases municipal government revenue. Generating revenues from land is crucial to the operation of municipal governments because, from 2002 to the present, the cost of public goods devolved from the central state to local states. Moreover, local state tax revenues from the central state have continually decreased.[25] This means that local states need to generate revenues to provide basic services. From 2000 to 2016 transactions surrounding land use right transfers generated an excess of 50 percent of municipal government revenues. During this period, there was a steady increase in the percentage of local fiscal revenues generated by municipal governments through land transactions from roughly 15 percent in 2001 to nearly 70 percent in 2017.[26] Even though the price of land fluctuates, municipal governments continue to operate and provide services through revenues gener-ated from local land transactions.[27] Decades of fiscal incentivization to generate revenues from land transactions transformed municipal states into multiscalar administrative complexes empowered to maximize fiscal extraction from land under their control.[28]

Presently in the fifth decade since the postsocialist transition began, generat-ing revenues through land transactions remains crucial to the functioning of municipal governments. And, therefore, processes of local state territorialization to generate revenues from land continue. Municipalities through the early to mid-2000s expanded to include vast peri-urban regions within their adminis-trative reach.[29] But municipal states were not able to readily control rural land or place it on the secondary land market for development. Rural areas within municipal regions, therefore, have become theaters for power plays between gov-ernment bodies over land.[30] Municipal governments are often in competition with township governments for control over these peri-urban lands.

In recent years, township governments have been losing ground to municipal governments who have found new *ecological* techniques at their disposal. The introduction of policy mandates for ecological protection and urban-rural plan-ning occurred simultaneously with stricter constraints on municipal finance. As such, the creation of development zones (*kaifaqu*)—a key technique of municipal territorialization and land-based profit during the 1990s and early 2000s—slowed significantly.[31] Since development zones are strictly regulated by the central state, the designation of ecological protection areas on rural land became part of a new set of techniques for municipal governments to generate land revenues while responding to central state mandates for environmental protection. Ecological protection land is legally ambiguous. It is one of many classificatory layers inte-grated into urban-rural comprehensive planning. New eco-developmental tech-niques stem from the introduction of the 2014 New-Type Urbanization Plan and central state mandates for demarcating ecological protection land in municipal regions. The New-Type Urbanization Plan has four main goals: promoting the orderly conversion of rural people into urban residents, optimizing urbanization patterns, enhancing urban sustainability, and promoting urban-rural integra-tion.[32] These goals align in municipal state efforts to zone rural land for ecologi-cal protection.

Ecological territorialization entails assigning overlapping functional land uses during the urban-rural comprehensive planning process in which at least one land use is "ecological." Additionally, ecological territorialization entails some form of ecological migration and constructing ecological infrastructure—the costs of which generally exceed municipal government budgets. To cover these costs, opportunistic municipal bureaucrats foster state-corporate alliances with organizations assigned responsibility for financing ecological construction on and managing ecological protection lands. Municipal government officials refer to this process as assigning responsibility to an organization (*fuze jigou*). The organization then becomes the proprietary owner (*yezhu*) of ecological land. Government officials assign responsibility to various organizations ranging from state-owned enterprises (SOEs); private companies; real estate firms; semiprivatized state-owned enterprises; and municipal-level government bureaus.[33]

These organizations not only provide institutional support for financing construction, but municipal states also generate revenues through their involvement. Part of the revenues from land transactions are used to compensate ecological migrants resettled in the process. Since municipal states aim to maximize revenues generated from land transactions, municipal bureaucrats are incentivized to minimize compensation capital to people being displaced and resettled. Similarly, organizations assigned responsibility aim to profit from their involvement in conservation-oriented development surrounding ecological protection areas. Assigning responsibility for ecological protection areas allows municipal states to enact policies that would otherwise exceed their budgetary constraints.

In the wake of forced ecological migrations, state-corporate relationships propel profiteering via conservation-oriented land development. Hence, processes of ecological territorialization entail consolidating control over rural spaces within the municipal state hierarchy and dispersing control in complex capillary forms.[34] These processes are steeped in ambiguities around licit and illicit developmental activity and organizational control. As Peter Ho writes, "Institutional indeterminacy [and] . . . the ambiguity of legal rules allows the land tenure system to function" in China.[35] Ho's words, written to describe national variations in land marketization during the 1980s and 1990s, are still applicable today to the ambiguities surrounding land designated for ecological protection.

Old Dian as an Example

Old Dian is an ecological protection area and tourist attraction on the outskirts of Kunming. The site's tourist infrastructure reflects cultural elements of the Indigenous Dian Kingdom, which reigned in China's southwest from the fourth to first centuries BCE. Statues of animal deities and farmers toiling behind oxen line the grounds. Though there was no admittance fee, tickets for boat rides were nearly a thousand RMB. Rows of outdoor kiosks sold local food, hats, bubbles, toys, and fishing nets to catch crawfish. Classical music sounded from ground-level speakers hidden among flowers that lined paved walkways. Pick-it-yourself gardens grew produce that could be taken home or cooked in on-site restaurants. Newly built commercial housing and single-family villa homes hugged the water line.

Before Old Dian was built, the municipal government, in consultation with township governments, created the urban-rural master plan. The plan demarcated land use functions across the municipal region. To meet central state quotas for ecological protection, planners zoned land with overlapping functional land use designations. In this instance, ecological land overlapped with agricultural land. Designating overlapping land use functions facilitated municipal government intervention. Rural people, living on land newly classified for ecological protection were enrolled in ecological migration. In the next chapters, I discuss the politics of land and housing compensation, as well as how residents navigate ecological migration. Resettlement paved the way for an organization to undertake ecological construction and conservation-oriented development.

The organization assigned responsibility by the municipal government for this site was a private company called Qicai Yunnan, a private subsidiary of a larger parent company. Resettlement housing was built with Qicai Yunnan's financial assistance. Within a year, villagers moved into nearby high-rise resettlement apartments. The municipal state charged a transfer fee to allocate land use for the ecological protection land to Qicai Yunnan. The company outsourced environmental design for the site's treatment wetland. They then financed its construction, as well as tourist infrastructure and an array of commercial infrastructure. After construction, the company acted as the umbrella corporation managing the area. The company's economic activities, however, remained under the surveillance of the municipal state hierarchy.

The commercial housing they built near Lake Dian's waterline transgressed the urban-rural comprehensive plan. This violation did not go unchecked. During an annual environmental survey, a municipal bureau assessment found the housing infrastructure already completed. The municipal government proceeded to levy a fine against Qicai Yunnan for violating ecological protection measures written into the urban-rural master plan.[36] Even though the municipal government fined Qicai Yunnan for the housing development, they allowed other economic activities to continue unabated, such as boat rentals, kiosks, and restaurants (figure 11).

In developing land demarcated for ecological protection, organizations like Qicai Yunnan not only provide crucial financial support for ecological construction, the costs of which can be substantial, but also generate revenue for the municipal government through fees associated with land use transfer. A relationship of mutual benefit forms between the municipal state and the organizations they partner with. Government officials, across contexts, referred to these

FIGURE 11.   An ecological protection area. Boats in the foreground can be rented. Commercial housing is visible in the background. Photo by author.

organizations as the proprietary owners (yezhu) of land. Yet, the power to plan and make claims regarding what activities violate the plan rests with the municipal government hierarchy. Urban-rural comprehensive planning and multifunctional land zoning, therefore, are techniques through which municipal states exercise this power. In these ways, opportunistic municipal bureaucrats turn central state mandates for urban-rural comprehensive planning and ecological protection zoning into mechanisms that not only satisfy central state environmental policies, but also justify municipal state acquisition of rural land for conservation purposes. Because the urban-rural comprehensive plan is internal to the state, municipal state actors are empowered to dictate what forms of development are allowed and which violate the plan.

In this case, the municipal government used the urban-rural master plan as a tool to levy fines against their corporate partner. The fine, however, did not deter Qicai Yunnan, which not only continued to develop commercial housing in ecological protection areas in the Lake Dian basin, but substantially expanded their commercial developments in ecological protection areas up through 2021.[37] Ecological territorialization in municipal regions, therefore, entails the opportunistic implementation of central state environmental policies via mutualistic, and at times confrontational, state-corporate partnerships. These partnerships generate revenues for the municipal state and extend control over rural land, previously under control of township governments and villages.

In the following sections, I discuss ecological territorialization as a generalizable process. I detail the ensemble of techniques through which municipal states wield ecology to consolidate power over land and disperse conditional land use rights to organizations.

Consolidation

Zhang Jie, the vice president of a municipal-level environmental planning bureau, characterized the New-Type Urbanization Plan as a "new paradigm of planning" wherein "multiple forms of planning merge into one" (*duoguiheyi*). In pursuit of what he and other urban planners called "spatial optimization" (*kongjian youhua*), multiple forms of planning, previously conducted independently were centralized under the municipal government. New-Type planning synthesized and centralized urban and rural land use planning, environmental protection planning, economic planning, and tourist planning. Previously, these planning processes were independent at municipal and township levels. But as municipal bureaucrats like Zhang explained, this new planning paradigm incorporated multiple bureaus and types of planning across the municipal region. Of key importance here is that under the New-Type Urbanization Plan, rural planning falls within the parameters of urban-rural planning processes, and therefore under municipal state control.[38] Centralizing planning in this way vests power within the municipal government hierarchy to demarcate ecological protection areas and determine land use functions on rural land within municipal regions.

Zhang Jie explained that municipal and township planners drafted parts of the urban-rural master plan independently before representatives discussed them in joint planning meetings over the course of the year. Historical ecological records were considered in proposing land use functions and locations of ecological protection areas (see chapter 2). These proposals were then incorporated into ecosystem models to determine landscape functions and regional carrying capacities. Discussing this, Zhang said, "in terms of environmental protection planning, such as delineating ecological red lines and environmental carrying capacity we calculate how much load the landscape can bear. Through calculating carrying capacity we create measures for environmental protection in the plan."[39] In some municipalities, such as Kunming, ecological protection areas were organized through tiered designations depending on how systems models projected areal carrying capacity. According to the plan, in tier one ecological protection areas no economic activity is allowed. Government officials discussed tier-two and tier-three areas, as having "cautious, chosen, or appropriate" developments that require approval from municipal planning bureaus.[40] In other municipalities, like Chengdu, designating ecological protection areas and land use functions occurred without tiered designations.

During urban-rural planning meetings, interbureau disputes over functional zoning were frequent. When disputes arose, members of municipal-level environmental planning bureaus mediated to ensure the appropriate percentage of ecological protection zones remained in the plan. High-level officials in municipal environmental bureaus and urban planning bureaus maintained veto power regarding locations of ecological protection areas and functional land use designations. Historically, environmental bureaus have been relatively weak. But the fact that they were able to exercise veto power in the urban-rural planning process indicates a strengthening of their relative position within the municipal government hierarchy.[41] At the top of the municipal government hierarchy are CCP cadres and appointed party officials. These high-level officials mediated any outstanding conflicts and made final decisions within the urban-rural planning process.[42]

Initially in 2014, municipal state planners considered central state mandates to demarcate 20 percent of land in municipal regions for ecological protection a problem. The key dilemma stemmed from squaring new environmental protection mandates with preexisting policies for maintaining agricultural land quotas and limiting construction. Rural land designations include agricultural land (of which there are several subcategories), village housing land, and village construction land. The 1998 Land Management Law and its later revisions required agricultural land assigned for development to be replaced with an equal amount of agricultural land under the policy of creating "balance between agricultural land occupation and reclamation" (*zhanbu pingheng*). This policy aimed to mitigate the net loss of farmland. Yet, despite this policy, agricultural land continued to diminish across jurisdictions due to urban and rural development. After experiments in 2006, the central state implemented a policy that "linked the increase in urban construction land with the decrease in rural construction land" (*zengjian guagou*).[43] In essence this policy aimed to bring about no-net-gain of construction land and retain the sum total of agricultural land. Agricultural land quotas became a transferrable asset between administrative units of the state. Through opportunistic zoning techniques state planners turned this problem into an opportunity.

Through multifunctional zoning in the urban-rural comprehensive planning process, state planners allotted a single tract of land multiple land use functions.

If a parcel of rural land was already demarcated as agricultural land, for instance, municipal planners either swapped an equally sized land parcel to agricultural land and demarcated the original parcel as ecological land or assigned multiple overlapping land use functions that overlayed ecological land use with another land use designation. Similarly, rural construction land could be swapped with urban construction land so long as the total amount of construction land did not increase.[44] Within the urban-rural planning processes, it is crucial that the total amount of construction land and agricultural land remain the same while zoning 20 percent of the municipal region for ecological protection. Even though agricultural land demarcations are supposed to be agriculturally productive, state planners claimed they could retain agricultural land classification so long as the land in question maintained perennial vegetative cover, such as forests, grasslands, or wetlands.[45] In the process of making the comprehensive urban-rural plan, planners overlayed previously existing green land designations with new ecological protection designations. As discussed in chapter 2, slum areas (penghuqu) could also be designated during the urban-rural planning process on land that overlapped with ecological protection areas. In interviews, state planners frequently discussed the urban-rural planning process as a way to "optimize" the spatial layout of the city and the countryside.[46]

Municipal governments are the regulatory face of the state regarding urban land, but under the CCP constitution, rural land belongs to villages and is often under township governments' de facto administrative control. Municipal states wrest control of rural land by first zoning land with multiple overlapping use functions and then, with ecological protection as justification, initiating processes of ecological migration. Ecological migration can involve land lease or purchase of land through negotiations between township governments, village councils, development institutions, and municipal representatives.[47] How municipalities orchestrate ecological migration in peri-urban areas varies across local contexts and within a given municipality. Indeed, underneath the veneer of a standardized conservation policy lies incredible variability in how peri-urban villagers' land and housing are incorporated into ecological protection areas.

Each form of peri-urban ecological migration entails a process of withdrawing access to rural land and spatially concentrating villagers in resettlement housing (anzhifang). Rural land can be purchased in one-time payments, leased by a government bureau or an organization assigned responsibility. Land can also be consolidated into a village shareholding corporation that manages a rural land lease and distributes shares of the land rents to members of the village collective. In most cases, villagers are relocated into resettlement housing that resembles urban high-rise apartments. Resettlement housing is frequently built on rural construction land or formerly agricultural land that has been swapped with rural construction land elsewhere. Total amounts of land classified as construction land must remain constant during the urban-rural planning process. Because the urban-rural comprehensive plan synthesizes land use functions and maintains quotas through land classification swapping, processes of ecological migration do not instigate a net gain or loss of rural construction land or agricultural land, at least not according to official state figures.[48]

Depending on financing and the pace of building resettlement housing, villagers are in some cases able to remain in village housing for extended periods of time without access to agricultural land. Rural housing is owned by villagers, but the rural housing land (*zhaijidi*) on which houses are built belongs to the village collective. Short-term use of this land is allotted to village households but is not legally owned by households.[49] Despite this, it can be enrolled in the politics of land valuation and compensation. After contracts are drawn up for land lease or purchase, ecological construction can begin on rural land. In some cases, as I will explain in later chapters, this occurs without all villagers signing contracts and agreeing to resettlement. The amounts of compensation capital offered for land are site contingent and can differ among the natural villages within a single administrative village.[50] There is a wide array of peri-urban ecological migration experiences contingent on the politics of land and housing valuation and compensation, which I discuss in the following chapter. For now, it suffices to reiterate that displacement of rural people is central to producing new frontiers of conservation-oriented development.

State planners considered both the concentration of rural people and the transformation of rural land to perennial vegetative landscapes as forms of social, economic, and environmental improvement. One official noted that

> when there is ecological construction, we must move villages out. . . . We have a record of those we need to move, if we don't move them, they will become like a village-in-the-city [*chengzhongcun*]. We give them an improved living situation. Previously the village did not have planning. Wherever the village headman said to build, there something was built. With this kind of comprehensive planning and planned construction, their living situation improves.[51]

This assertion typifies a shared sense among state planners that urban-rural comprehensive planning and ecological migration bring about socio-environmental improvements. In considering the outcomes of ecological migration, state planners expect urbanization to improve rural people's economic prospects, living conditions, and livelihoods. In cases of ecological migration wherein rural land is leased, state planners claim that this contractual arrangement provides a transitional period for villagers to adapt to life without access to land while receiving annual land rents.[52] According to the logic, villagers can transition out of farming by pursuing other economic opportunities. One government official stated this logic succinctly, saying, "We want rural people around these protected areas to go into the city to work, especially rural people in peri-urban areas. We need to help them to transition into urban labor markets and into urban housing."[53] Mechanistic approaches to social and environmental planning, however, don't simply produce the outcomes planners project. The lived experiences of ecological migration are much more varied than municipal planners conveyed.

Urban-rural comprehensive planning processes facilitate the consolidation of municipal government control over rural land and the socio-spatial reorganization of rural people's access to land and housing. The urban-rural master plan, therefore, is a mechanism for municipal states to justify resettling rural people and consolidating control over rural land. The full contents of urban-rural master plans are internal to the state. Official state websites publicly share written descriptions and a limited number of maps from the plan. Internal to the state, the plan is a blueprint for state interventions toward socio-spatial optimization.

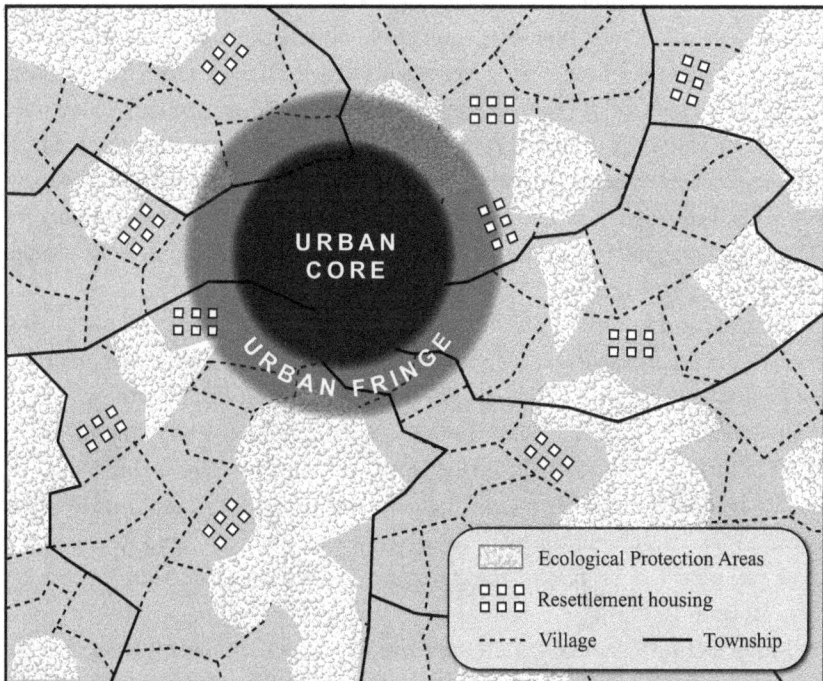

FIGURE 12. Conceptual diagram of ecological territorialization within municipal regions.

The local state can make claims and compel action in accordance with a plan, which nonstate entities cannot fully access.

Figure 12 is a conceptual diagram that represents ecological territorialization processes. The outer edges of the figure are the boundaries of a municipal region. Within the municipal region are ecological protection areas designated on rural land and resettlement housing complexes.

The figure provides a sense of the scale of land demarcated for ecological protection and processes of resettlement within municipal regions. In the Kunming municipal region, for example, there are more than one hundred ecological protection areas.[54] In order to transform land in alignment with the urban-rural master plan, municipal states assign responsibility to partner organizations for financing ecological construction and land management. This dispersion of responsibilities occurs after urban-rural coordinated planning.

Dispersion

Dispersion entails processes of distributing responsibilities and conditional control over ecological protection land to organizations. The responsibilities organizations take on include financing ecological construction and postconstruction land management.[55] Municipal governments disperse land control by allocating or granting land use in ecological protection areas to organizations. They refer to these processes as assigning responsibility to organizations who become proprietary owners (yezhu) of ecological land. Through extensive interviews and site visits, I catalogued several different organizations assigned responsibility for financing, constructing, and managing ecological land, including state-owned enterprises; municipal-level government bureaus; private companies; real estate companies; and semiprivate state-owned enterprises. The right to utilize state-owned land is a leasable asset. It operates like a legally transferable property right for land, albeit with use restrictions put in place by the municipal state. Municipal governments regulate the right to build on and use land. According to article three of the 1990 Provision Ordinance for Granting and Transferring Land Use Rights over State-owned Land in Cities and Towns, any company, individual, or organization can obtain the right to use land and engage in land development after paying the appropriate land premiums, which correlate with the market price of land.

Municipal governments grant land use to entities through the payment of land premiums. In contrast, state institutions can mitigate fees for land transfer if the municipal state allocates land to them.[56] State-owned enterprises are readily allocated land use rights, without paying the full land premiums. They either pay a reduced land premium or the premium is waived. This is because SOEs are formal branches of the state that have historically provided infrastructural services on which municipalities rely. It is not uncommon for state-owned and state-holding enterprises to contribute to fixed asset investments in municipal regions across sectors including infrastructural provisioning. Over the last decade, SOEs accounted for roughly half of all investments in municipal regions. Private organizations, in contrast, are granted land use through public bidding (*toubiao*) and full payment of land premiums. Taxing these land transactions generates revenues for the municipality and simultaneously reduces municipal expenditures as various organizations take on responsibilities. Once proprietary owners are assigned responsibility for ecological land, both state and private organizations respond to market demands to capitalize on land rents.

In interviews, planners would repeatedly tell me to look for the proprietary owner to understand who had control of ecological protection land.[57] There are multiple ways to express ownership in the Chinese language. The word used by municipal bureaucrats for proprietary owner—yezhu—denotes a land management and use right but not an alienation right. Officials used a different word—dizhu—to express sovereign control of land, in this case the condition of being a de facto landlord. Municipal government bureaucrats reserved the term dizhu for themselves. The proprietary owner is the organization assigned responsibilities for financing ecological construction and managerial activities within parcels zoned for ecological protection. The utilization of the language of ownership in this context indicates the indelible role of organizations in territorializing rural land. Organizations obtain land use rights, but sovereign land ownership remains vested in the state.

Through dispersing responsibility to organizations for ecological land, municipal states strengthen control over peri-urban land in capillary forms. The municipal state enrolls organizations in the context of limited municipal finances and economic opportunism. Municipal government budgets cannot cover the costs of ecological construction and management in ecological protection areas within municipal regions. As noted above, this is in part because tax allocations from the central state remain low. Additionally, since the 2000s, government bureaus have been barred from obtaining loans from commercial banks, which they could use for such purposes. Hence, municipal governments benefit from fostering partnerships outside of the municipal hierarchy. One official put this state-corporate relationship quite succinctly. In the context of discussing how responsibility was assigned to an organization for building a treatment wetland in an ecological protection area he said, "Whoever gets the investment decides how to build the wetlands. Whoever builds the wetlands governs the wetlands."[58]

TABLE 1 Transitions in land control through ecological territorialization

TYPES OF LAND "OWNERSHIP"	BEFORE ECOLOGICAL TERRITORIALIZATION	AFTER ECOLOGICAL TERRITORIALIZATION
Yezhu: A land use right, proprietary control	Villagers and village collective	State, semi-state, and private organizations
Dizhu: Sovereign land control, landowner, de facto landlord	Township government, appointed cadres, and elected members of village council	Municipal government hierarchy

Proprietary owners transform land in accordance with the ecological land use functions outlined in the urban-rural coordinated plan. For instance, a proprietary owner could be responsible for building a treatment wetland or planting trees as part of an afforestation effort. Their responsibilities correspond with the ecological function assigned to the land parcel. The organization is then subject to oversight and environmental monitoring from the municipal government hierarchy.[59] But proprietary owners also have vested interests in profiting from ecological protection land. Proprietary owners, predominantly, construct sites that serve conservation functions outlined in the urban-rural plan and their own economic interests.[60] Planners emphasized how proprietary owners often construct ecological sites that emphasize aesthetic landscape functions (*jingguan gongneng*) to attract tourists. One mid-level government official explained this is "because the object is to get people to experience the ecology of the place."[61] Another mid-level government official explained how his organization utilized parts of the ecological protection areas they governed like development zones (*kaifaqu*).[62] This institution became the proprietary owner of two large-scale ecological protection areas. For the organization to successfully finance infrastructure for each, they treated portions of ecological land like development zones.

Organizations that are granted responsibility for these lands find variegated economic geographies under their purview. Each organization can act as an umbrella corporation contracting out spaces within the ecological protection areas they control. Controlling ecological protection land provides opportunities for generating capital through land rents, commercial forestry, commercial housing, state subsidies, and tourism. Some proprietary owners build commodity housing and resettlement housing.[63] Others construct commercial housing within or adjacent to ecological protection areas. In addition, many organizations sublease spaces within ecological protection areas for entrepreneurial activities. Furthermore, state subsidies are available for ecological construction from the central state. These subsidies serve as economic boosts to proprietary owners. Finally, proprietary owners benefit from tourism, including subleasing land within ecological protection sites to enterprises that cater to tourists. Some sell access to the ecological area through, for instance, entrance tickets or parking fees.

Becoming a proprietary owner requires managing market risks. In many cases, organizations require large amounts of financial capital to construct and manage sites. One manager explained how his organization

> receives a plan from the urban planning department, which indicates where particular wetlands must be built. [Our organization] builds according to the plan, but the specifics of how to build it is up to us. We must put the money forward ourselves. They can give us a subsidy from the central state or the province. Now there are many subsides for this. The wetlands we are making are costly . . . the overall investment was over 10 million, actually more than 13 million RMB [US$2 million].[64]

These figures provide a sense of the economic risks involved in proprietary ownership, which motivate proprietary owners to profit from ecological construction.

Each site is funded independently, and financing is contingent on the financial arrangements of the proprietary owner. Sources of financing span state subsidies, private financing, public-private partnerships, debt financing, or combinations of these. Through public bidding (*toubiao*) the municipality can grant land via leases to numerous organizations with varying capacities.[65] One manager of an organization assigned responsibility noted how his company had more than a thousand employees and seven subsidiary companies.[66] This reflects the high capacities of some organizations involved.

Organizations compete for financial assistance from the state. The vice president of a bureau involved in environmental planning stated that

> there are more than one hundred urban ecological projects areas [in the municipal region]. . . . Financing was centralized under the Thirteenth Five-Year Plan, with active support from national and provincial funds. We had 6 billion RMB for governance and environmental protection alone. But, organizations also compete for this capital. We have to compete for shares of national and provincial support. . . . The remainder of the capital we need, we garner from the support of public-private partnerships.[67]

When discussing public-private partnerships, government officials would often use the acronym PPP, or a joint state-private operation (*gongsi heying*), which

included the involvement of semiprivatized SOEs, as well as wholly private entities.[68] The official continued discussing ecological protection area financing, noting that

> state-private partnerships [gongsi heying] are widely sought after. We
> also consider private financing. These are different channels for financ-
> ing adopted according to each ecological protection project. They start
> by designing the project, making it official, and providing an expert
> review. When ready, organizations go on to find financing. Once they
> find it, then it is built. Now as for assigning responsibility over land, this
> is divided between different organizations.[69]

If financing comes from state-owned enterprises, private capital, or semiprivate
enterprises, the municipal government can reduce budgetary expenditures while
responding to central government conservation mandates.[70]

When municipal bureaus are assigned responsibility, they can also draw on
state subsidies and municipal revenues to contract services. Since the 2000s,
however, government bureaus were prohibited from obtaining direct commercial
bank loans. In cases in which construction costs exceeded subsidies, which was
every case I encountered where a municipal bureau acted as proprietary owner,
construction was outsourced to a partner company. A mid-level municipal official described the financial sources for developing urban ecological protection
areas as a mix of capital allocated to his bureau from the central and provincial
state. The rest of the capital, he said, came from land transactions within the
protected area orchestrated by a corporate partner.[71] One manager of an organization assigned responsibility described how "the capital comes from money
earmarked for infrastructure, repairing roads, water, and electricity . . . in addition
to selling land."[72]

Many municipal state planners indicated that the sale of land was a crucial
source of capital for financing ecological construction. One municipal government official remarked how

> the [name redacted] investment company is in charge of recruiting
> finances for our urban ecological protection area. . . . Financing may
> be allotted to the [name redacted] submunicipal district governmental
> bureau. . . . We call this the "first party" [jiafang] of the area, and they
> become the proprietary owner [yezhu]. The financing that is available
> is also struggled over between proprietary owners [yezhu]. There are
> more than one hundred different ecological protection area projects
> within the city. The responsibility over them is dispersed differently in
> each place.[73]

This quote illustrates how organizations compete for limited state subsidies. Because these subsidies are limited, the sale of land and investment tenders become important venues for raising capital. In effort to increase state subsidization, some proprietary owners applied to join the national park system, which would elevate their ecological protection area from a municipal-level to national-level conservation area. In the 2010s, China began implementing a national park system with substantial central state subsidies. The nascent process is ongoing. Although the organization was unsuccessful in their bid for national park status, their proposals illustrate that organizations are willing to undertake substantial efforts to obtain state subsidies. One mid-level municipal government official, whose bureau took on responsibility for an ecological protection area and put forward the bid to become a national park, stated,

> Now in China the country supports ecological construction more than anything else.... Humans are one aspect, and the other is environmental improvement, for which state subsidies are relatively significant. Each year after an annual inspection, the state will be able to cover our basic environmental maintenance governance expenses. But if our site is designated a national level park, this place will be able to generate income on its own. We can make the area into a tourist attraction as long as we really focus on environmental protection.[74]

This government official highlighted the political-economic incentive to generate revenues from conservation-oriented development.

Garnering proprietary ownership of ecological protection areas can be a path for organizations to profit from land. However, many proprietary owners noted the challenges of land-based profiteering. The challenges stem, in part, from development restrictions placed on protected areas. Second, central state and provincial state subsidies linked to ecological construction are limited. Yet, there is a strong market impetus to generate revenues through land. One proprietary owner, in illustration of market pressures, noted how "there are many subsidies available because [the government] considers this very important. But they will not be there for the long-term. The sites still need to run independent of subsidies."[75] The manager explained that in order to finance ecological construction and maintain the ecological protection area his organization required a mix of state capital support as well as revenues generated from the ecological protection area. He said,

> The government offers us 1.5 million RMB a year [in subsidies] for financing our ecological construction and management. But in reality, the capital should be around 3 million. We run in a deficit, but we only

run a slight deficit currently because we can get a profit [from the eco-logical protection area]. We get funds from the parking lots, we rent out areas for service provisioning, and in another two years we will make more profits. Then we can raise the prices for parking and leasing fees.[76]

Proprietary owners aim to finance ecological construction projects through a combination of formal state channels and efforts to turn a profit from ecological land. The financial demands of ecological construction projects and land management, in conjunction with the drive to profit from land rents, incentivizes organizations to violate environmental protection measures outlined in the urban-rural master plan. Despite the fact that organizations can be held in check by municipal states for development that falls outside the plan, it is not uncommon for proprietary owners to push and exceed the boundaries of what municipal states will permit.[77] If and how proprietary owners are brought into check depends on the severity of the violation, the capacities of municipal bureau oversight, and the relationship between bureaucrats within the municipal state hierarchy and those in organizations assigned responsibility for ecological protection land.

* * *

China's political-economic system has been aptly described as "capitalism with Chinese characteristics"—a balancing act between state-directed entrepreneur-ialism and market forces.[78] Market processes, in turn, are embroiled in the exercise of state power. In the early 2000s, municipal governments undertook forms of urban entrepreneurialism and land territorialization through agglomeration-oriented developments, which Hsing theorizes as the urbanization of the local state.[79] Under this mode of governance, urbanization became central to municipal government profiteering and local state formation. In recent years, ecological territorialization has become key to producing new frontiers of conservation-oriented development and municipal state consolidation of power over rural spaces.

Ecological territorialization is distinct from the urbanization of the local state in three ways. First, it is a form of state territorialization motivated by socio-spatial optimization and conservation. It is operationalized through processes of urban-rural coordinated planning and multifunctional land zoning. Second, it facilitates municipal state consolidation of control over rural spaces by targeting peri-urban land and rural populations within municipal regions. Third, assigning responsibility for ecological protection land to organizations facili-tates forms of development that are dually oriented toward conservation and economic interests. Extending the reach of municipal power and generating municipal revenues are predicated on tense market-based mutualisms with organizations assigned responsibility for ecological lands.

Producing these eco-developmental frontiers entails widespread displacement of peri-urban residents who undergo ecological migration, the effects of which are visible on the landscape. High-water marks of displacement can be seen, for instance, in walls of corn that come to an abrupt stop on the borders of eco-logical protection areas. Stark juxtapositions of piecemeal agriculture with aes-thetically designed conservation sites are increasingly common across China's peri-urban landscapes. As I walked through the infrastructural debris of one such site, I came across stacks of doors. Tattered "prosperity" signs hung upside down on metal door frames flailing in the breeze. Among the piles of smashed concrete and rubble, doors were the only remnant of village houses still identifiable. A stack of doors provided a sense of how many homes were once here. The sound of pounding sledgehammers and hydraulic breakers reverberated across the few remaining houses in a neighboring village.

State planners promised new doors. They promised improved housing in resettlement complexes. They considered the concentration of villages and scien-tific ordering of space as forms of eco-developmental improvement. From where I stood listening to the sound of demolition equipment, I could see high-rise resettlement complexes on the horizon. State scientists and planners' vision for an eco-developmental future seemed to be materializing across the landscape. Vertical stacks of doors from rural houses and nearby high-rise housing signified an urbanizing village—at least from the vantage of state planners.

But how were ecological migration processes shaping rural peoples' relation-ships to land, housing, and livelihoods? The next chapter draws on interviews, photovoice, and participant observation with ecological migrants to detail how the volumetric politics of land and housing valuation shape the ways they navi-gate resettlement processes and their aspirations for upward socioeconomic mobility.

Part II

ECOLOGY AND SOCIAL TRAJECTORIES

ECOLOGICAL MIGRATIONS, VOLUMETRIC ASPIRATIONS

The small white fish moved its tail slightly, then laid still on the earth, opening and closing its mouth. How much longer would it survive out of water? On the banks of Lake Dian, a half-dozen peri-urban villagers cleaned whitebait from their nets in an isolated inlet shrouded by willow trees. In one smooth movement, they plucked the nearly translucent fish, cleaned green algae from nets, and neatly rolled them up.

A middle-aged woman wearing a wide brimmed hat and a floral long-sleeve blouse with arm covers up to her elbows introduced herself as Li Mei, then promptly asked to take a selfie with me. I asked how they planned to use the fish. Li said they planned to sell the catch at the market. If there were no buyers, they would eat it themselves and share some with neighbors.

Li said she and her friends from the village came to this section of the lake to fish for whitebait every year. But this year was different. The municipal government recently zoned their village land for ecological protection, including the tract of land where we then stood. The comprehensive urban-rural plan demarcated this place as a wetlands. Li's farmland was purchased and transformed into an artificial treatment wetland. Agricultural fields were dug up and filled with water. New nitrate absorbing plants were brought in to mitigate wastewater pollutants from a nearby water treatment plant before flowing into Lake Dian.

Around the corner from the willow trees where we stood with fishing nets, tourists strolled through treatment wetlands along finely manicured walking paths. The proximity to the city attracted thousands of tourists daily. Peri-urban areas with newly made conservation sites such as this one, offered respite from urban life. Tourists biked over newly paved bike lanes on land that, the year prior, was lined with agricultural produce. They posed for endless pictures with nature, scarves fluttering in the breeze as they stood in front of an aesthetically manicured landscape. When walking through the wetlands park, I was often asked to pose with tourists taking photos with selfie sticks. It became routine. Once with sunglasses on. Then sunglasses off. One from a side angle. Another looking off into the distance. Tourists commented about the beautiful features of the ecological protection area. Streams of picture-taking tourists marveled at recently planted mitigation forests and seasonally changing botanical installations.

From my outsider's perspective, it seemed that peri-urban villages were rapidly dissolving in the wake of ecological protection zoning. Villagers like Li faced ecological migration (*shengtai yimin*)—state-directed resettlement in the name of conservation. The process of resettlement, for many, revokes access to rural land and housing. State planners and scientists explained resettlement processes as routine. For state planners, resettling rural people into urban high-rise apartments is a means to optimize socio-environmental and socio-spatial relations. But it was evident from encounters with villagers like Li, who no longer held rights to her agricultural land but still lived in her original village home, that ecological migration processes unfolded piecemeal and unevenly.

Restrictions on land use accompanied newly zoned ecological protection areas, effectively halting agricultural production, fishing, and according to the comprehensive urban-rural plan, "any form of human activity" for rural people who historically relied on land to support their livelihood. But there was erratic enforcement of these new land use restrictions. And for the high price whitebait could fetch on the market, fishing was worth it for Li and her friends. Afterall, the land and water were still there, just technically no longer theirs.

Before Li's ancestors lived on land, home was on the water. Some of the oldest living members in this village spoke about how they became farmers from fishers, but never stopped fishing. From the late nineteenth century up through the early twentieth, entire families lived in wooden boats on Lake Dian with an open bow and stern. A low central awning offered protection from the sun and rain. Households paid boat-docking fees in the form of fish and labor to landlords. In the early 1900s, boat-dwelling fishermen moved to land. A handful of families set up tents on the land and slept in them. Currency replaced fish. A village grew.

"We have always fished. Our village used to all be fishers. But now there are just a handful of us who continue," Li said. Claims such as these came from stories that were learned. I learned them too, over the years I visited Li and other peri-urban villagers facing ecological migration in the municipal regions of Kunming, Chengdu, and Dali. As the last of the nets were rolled up, I offered a hand hauling the catch back to Li's home.

Li's home stood one lot away from the main intersection of the only crossroads that ran through the village. A red metal door with two paper posters of the protector deity Guanyu marked either side of the entrance. Concrete walls and floors showed 1980s renovations. The entryway was filled with unused farming tools for separating seed. It opened into a main room with a ground-level table brimming with homemade snacks. Inside was a tattered sofa covered in cloths of various colors, a water dispenser, and a sleek black TV. A red-starred, hammer and sickle calendar hung on the wall with the faces of Mao, Deng, and Xi—a gesture to continuity.

Her front yard was a dirt road leading east and west. To the west lay the ecological protection area. In it, a new treatment wetland replaced agricultural land. The wetlands merged with the banks of Lake Dian. Newly built villa-style housing (*bieshu*) bordered the wetland to the south. The proprietary owner of the ecological protection area (see chapter 3) had already sold the housing units, mostly to government employees. To the east, high-rise resettlement housing (*anzhifang*) complexes and a new resettlement site under construction marked Li's imminent future. Guerrilla gardens hid in groves of newly afforested land. One supported a plastic greenhouse, defiantly incubating lines of cabbage despite new prohibitory land use regulations.

Li explained that the entire village was going to move out of their homes into high-rise resettlement complexes but did not know when. Awaiting notification, she and others in her village lived in a medial state. Li did not have access to agricultural land, but still had her house in the village, albeit with the proviso that she will eventually be offered a contract to vacate and move into resettlement housing. The resettlement complex construction site was visible through the wreckage of a partially demolished three-story house on the north end of her village. The top two stories had been partially lopped off by an excavator that rested along the side of the road. Through the hanging bricks, a multitude of cranes on the dusty horizon were in the process of making buildings taller than the first two resettlement complexes in adjacent blocks. According to state plans to urbanize the rural population and socio-spatially optimize the municipal region, these thirty-story high-rises were to be filled with peri-urban ecological migrants.

As the process of ecological migration began to unfold, the valuation and compensation of rural land and housing were at the forefront of Li's concerns. Li hoped to be compensated with a resettlement apartment unit on a low floor. She hoped that the contract for her village housing could afford her an extra apartment unit that she could lease out. She had heard of other villagers leasing extra units after moving into resettlement complexes. Li aspired to do the same. She hoped the compensation for land and housing would be enough to sustain her family as they transitioned from the rural life that they knew into an "urban" life, the content of which to Li sounded promising, but remained unknown. No longer satiated by whitebait, she hoped to catch bigger fish.

Volumetric Politics of Peri-Urban Ecological Migration

Ecological migration entails the involuntary resettlement of people, almost exclusively rural people, as part of state-led efforts to conserve or restore land. Ecological migration emerged as an official state term in the context of large-scale antidesertification and grassland conservation campaigns during the 1990s and early 2000s, particularly in western China.[1] In that context, the term connoted state-directed movement of herders and farmers into concentrated resettlement areas. It also entailed either revoking or severely curtailing traditional forms of land use and access to land. There has been comparatively little engagement with analogous displacement processes underway in rural areas within municipal regions. As the previous chapter notes, municipal regions are areal administrative units containing multiple subdivisions, including urban districts and extensive rural areas. By peri-urban, I mean porous areas of transition between urban and rural land uses, classifications, or characteristics that are proximate to municipal regions.

While "peri-urban ecological migration" is not an official state term, municipal state planners utilize the term *ecological migration* to discuss processes of displacing and resettling people who live on rural land in municipal regions. The process is initiated by the incorporation of rural land and housing into ecological protection areas during the urban-rural comprehensive planning process. Peri-urban ecological migration indexes similarities with ecological migration processes in China's West. Millions of rural people experience peri-urban ecological migration processes, however, far outnumbering those in China's West.

Since the 2014 introduction of New-Type Urbanization planning, the central state mandated that 20 percent of land in municipal regions be demarcated for ecological protection and that rural land be included in the urban-rural planning process. These policies aligned with national efforts to urbanize 100 million rural people, thereby accelerating the transformation of China's small-holding agricultural population into an urban industrial workforce. In the previous chapter, I discussed how municipal states' opportunistic implementation of ecological protection zoning policies facilitates ecological territorialization. This chapter details the spatiotemporal politics and lived experiences of peri-urban ecological migrations.

The transitional processes initiated as Li's rural land was incorporated into an ecological protection area raise several questions. As a multigenerational farmer and fisher, how would Li make a living without access to her agricultural land? In addition to land, what other spaces matter for ecological migrants as they navigate displacement and resettlement? How do peri-urban ecological migrants marshal rural land and housing valuations for their own benefit? What kinds of individual and collective social conduct matter to these processes? The answers to these questions eschew a singular story. Indeed, under the veneer of centrally orchestrated environmental protection and urbanization processes, there is a great deal of variability.

Crucial from the standpoint of Li and others facing ecological migration is the fact that valuation of rural land and housing can take multiple forms. Land can be valued monetarily and compensated via land sales or land leases lasting several decades. Housing can be monetarily valued and sold or valued as an exchange relation in a contract for newly built *urban* resettlement housing. These monetary and spatial valuations can be negotiated between municipal states, development institutions, township governments, and village councils or corporatized villages. Land and housing compensation can take the form of payments based on the duration of time between moving out of village housing and into urban resettlement housing. Land and housing valuation and compensation processes, therefore, are arenas of political contestation, as are the timetables within which and governmental hierarchies through which compensation is meted out. These are just some of the spatiotemporal valuations that matter for those navigating displacement. Peri-urban ecological migration, as this chapter reveals, entails myriad forms of politically contestable land and housing valuation processes. The spatiotemporal politics of land and housing valuation, I argue, shape ecological migrants' aspirations for upward socioeconomic mobility and uneven social trajectories.

To conceptualize how spatiotemporal politics of land and housing valuation matter for ecological migrants, I draw on and advance geographical concepts of verticality and the volumetric.[2] Architect Eyal Weizman, writing in the context of Israeli occupation, brought attention to how a "politics of verticality" is enrolled in banal architectural forms, such as housing developments and underground tunnels. These architectural forms not only displace people in jigsaw fashion but interconnect occupied territories across spatial dimensions. One of Weizman's key insights is that spatial politics of displacement operate across a multiplicity of vertically layered territorial planes.[3] Weizman distinguishes between territories layered horizontally across earth surfaces, the ground below earth surfaces, and the air above. He argues that territorial politics of occupation and displacement operate across these vertical spaces. His work propelled a vertical turn in geographical scholarship, particularly in relation to the built environment.

During the 2010s, scholarly works engaging vertical dimensions of the built environment and territory across heights, depths, and volumes came to be articulated through the term *volumetric*. Volumetric refers to spatial dimensions and measures of volume, often linked to territorial or sovereign claims. In this vein, geographer Stuart Elden, focusing on military geographies, argues for broadening areal dimensions of territory beyond purportedly horizontal frames.[4] There is much to be gained, he contends, by viewing areas as volumes. Volumetric geographies entail multiple spatial dimensions around which political claims are made and political processes play out. Elden's intervention precipitated scholarly works that foreground the state in voluminous geographies of aerial control.[5]

Urban geographers shifted from questions of how sovereignty is exercised volumetrically to how vertical and volumetric relationships shape urban spaces and urban experiences. For instance, *Vertical* by Stephen Graham is emblematic of scholarship that looks "above" and "below" horizontal ontologies to consider how vertical relationships materialize in the urban realm. Graham articulates the volumetric as "relations between layers and levels within volumes of geographic space."[6] Building on these insights, I deepen and extend scholarship on verticality and volumetric geographies in new directions. First, I theorize multiple overlapping relations between horizontal and vertical spaces and temporal dimensions as internal to volumetric relations. Second, I focus not only on volumetric experiences in relation to urban life, but also in relation to rural life. Third, I ground the volumetric in lived experiences, not simply in aerial visions from above.

Conceptualizing temporalities as constituent of the volumetric broadens its theoretical scope. I support this by demonstrating how relations of height, depth, surface, and volume intersect with temporalities of labor, built environments, domestic spheres, gendered relations, social mobilizations, and livelihoods in transition. In this, I embrace volumetric urbanisms' attention to vertical spatial relations across horizontal planes, heights, and depths. My conceptualization of volumetric politics, however, also engages intersections of temporalities with spatial relationships. Additionally, I point out how the volumetric is meaningful not only to the urban, but to urban-rural relations and processes. This departs from scholarly engagements that treat verticality and the volumetric as predominantly urban phenomena. My conceptual broadening reflects the empirical character of peri-urban ecological migrations in China.

It became clear from Li's experiences, and other per-urban ecological migrants like her, that the urban and rural are deeply relational and constituted through process-oriented relations.[7] The volumetric is significant not merely to urban settlement types, but to variegated socio-spatial processes that remake the urban and the rural in relation to one another.[8] In these ways, the countryside and the city are mutually constitutive.[9] Detailing this relational co-constitution in the context of China addresses calls by Global South urbanists, such as Ananya Roy and Jennifer Robinson, regarding the need to theorize urban social relations beyond Euro-American experiences.[10] In focusing on urban-rural relationality and the lived transitions of rural people as a lens to reflect on urbanization processes, this analytic moves beyond traditional places and relations to theorize anew the urban.[11]

The third point of departure is a reorientation of volumetric perspective. Scholarly work on verticality and the volumetric tend to provide God's-eye views from above. Verticality is presented from the standpoint of the planner, the military strategist, elites who bypass ground-level plebian mobilities in private helicopters, or satellite areal images that gaze down from above. By focusing on volumetric experiences from "below" as villagers navigate municipal-state-directed projects of ecological migration, I depart from prevailing vertical imaginaries in geographical scholarship. This shift in focus provides a subaltern-centered corrective to vertical geographies of the city.

These interventions reveal how volumetric geographies are not only crucial to state territoriality, sovereignty, and the urban experience, but are at the core of rural politics, rural-urban transitions, displacement, and resettlement. In this account, I focus on spatiotemporal measures and calculations of land and housing volumes that matter to peri-urban ecological migrants. What makes the stakes of volumetric politics distinct and so important lie in the contestability of land and housing measures, the slipperiness of calculability, and the experiential variability of resettlement processes. Volumetric politics shed new light on uneven socioeconomic trajectories of displacement and forms of counter-conduct.

In the introduction of this book, I drew on the work of Michel Foucault to define counter-conduct as the ways that people struggle with and against governmental processes aimed at conducting society.[12] There are two senses in which I discuss counter-conduct in this chapter. The first is through struggles, negotiations, and compromises surrounding how people act individually or mobilize collectively to maximize compensation capital. For instance, in some cases villagers corporatize to effectively manage shared assets from land. In other cases, ecological migrants collectively protest over amounts of compensation for land and housing volumes. These political formations take shape in the context of a speculative real estate complex, wherein state and private actors vie for control over land for conservation-oriented development. Within this context, rural people also strive to maximize compensation from rural land and housing volumes. But rural people's bargaining positions are uneven. Unevenness is, in part, shaped by preexisting social inequalities, as well as how rural people organize, if they organize at all. Since the process of ecological migration can be coercive, as I detail in chapter 6, there is an underlying sense that the state, and those that act on behalf of the state, may deploy their monopoly on physical force. Despite this pervasive concern, villagers that collectively organize fair comparatively well. In the cases discussed in this chapter, counter-conduct is often aimed at maximizing the value of land and housing. But there is a second sense of counter-conduct that relates to the aspirational.

The second sense in which forms of counter-conduct articulate with volumetric politics is through ecological migrants' aspirations for upward socioeconomic mobility. These aspirations find expression in how migrants *utilize* land and housing compensation capital. In this vein, I bring attention to how desires, particularly those related to lived senses of place and belonging, shape how people utilize compensation capital. In the eyes of state planners, rural people are supposed to move into resettlement housing and enter urban labor markets. Yet, because of myriad forms of counter-conduct their transitions diverge significantly from this linear prescription.

Senses of place and belonging inform how rural people imagine, pursue, or resist vertical life in high-rise resettlement housing. Many who resist use their compensation capital to acquire alternative housing in rural environs and to pursue new economic opportunities in agrarian sectors. How rural people utilize compensation capital and where they choose to do so is, in part, informed by where they feel like they belong, what economic opportunities they wish to pursue, their familial obligations and social positionalities, and how they imagine their future. Within this experiential and emotive sense, temporalities of displacement and resettlement matter greatly. Regular compensation payments, for instance, provide supplemental income for some migrants who pursue agrarian livelihoods instead of becoming industrial wage laborers in cities. Additionally, the valuation of time between moving out of rural housing and into resettlement housing can become a source of capital accumulation. Temporalities of displacement and resettlement are important not merely because of their economic outcomes. Age too mediates the experience of adapting to high-rise resettlement housing. Fear of vertical life, for instance, is pervasive among elderly villagers awaiting resettlement.

In what follows, I chart the volumetric politics of peri-urban ecological migration. I highlight *horizontal* relations to land proprietorship, *vertical* relations to housing, and *temporalities* of displacement and resettlement. Through the experiences of Li and other peri-urban villagers, I illustrate how volumetric politics shape processes of becoming richer, moving into poverty, and finding oneself, at least for a time, somewhere in between.

Horizontal Relations to Land

In the summer of 2015, my daughter Akira and I attended a funeral in Li's village. Close kin wore white shrouds and walked the deceased through the gravel streets. Stone lions burned incense marking the north and south entrances to the village. The open spaces allowed for a procession of the deceased to homes of family members and close friends. Fireworks cracked loudly clearing way for the procession. "A funeral procession in a high-rise resettlement complex would require a lot of elevator rides," Li joked.

When I returned to Li's village in 2016, she was gone. After several visits to her home, padlocked from the outside, I called her phone. No answer. A call the following week retrieved her voice on the other end. "When will you be back to the village," I asked. "I am not coming back anytime soon," she said. "I rented land in Yiliang. I am farming here now. I have to stay in Yiliang, otherwise local villagers might steal my equipment."

Months later, as I walked through the same village to visit another household, a grey car stopped next to me. The window rolled down. Li and her husband Tao Jiang peered out at me. They asked me to accompany them back to their home. Once there, Li told me that Tao had a farming accident and injured his finger. They returned to their village home to visit the local hospital and recuperate. We cooked fish from Lake Dian for lunch and talked about their new entrepreneurial project in Yiliang.

After their village was zoned for ecological protection, the municipal government purchased Li's agricultural land for 100,000 RMB (US$16,000).[13] Li utilized the bulk of the capital from the land sale to sign a three-year-minimum binding lease with a village council in Yiliang, a subcounty within the Kunming municipal region. There she rented four aquaculture ponds (*yutang*) on forty mu (about 2.6 hectares) of land with her husband.[14] The annual land rent was 20,000 RMB (US$3,200). Li and Tao paid three years of land rents up front to obtain the contract. They utilized over half of their compensation capital on this agricultural land lease. As they talked about how they used their land compensation capital, Tao looked across the table of fried fish and said, "A farmer without land is not a farmer. Just like a fish without water, you can't survive. But if you have land, you can eat forever." Even though Li and Tao were in the midst of a prolonged ecological migration process, they were certain that they wanted to continue farming.

In Yiliang, Li and Tao were learning a new agricultural enterprise—aquaculture husbandry. They tended freshwater crayfish and other fish varieties in artificial ponds (*yutang*). Nearly all their time was spent in Yiliang. To stay there, they built a simple lodging out of concrete blocks on a walkway between two fishponds. After selling their land, commercial fish production was their primary livelihood endeavor. But it was not the only one.

Li took another portion of the compensation capital and invested in a rental kiosk within the newly made ecological protection area, which was once her farmland, now a treatment wetland. She rarely opened for business, except for major holidays like Spring Festival or National Week, when tourists flocked to the wetlands park. During these weeks, Li returned from the neighboring county to sell fish. She would either use the commercial space she rented within the ecological protection area or set up a kiosk near the entrance of the wetlands park. Through the capital influx from the sale of agricultural land, Li and her husband transitioned from subsistence land-based production to petty commercial production coupled with entrepreneurialism in the ecological protection area.

The transformation of Li's village land to capital and capital to new forms of land-based production illustrates how villagers utilize land compensation for new entrepreneurial endeavors. In Li's case, she used the capital generated from her village agricultural land to continue land-based production through an inter-village land lease. This facilitated upward socioeconomic mobility as Li and Tao entered a class of semi-autonomous producers and petty merchants—a transition experienced by many in their village. Those forced to sell land received one-time capital influxes that facilitated petty entrepreneurialism and intervillage land leases. In addition to land sales, land leases are another volumetric relation to land that mediates social differentiation and livelihood transitions.

Months after visiting Li, Akira and I drove parallel to the Cangshan Mountains toward a cluster of villages in the Dali municipal region. These villages started leasing their agricultural land to a municipal bureau after it was zoned for ecological protection. The municipal state then assigned responsibility to an organization to transform the farmland into a treatment wetland. The wetland is designed to mitigate pollution from tributary waters flowing into Lake Erhai, Dali's largest freshwater lake. Akira and I visited these villages often and made the rounds to see villagers we knew.

We planned to meet peri-urban villager Wang Zhihong and waited outside his house near the treatment wetland. Construction trucks hauled dirt and materials to lay walking paths. As Akira and I waited and watched concrete dry, Wang pulled up in his truck. A dozen women arrived soon afterward on foot and started to unload garlic shoots from the back container, weigh them, and tie them into bundles. Men watched and smoked. Akira decided to help, carrying two bundles a time. I talked with Wang who explained that these newly landless ecological migrants worked for him as day laborers. They could earn 100 RMB (US$16) a day working the garlic harvest and half that figure for assisting with his agricultural wholesaling enterprise.

FIGURE 13.   Akira, the author's daughter, helps prepare the harvest for transport to Dali. Photo by author.

Wang's household received 8,000 RMB (US$1,300) annually as compensation from a bureau of the Dali municipal government for leasing their agricultural land. Wang claimed that, if he were growing agricultural produce, he could make around 5,000 to 6,000 RMB from a single mu of land, but with all the needed inputs and time, the profits would only come to around 3,500 RMB (US$600) per mu. Leasing agricultural land effectively cut rural people off from autonomous land-based production. This "freed" labor to transition into migratory streams, wage labor, or other entrepreneurial enterprises.[15] Land leases provided an economic cushion to cover basic living costs and housing maintenance expenses, which allowed many in this village to transition into new jobs. Reflecting on the arrangement Wang said, "If we still had our land, we would just be farming all day. Now we really have a great opportunity to improve ourselves." Wang's newfound mobility and aspirations for socioeconomic improvement took shape in relation to compensation capital in the form of an annual distribution of land rents from the municipal state.

As part of his livelihood transition, Wang began transporting agricultural produce between nearby rural storehouses and other areas within the Dali municipality. The 8,000 RMB per annum was enough to maintain basic expenses while he became an agricultural middleman. Wang's village is a case of how land-leasing

FIGURE 14.   A peri-urban villager working as an agricultural day laborer. *Source*: Photo taken by a peri-urban villager and reproduced with permission.

relationships to the local state spurred labor mobility. Through volumetric relations to land and the utilization of compensation capital, Wang's socioeconomic position shifted from a semi-proletarianized wage worker into a wholesaler. He leased his land to the state, hired seasonal labor, and maintained the flexibility to sell his own labor.[16] For most peri-urban villagers in these villages, annual compensation for land was enough to shift from subsistence agricultural production to semi-proletarianized wage work. Involuntary land leases freed labor from land, thereby allowing Wang to employ local villagers as day laborers. These volumetric relations to land contributed to reducing the risks of labor transitions.

Annual payments for land-leasing, however, did not provide enough financial support for families with children and elderly to care for. Accordingly, many villagers aged twenty to fifty entered migratory labor streams as near as Dali or as far as Shanghai.[17] Familial and economic needs shaped decisions to take on temporary wage labor positions. Villagers in peri-urban Dali frequently spoke about their experiences of livelihood transitions brought on through ecological migration processes. Wang's experience, much like Li's, entailed upward socioeconomic transitions linked to the utilization of compensation capital. Upward socioeconomic trajectories were also widely discussed among ecological migrants in peri-urban Chengdu where corporatized villages obtained favorable compensation for rural land and housing.

Several weeks after our visit with Wang in Dali, Akira and I hitchhiked through northern peripheries of the Chengdu municipal region to an ecological protection area. At this site, agricultural land was transformed into a treatment wetland, but the site had different forms of land valuation and compensation than the two examples noted above. Villagers here corporatized and, with mediation from their corporate affiliate, signed a contract with the municipal government to lease their rural land, which was designated for ecological protection.[18] The corporatized village, business partner, and the proprietary owner—a private company tasked with ecological construction—negotiated a contract that included villa-style housing (*beishu*) for villagers, as well as annual payments at prime rates for leasing land. Peri-urban villagers at this site in Chengdu, and others like it, frequently used the term "moving into riches" (*ban fuyou*) to describe how they collectively organized around land and housing valuation to gain favorable compensation. Their compensation for land and housing volumes precipitated upward socioeconomic mobility.

As the Chengdu municipality incorporated their rural land and housing into an ecological protection area, these corporatized villagers transitioned from dual-employment households to petty bourgeoisie. Many turned their new resettlement homes into teahouses, restaurants, and rural-themed restaurants (*nongjiale*). In addition to deriving an annual share from the village corporation that managed the land lease, ecological migrants at these sites in Chengdu generated income from businesses run from their resettlement housing. In this, their domestic spaces doubled as spaces of exchange and production. Their successful navigation of volumetric politics facilitated capital accumulation through processes of displacement.

Political-economic theorists commonly consider displacement to result in socioeconomic losses for the dispossessed. Land dispossession has been theorized as both a process of removing labor from land and as an original moment of accumulation for elites referred to as "primitive accumulation" or "original accumulation."[19] David Harvey, intervening within the Marxian variant of this theory, conceptualized "accumulation by dispossession" as ongoing processes of dispossession necessary for capital accumulation.[20] For Harvey, accumulation by dispossession entails state- and elite-driven commodification, privatization, and financialization. Michael Levien, building on this political-economic framework, argues that land dispossession is a key structural force that produces social inequality.[21] Drawing on extensive research on special economic zones in India, Levien makes the case that as state and private actors seize control of land for the purposes of development or real estate speculation, rural people dispossessed from land are proletarianized and impoverished. In his formulation, displacement breeds poverty. Yet, for Levien, the process of dispossession doesn't necessarily produce development or capital accumulation. When capital accumulation does occur, it is limited to local and extralocal elites. For Levien, displacement from land is a form of coercive redistribution that structurally conditions proletarianization and produces poverty.

While a host of studies support this formulation, the experiences of China's peri-urban villagers' "moving into riches" confound the maxim that displacement necessarily produces poverty. The fact that some villagers, instead, accumulate and experience upward socioeconomic mobility through displacement processes unsettles longstanding structural formulations. Displacement, in these cases, did not necessarily produce poverty. Instead, these cases show how volumetric politics of valuation and compensation figure into differentiated socioeconomic trajectories. I consider processes of generating wealth and obtaining upward socioeconomic mobility through displacement from land and housing as *accumulation through displacement*. Peri-urban villagers can not only become wealthier through displacement, but they *aspire* to accumulate through successfully navigating the volumetric politics of land and housing valuation. In this sense, volumetric politics is a useful conceptual lens for engaging political economy, urban-rural relationality, and forms of counter-conduct.

In each of these cases, peri-urban villagers achieved some degree of accumulation through displacement, albeit through divergent ways of navigating volumetric relations to land. Li and Tao invested their displacement capital into land-based production in a nearby village and petty entrepreneurial endeavors. Wang's annual land rents covered basic living expenses, thereby spurring labor mobility and his new agrarian entrepreneurial endeavors. Corporatized villages within the Chengdu municipal region moved into riches. Their collective action to partner with a corporate entity resulted in annual payments for land rents at prime market rates and new villa-style resettlement housing, which double as sites of production.

Certainly not all villagers undergoing ecological migration, however, move into riches or experienced the kinds of upward socioeconomic trajectories highlighted in this section. The following section delves into vertical relations to housing by juxtaposing ecological migrants who moved into riches with those who experience acute socioeconomic and emotional loss as they are displaced from rural land and resettled into high-rise resettlement housing.

Vertical Relations to Housing

As we ate lunch at Li's house, I remarked that it had been two years since we first met on the banks of Lake Dian, yet Li still did not know when she would be resettled into high-rise resettlement housing. "We don't have a housing contract yet," she explained. "We don't know yet what will be included, but since they instituted a building moratorium [on village houses] I have doubts that we will be compensated for sky fees [*tiankongfei*]." Li explained that each housing acquisition involves measurements of the built dimensions of rural housing, building materials, and floor space. This process involves measuring and ascribing value to the dimensions of rural built environments. As contracts are drawn up, valuations are formalized into contracts for housing sales. Measures related to the physical infrastructure of houses, however, are not the only spatial dimensions valuated. Vertical spaces above and below the house can also be ascribed value.

Sky fees entail the valuation of yet unbuilt, vertical housing space. This is a volumetric valuation of the air above the house where there is no built structure tabulated in relation to the interior floor space and infrastructural materials of the house. Sky fees are a measure and valuation of potential housing space. They are based on the condition that a household could have built additional floors at some future time on their rural homestead. Sky fees, therefore, correspond to projections of future vertical floorspace. When valuated, households are compensated for relinquishing the possibility of building an additional floor sometime in the future. Since, the original rural house will be dismantled, additional floors will never be built. Moratoriums on building additional floors go into effect after rural housing land is zoned for ecological protection. Measurements of Li's house were taken by a development institution after conservation zoning. But they had yet to negotiate a housing contract. Li waited. And, as she waited, she remained skeptical that sky fees would be included.

At another ecological protection area near Li's village, villagers negotiated for sky fees. Each villager was compensated for an additional vertical floor, the measures for which were based on measurements of the first floor and the infrastructural materials of the village house. In this village, housing compensation did not take the form of monetary currency. Instead, each household was compensated in the form of floor space in an urban high-rise resettlement apartment complex. The extra square footage within the resettlement complex allowed some households to procure an additional unit or, depending on the square footage and materials of their original village home, multiple units in a resettlement complex. Many ecological migrants at this site took on rentier status—accumulating through displacement—as they leased out the additional unit(s) in the resettlement complex to third parties.

Subsurface housing fees (*dipifei*) are analogous to sky fees. Subsurface housing fees entail the valuation of the ground underneath a rural house, yet another volumetric valuation. The land beneath a village house is rural construction land to which a use right is distributed to registered households within a given village. Like sky fees it is not a built addendum to the house, but the surface on which the house stands. From the vantage of valuating along a vertical axis, there can be both the valuation of space above the house and the earth beneath. Both sky fees and subsurface fees are volumetric insofar as they are measures and calculations of height and depth related to housing and housing construction land.

These volumetric valuations shape socioeconomic transitions and forms of social differentiation. For example, Zhang Lin moved into the Cherry Blossom resettlement complex after his village land was purchased for conservation. His corporatized village succeeded in obtaining a good price for their land. They also negotiated for sky fees and subsurface housing fees to be paid, not in the form of money, but as additional housing space in a new high-rise resettlement complex. Zhang's rural housing had substantial floor space and multiple stories. His compensation capital was substantially more than cases where subsurface housing fees and sky fees were not granted.

The dimensions and materials of his original village home were valuated and compensated in the form of resettlement housing space. Zhang's family decided to lease the extra units and collect monthly rents. Through the valuation of their village land and housing, which included sky fees and subsurface fees, they were compensated with multiple units in the resettlement complex. This facilitated their transition to urban high-rise life and rentier status as comparatively well-off

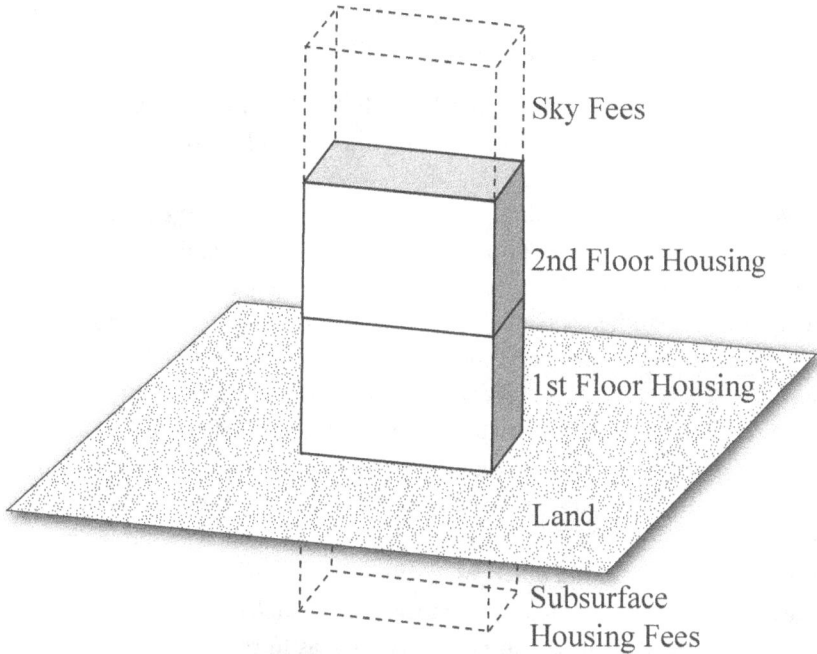

Sky Fees

2nd Floor Housing

1st Floor Housing

Land

Subsurface
Housing Fees

FIGURE 15.   Spatial rendering of volumetric forms of land and housing valuation.

resettlement complex landlords. Zhang and his family moved into riches by accumulating through the process of their own displacement.

Wearing glistening sunglasses and a blue Mao suit, Zhang lit a cigarette in the courtyard of the resettlement complex. He smiled looking up into the sun and said "I don't have a care in the world, I'm set for life." Altogether his family owned fifteen, one-hundred-square-meter apartments in the Cherry Blossom high-rise resettlement complex. They rented out more than half of the extra apartment units for an excess of 5,000 RMB a month (US$800).[22] This case shows how the vertical and volumetric valuation of rural spaces shaped livelihood transitions in relation to urban housing spaces. As Zhang's rural land and housing took the form of urban housing, his household transitioned from semi-proletarianized farmers to urban landlords. Zhang was not only happy to have *moved up* socioeconomically, but also spatially.

> We can't light incense in the apartments like we could in the village. But I am alright with that because these apartments are so modern and civilized. They have electricity and modern electrical outlets. My wife is in a wheelchair now. She uses the elevator to get in and out of the apartment, which is very convenient. The best part is that my children can

have a modern life and they don't have to bear the hardships [*chiku*] of toiling in the fields anymore.

Zhang commented at length about how his families' lives improved as they moved into high-rise resettlement housing. Not all ecological migrants experienced ecological migration as Zhang did, however.

Volumetric politics of valuation vary across sites. As does the distribution of compensation capital. Land ownership is ambiguous and underdefined in law, which makes the forms through which land is *valued* and *compensated* deeply political. Sky fees, when obtained, are distributed directly to the registered household because they are a form of compensation directly linked to personal housing ownership. However, village construction land is distributed for the purpose of home building to each household.[23] The distribution of subsurface housing fees, therefore, takes place through the village council and often behind closed doors. In some cases, subsurface housing land was compensated and dispersed across rural households. In other cases, there was no compensation for subsurface housing space. In still other cases, subsurface fees were granted, but the village council did not distribute the compensation capital, thereby marking a form of elite capture. If granted, but not distributed, as in the case of elite capture, already existing forms of class stratification become more pronounced. As these examples illustrate, volumetric politics shape social differentiation and uneven experiences of ecological migration. This is evident through a comparison with ecological migrants resettled under starkly different conditions. As their rural spaces became incorporated into conservation areas, undercompensated ecological migrants experienced downward socioeconomic trajectories.

The "refugee district" (*nanmin xiaoqu*) is the name residents gave to their resettlement community in North Kunming. Ecological migrants in the refugee district were compensated for land and housing jointly with just one apartment unit and monthly payments of 500 RMB (US$85) for twenty years. This monthly compensation is barely more than the national low-income welfare subsidy (*dibao*). Most of the people living in the refugee district resettlement complex moved there when their land was zoned for ecological protection. Each household, regardless of the number of family members, type of housing materials, or measures of rural housing space, was issued a fifty-square-meter unit in the resettlement complex. I met many families in the refugee district that lived in a single resettlement apartment unit with upward of ten family members.

"We live like dogs here. There is shit all over the place. The ground level is not maintained, the concrete walls are thin, and the ceilings are leaky. Everything here is of poor quality, and the elevators always break down," one resident exclaimed emphatically.

We pay a property management fee [*wuguanfei*] of 1,000 RMB a year, but it takes the management a long time to fix something. They only compensate us 500 RMB a month, and we have to pay 1,000 RMB for poor quality property management. In addition, if something breaks down in our apartment unit, like the toilet or if there is a problem with the sink, we have to pay a special repair fee [*zhuanxiufei*]. Our compensation is not even enough to cover the basic living expenses in the resettlement complex.

Tenants routinely waited months for repairs. Those living in the refugee district were particularly upset when talking about the conditions in which they lived and how village sociality changed after they moved into the high-rise resettlement complex.

Song Lan, a middle-aged ecological migrant, spoke about how she broke her ankle as she tried to walk out of a lopsided elevator. "The elevators don't stop flush with the floor. The floor surfaces and the elevator surfaces are all misshapen, with bumps and slants. They are not flat at all." Song, and others in the resettlement complex, were injured simply by exiting or entering their resettlement apartment units. Song talked about how she shared her single fifty-meter unit with her two sons, their wives, and their children.

Our village houses were so big and comfortable, who would want to move into a high-rise apartment? This is not enough space. Our lives totally changed since we moved. Here in the high-rise people don't care about you. In the village people said "hello" and would stop in the street to talk. Houses were open and you could come over anytime. Now people just look at you. But they don't care about you. Back in the village we had plenty of space. We could even rent out extra rooms. Before we were landlords—now we are slaves to housing rents [*women yiqian shi fangdong, xianzai women shi fangnu*]. And with all the apartment fees there is so much pressure for us all to work that we have to figure out special arrangements to take care of the babies. It is too much.

This household had six adults and two babies living in a fifty-square-meter unit on the twelfth floor—a domestic situation, which contrasts significantly with the spacious village home from which they moved.

Juxtaposing the case of Cherry Blossom resettlement complex landlords, who moved into riches, with ecological migrants in the refugee district, who moved into conditions of socioeconomic hardship and emotional stress, brings into sharp relief how volumetric politics matter. Not only does the juxtaposition highlight the role of volumetric politics in shaping uneven socioeconomic trajectories and social differentiation, but it additionally points to the domestic sphere as a site of exchange value. Uneven valuation and compensation along vertical axes were not the only ways that verticality mattered for those awaiting displacement. Many harbored fears of what life would be like in a high-rise resettlement apartment.

Fear of vertical living was prevalent across urbanizing villages, especially among elderly villagers. The more interviews I conducted in peri-urban villages and resettlement complexes, the more I heard elderly people talk about the specter of vertical life as a source of fear. Many elderly people feared being lost in the high-rise. They were afraid of being unable to find their housing unit in blocks of identical apartments. Many expressed fears of heights. Units close to the ground floor were highly sought after. Because of this, development institutions tried to use low units as an incentive to attract villagers to sign housing contracts early on in the process. Others were afraid of riding in elevators. They were as reluctant to trade *their* soil for *shared* concrete as they were to trade open streets for vertigo-inducing apartment windows.

These fears were not without basis. At one resettlement complex in North Kunming, six elderly residents died within the first month of moving in. An announcement from the residential apartment complex managers of "no discernable cause of death" catapulted this phenomenon into lived folklore. Villagers across the municipal region awaiting their move into high-rise resettlement apartments reimagined this story in their own words to me over and again. This collective reimagining and storytelling contributed to the psychological stress and anxiety of forfeiting village life for an uncertain future in an urban resettlement apartment. For many who made the move into resettlement complexes, anxieties remained as they struggled to transition into high-rise life.

Living in a high-rise resettlement complex reconfigures the material practices of daily life, especially for the elderly. While Zhang lauded the elevator that transports his wheelchair-bound wife to and from their apartment, others felt that navigating resettlement infrastructure was a challenging endeavor. I met an elderly woman who was repeatedly lost, wandering inside the resettlement complex. I asked which apartment unit she lived in to help her return home. "I don't know," she said. "My son brings me down to the courtyard, but I can't find my way back on my own. I wait here until he brings me back to my apartment later in the day." I met many more elderly people, who were brought down to the courtyard of the resettlement complex in the morning by their caretaker, picked up for lunch, brought back down for the afternoon, and escorted home in the evening. Unable to navigate the resettlement complex on their own, these elderly people's daily routines relied on the labor of others. Once retrieved, many returned to poorly constructed resettlement apartments.

FIGURE 16. A resettlement apartment complex for peri-urban ecological migrants. Photo by author.

The resettlement complexes where I conducted research exhibited significant infrastructural breakdowns and long-term stoppages in services. Gas, electricity, and elevators, for instance, were unreliable. Despite being newly built, resettlement complex infrastructures functioned poorly. Ecological migrants suggested this was because developers cut corners in effort to turn a profit. As a result, many resettlement apartments deteriorated quickly.

At the refugee district resettlement complex the elevators were constantly breaking down. Electricity outages were common. And gas was intermittently shut off for weeks at a time. Yu Liang, an octogenarian ecological migrant, lived in the refugee district resettlement complex on the sixteenth floor. When the electricity was out or the elevator broken, the only way to get out of the building involved walking fifteen flights of stairs. Those same stairs were her only way back up to her unit. At night she illuminated the dark stairways with a flashlight for safety. As she talked with me in the refugee district courtyard about the apartment infrastructure, she recounted how just that week, after a trip to the market and a slog up to the sixteenth floor, she was stuck without electricity or gas, vegetables and raw pork in hand. With no gas to cook, without an operating refrigerator to keep the meat cold, and without a working elevator, her only option was to walk back down and look for an alternative place to cook.

Temporalities of Displacement and Resettlement

After we finished eating lunch, Li invited me to visit her aquaculture project in Yiliang. And we made plans for a time that would work for us both. I followed up to ask if she had any idea when her resettlement housing may be completed. "I am not sure," Li said. "But they are probably delaying the housing contract and moving us out of our village homes until they finish the resettlement apartments. This way they can avoid paying 'transition fees' [*guodufei*].[24] It might be several more years before we receive a housing contract." Transition fees are monies paid in monthly installments for the time between when villagers move out of their village homes and into resettlement housing. This volumetric measure is tabulated in relation to the square meter housing space of the village home for the duration of time that elapses between when rural housing is purchased and rural people move into resettlement housing. Its purpose is to mitigate interim housing expenses.

In Li's case, she awaited resettlement housing while retaining ownership of her original village home. In other cases, rural housing is demolished before resettlement housing is built. There can be a significant amount of time between when peri-urban villagers sell their rural home and when they move into resettlement housing. Some ecological migrants have years to grapple with becoming landless peasants (*shidi nongmin*), as they occasionally refer to themselves.

Transition fees are another form of volumetric valuation that effect uneven socioeconomic trajectories of displacement. For example, one villager in Chengdu whose original rural housing space measured 242 square meters was contractually awarded transition fees at a rate of 10 RMB per square meter. They received transition fees of 2,420 RMB (US$400) per month as they awaited the completion of resettlement housing. In this case, the villager waited four years, thereby accumulating over 100,000 RMB. Transition fees were paid by the development institution tasked with constructing resettlement housing. The development institution was contractually obligated to pay transition fees each month until ecological migrants moved into their resettlement housing. Yet, analogous to the other forms of volumetric valuation discussed in this chapter, transition fees are politically contestable.

In one peri-urban village, houses were razed soon after they were zoned within an ecological protection area. Villagers awaiting the completion of resettlement housing initially received transition fees of 14 RMB per square meter each month in relation to their original housing floor space and infrastructural materials. After two years of waiting for the resettlement complex to be finished, a stipulation in their housing contract doubled this figure. Many of these peri-urban villagers had five floors of original village housing space and rented out the extra floors. Those who had multiple floors were given transition fees of 2,000 RMB per floor, a flat rate. Households with five floors initially received transition fees of 10,000 RMB (US$1,600) per month. After two years, the stipulation in the contract became active and the new figure for transition fees became 20,000 RMB (US$3,200) a month. These volumetric valuation and compensation practices sharpened social differentiation between villagers that originally owned multiple floors of village housing compared to those that did not. The valuation of original village housing space through transition fees enriched villagers who were already comparatively well off before ecological migration processes began.

One month, without warning, the development institution stopped paying transition fees. Ecological migrants had to begin paying for their own accommodation without contractually obligated financial support. Although the development institution owed back payments of transition fees, they demanded that residents pick up the apartment keys (*jie yaoshi*)—a process that establishes they have moved into the resettlement complex. Ecological migrants were concerned that doing so would abdicate the development institution from paying overdue transition fees. Soon-to-be fully resettled ecological migrants found additional move-in surprises. If they wanted a parking spot, for instance, they would have to purchase it. The development institution began selling parking spaces in the resettlement complex to residents for exorbitant prices. Alternatively, they could rent parking spots at twenty- to thirty-year intervals at a prorated rate for the duration of the lease. For many awaiting resettlement and overdue transition fees, this was the last straw.

In March 2017, a group of roughly three hundred peri-urban ecological migrants took to the streets of Kunming to protest. Police arrested protestors as they mobilized from the resettlement complex to the steps of a municipal government bureau office. Within several days all were released. But there was still no resolution. After another month passed and another protest drew wider attention, the developer relented, offering a portion of the overdue transition fees and promising the remainder in the future. I went to the resettlement apartment units to talk with ecological migrants about their decisions to move into the high-rise resettlement apartment. After protesting and receiving a portion of the overdue transition fees from the developer, some who accepted the keys and moved into the apartment felt assured they would eventually receive the remainder.

Others, however, were upset about more move-in surprises. For instance, they had to pay a rental fee for the elevator to move their belongings into the apartment. Although the fee was a mere 10 RMB a day, the developer demanded residents pay for two months, even if the move lasted only a few days. Some discovered, as they moved in, that their resettlement housing was not yet finished. The gas was still not connected to the apartment buildings. So they could not cook. Those that agreed to move in at this stage were few. One resettlement migrant said he felt like he was living in a "ghost apartment." "Our dead ancestors are crawling out of the earth and there still aren't enough bodies to fill these empty resettlement apartments," he exclaimed. The standoff between those who had yet to move in and the developer remained unresolved.

In cases where housing compensation was determined per household, reconstituting a single household into multiple households, even temporarily, could increase compensation. To maximize compensation capital, some families adopted tactics of temporary familial separation.[25] Couples who strategically reconstituted their household through temporary divorce, referred to the process as "fake divorces" (*jia lihun*). Ecological migrants that used this tactic were able to receive additional resettlement housing. Many rented out the additional units or sold them and lived in one unit as a "divorced" family, thereby accumulating by redefining the familial conditions of their own displacement and resettlement.

After a period of maintaining two households, couples often planned to remarry. For many, the legal divorce proceedings were worth the additional housing they received as compensation. Though for Xun Yang, things worked out differently. After deciding on a fake divorce to maximize compensation, both her and her former husband were compensated as individual households. Each household was provided with their own housing unit. Living in the resettlement complex apartment was the first time in Xun's life that she had a place of her own. She found that she enjoyed her new sense of freedom. What, at first, she imagined as a temporary arrangement to maximize compensation, took on new longevity. Ultimately, she decided to end the relationship with her former husband. For ecological migrants like Xun, moving into urban resettlement housing offered newfound freedoms from gendered expectations of marriage and a sizable economic boost. Xun not only accumulated through strategically navigating the volumetric politics of displacement but found new individual freedoms.

In contrast, ecological migrants who moved into the refugee district found new financial constraints in which their life spans figured centrally. Six hundred RMB (US$90) per month became the new sum of compensation for both land and housing after their collective protests repeatedly shut down key intersections during peak traffic. Each resettlement migrant continues to receive 600 RMB a month for twenty years unless they die within the twenty-year compensation period. Postmortem compensation goes to the next of kin and the amount is half of what it would be if the original family member were still alive. Postmortem compensation cuts literally reduce by half the amount of remaining compensation capital on death. Those born after the move into the refugee district receive no form of compensation for what would have been their rural land.

For ecological migrants living in the refugee district, time is money. For the youngest of them, time would have been money. For those no longer living, time was money. As refugee district ecological migrants transition from life to death, their compensation is literally cut in half. Born after the move, and there is no compensation. For those in the refugee district, socioeconomic hardships and emotional loss accompany both death and a new urban life.

* * *

As I sat between Li and Tao at their new fish husbandry project in Yiliang, fishing pole in hand in the summer of 2017, I listened to Li talk about her hopes embodied in places both old and new. She wondered how her village house would be valued and compensated. She hoped it could be exchanged for a substantial amount of resettlement housing space. Li still did not have a housing contract. She spoke about her new entrepreneurial project and interim home. She hoped she could keep the formula for maintaining water oxygenation at the proper levels to raise another lucrative fish harvest. Li reflected sentimentally about her home back in the village. It was the home in which she was born and raised. A home that would soon be razed. Perhaps it would be turned into a pile of rubble or bedrock for vegetation. Or maybe it would be underwater as an extension to the treatment wetland, or the site of new villa-style housing.

We caught fish, all too small, and threw them back into the water. We put a loach in a small plastic bottle for Akira to observe. Unsatisfied, she demanded to fish herself. We gave her a pole, and she sat down to try her luck fishing next to

Li's interim house between the fishing ponds. I looked at the structure they had built. It was a ten-foot-high stack of concrete blocks and a tin roof. Two rooms: one for cooking, one for sleeping. Drywall interiors were left blank. One black chair. No fridge. A hand-action well pump provided water. A red door locked from the outside with an oversized padlock. No protector deities marked the door.

As we fished, we watched a funeral procession move slowly down the street carrying the deceased. A blown-up portrait accompanied the casket along with flowers, white robes, and a white shroud. This was a new village for Li. She didn't know the deceased. The procession was long. As it passed, we wondered aloud who the dead had been in life. Deafening fireworks chased the spirits away. We watched the procession go by without rising from our chairs.

There was quiet for a moment. "This aquaculture project has to be successful," Li said, finally breaking the silence. I sensed concern in her voice. She invested most of her compensation capital into this enterprise. If it failed to be profitable, her land's value repurposed as an aquaculture project in a new village would be lost. She would still have the kiosk in the treatment wetlands. She could potentially run a business out of her home, Li mused, at least for a while. But it was a home with a countdown to demolition. It was a home no longer part of her daily life. A symbol of the transitional process, it was locked and dormant. Each time I walked past, as I went to interview others in her village, I felt a palpable sense of the slow disintegration of village lifeways. The making of an ecological protection area had brought on a multiyear process of transition for peri-urban ecological migrants like Li. First land was gone. Her labors adapted. Her home was next. With land no longer tilled, laboring bodies dispersed, home vacant—a village emptied.

As I listened to Li and others like her, however, it became evident that rural life and rural spaces didn't simply disappear in the wake of ecological protection zoning and state efforts to urbanize rural people. Instead, volumetric politics of valuation and compensation are key to urban-rural transformational processes that include the reorganization of labor, livelihoods, and built environments. Rural spaces take on exchange value and new material forms in relation to what they once were, how they are valuated, and how rural people politically mobilize and utilize compensation capital. Ecological migrants, like Li, remake their lives through the valuative terrain of volumetric politics. Those who successfully navigate these spatiotemporal politics, to varying degrees, move into riches as they accumulate through their own displacement. Yet, as this chapter demonstrates, the trajectories of peri-urban ecological migrants are highly uneven.

The following chapter turns to questions of how unequal social positions shape villagers' access to rural spaces in transition and the spatial production of rural aesthetics. How do peri-urban villagers navigating displacement draw on a rural-ecological aesthetic for their own socioeconomic benefit? What roles do class, ethnicity, and gender play in how they do so? The next chapter engages these questions through two figures navigating displacement from opposite ends of the same village.

RURAL REDUX

At the border of an urban ecological protection area, a sign stood in front of a long gravel road advertising a restaurant called Green Fields. Birds of paradise lined one side of the road while *zhongshansha* (*Taxodium zhongshansha*), a flood-tolerant cypress tree native to China's east coast, lined the other. The trees led to a high-gated entrance of a two-story walled factory complex. The sign described Green Fields as an ecological garden (*shengtaiyuan*) and *nongjiale*. Nongjiale is a term that refers to restaurants, guesthouses, and entertainment venues that provide rural-themed fare and experiences.[1] Although highly variable in size and character, they draw on rural tropes in their cuisine, decor, and services.[2] They cater predominantly to urbanites, whose disposable income increased significantly over the 1990s and early 2000s and whose nostalgic desire to experience rural life intensified in the wake of rural-to-urban migration and urbanization.[3] The industry is fueled not only by a pervasive sense that traditional ways of life are disappearing but also that rural life is closer to nature. Through direct experiences with the rural, popular imaginaries hold, urbanites can reanimate their connection with nature and ameliorate modern urban malaise. Growing in number since the 1990s, nongjiale are common across peri-urban areas where the city and countryside meet and intermingle. Many nongjiale operate within the domestic spaces of rural homes.

Green Fields was spacious with a private road that leads to two-story L-shaped buildings adjacent to the banks of Kunming's Lake Dian. Dining areas were filled with tables cordoned off by intricately laced waist-high bamboo, which facilitated a bit of privacy but were open enough to allow larger parties to converse across sections. A spacious room within the gated entrance was filled with art made from natural objects. Rocks with anthropomorphic forms and sedimentary features were placed next to a large Guanyin statue carved from wood. The L-shaped buildings merged with an awning of green foliage to cover open-air mah-jongg tables shaded by trellises. A pond next to the tables was stocked with fish. Guests could fish and have their catch prepared according to order. Several long wooden fishing boats rested between the fishing pond and dilapidated factory buildings. Generations ago, these boats housed whole families across Lake Dian.

The first person I encountered was Bo Ximing, the garrulous owner of Green Fields. The afternoon we met, he invited me in for tea. And over the years, we drank tea and talked about how he transformed the remains of a run-down township-village enterprise (TVE) factory into the nongjiale—Green Fields. Through our conversations about his roles in village government and rural industry, I learned how he acquired the postindustrial rural infrastructure and land on which he lived in leisure.

Outside the gates of Green Fields, footpaths led into a manicured treatment wetland park. On the other side of the ecological protection area, near the southern border of the newly built treatment wetland was another nongjiale. An unfenced free-standing concrete house supported thin red characters reading simply—"nongjiale." I first met the proprietor, Wang Jiaqiang, as he was cleaning fishing nets and a two-pronged inflatable fishing vessel. He invited me to his nongjiale, an invitation extended widely as part of his adapted trade. A middle-aged multigenerational peasant, Wang lost access to his farmland when it was zoned for ecological protection. Without farmland, Wang transformed his house into a nongjiale and became a purveyor of rural-themed leisure services. Part of his daily routine involved walking through the conservation area just outside his home to attract guests.

Wang's home, roughly twenty meters from the banks of Lake Dian, was snugly set between two village houses. A narrow walkway between led to tanks where he kept fish caught from the lake. To the left, en route to an open pit-squat toilet were small cages for ducks and chickens, recently made illegal by prohibitions on rearing animals in the conservation area. To the right, inside the red metal front door, was a set of concrete stairs. Underneath the stairs, was a large glass-door refrigeration unit where customers could choose vegetables for their dishes. A wooden steamer and a large wok filled the kitchen. Three patched couches were seating for two dining tables upstairs. A third table stood in the corner next to a TV, on the wall were paintings of agricultural landscapes, and in another part of the room two mah-jongg tables were separated by strings of hanging beads. We laid out Wang's fishing nets to dry in the sliver of sunlight streaming through the surrounding houses as we talked. Wang explained that he turned his house into a nongjiale soon after his land was purchased to make an urban ecological protection area. But running a nongjiale was not enough to support his family financially. Despite recent moratoriums on fishing in Lake Dian, Wang continued to fish daily. Fishing remained an important part of his livelihood. He sold fresh fish from his home and ran a nongjiale specializing in rural dishes.

The contrast between the form and function of Wang and Bo's respective nongjiale is stark. Both exemplify a rural-ecological sublime, an aesthetic wherein people portray rural natures in relation to ecology. Bo and Wang are both aware of how to produce aesthetic forms that tap into popular imaginaries of rural nature. Yet there are key differences in how they produce a rural-ecological sublime, the means through which they do so, and what the "rural" signifies to each.

Since Bo's and Wang's agricultural land became part of an ecological protection area, former agrarian spaces became inundated with tourists. In the midst of this dramatic change, aesthetic forms related to rural and ecological natures figured centrally in how Bo and Wang refashioned their respective livelihoods, built environments, and senses of self. Their spatial practices navigating access to rural land and infrastructure, however, were highly uneven. Detailing the intersection of rural aesthetics and social difference, this chapter sheds light on differentiated practices of navigating displacement from opposite poles of the same village.

In this chapter, I draw on interviews, observations, oral histories, and photovoice to explore the aesthetic spatialization of difference in landscapes of rural dispossession.[4] Bo Ximing is an elite villager and part of what could be thought of as the capitalist employer class. Wang Jiaqiang is a multigenerational peasant.[5] In highlighting figures differentially positioned on a class spectrum, my intention is not to reproduce a structuralist reading of class or to reify class categories, but instead to highlight aesthetic spatializations of social difference and socioeconomic inequality. Through juxtaposing Bo and Wang's spatial practices, I show how, within differentiated categories of displacement, there are divergent ways of accessing space, mobilizing aesthetics, and remembering and re-creating rural pasts. Each figure represents different senses of the rural past. Their spatial practices emplace versions of the rural in landscapes of uneven displacement.

Differentiated Aesthetic Emplacement

Pierre Bourdieu, writing in the context of the mid-twentieth-century French peasantry, describes what he calls the "em-peasanted" body, "burdened" with traces of rural attitudes that come from living a life of agrarian labor.[6] For Bourdieu, class is visible in bodily comportment, in actions and inactions. For him, the "slow" peasant gait and "lumbering" bodies constitute "techniques of the body."[7] Importantly, these embodied identifiers of difference are visible to others. He intuits this through observations of dance culture in the French countryside. Aging French peasant bachelors don't dance, unless asked out of pity. Unfamiliar with modern "urban" dances, their opportunities to meet women are stifled, thereby, contributing to rising rates of bachelorhood. More to the point, Bourdieu argues that peasants' "wretched consciousness" of their bodies is the manifestation of acute awareness of class difference. Their rural class awareness is indelibly expressed in embodied actions and the inability to dance in urban styles. For Bourdieu, class difference is written into aesthetic forms of peasant bodies. Life prospects bear the imprints of, and are therefore structured by, this internalization of difference.

In this chapter, I depart from Bourdieu's reading of rural class aesthetics as an embodied burden from which one cannot escape.[8] Instead of being structurally emplaced in a way that incapacitates agency and prompts ennui for rural men, as Bourdieu contends, villagers in China actively harness rural aesthetics for their own ends. China's villagers are acutely aware of the value in producing rural aesthetics. And villagers often portray the rural and ecological in relation to one another. This is often expressed as "primitive ecology" or "original ecology" (*yuanshi shengtai* or *yuanshengtai*), which I discuss below. Rural citizens draw on aesthetic tropes unevenly, in the context of already differentiated positionalities. Villagers' active production of rural aesthetics not only reproduces social differences, but also contributes to the differentiated emplacement of rural-ecological aesthetics in landscapes of rural displacement.

In previous chapters, I illustrated how ecology is deeply political. Ecology is embroiled in the politics of scientific knowledge production, state socio-environmental planning, and eco-developmental aesthetics. Shared aesthetic senses within state scientific and planning circles, I demonstrated, are crucial to uneven power relations and the spatiotemporal politics of displacement. But the ways state scientists and planners configure ecology and rural natures are not the only things that matter. Rural people navigating displacement actively draw on ecology and rural natures in the reorganization of their livelihoods and daily lives. And, importantly, they deploy symbolic elements for their own socioeconomic interests. In doing so, they reflexively reproduce aesthetic forms that look and feel rural for tourist consumption, thereby reifying rural difference for consumers seeking authentic rural experiences.[9] Consequently, rural people's spatial practices reify urban-rural difference—a form of social differentiation key to state governance.

Geographer D. Asher Ghertner, drawing on Michel Foucault and Jacque Rancière, theorizes aesthetics as a shared distribution of senses crucial to the operation of government. Ghertner illustrates how state-sponsored aesthetic symbols resonate within segments of Indian society that internalize and imbue them with meaning. He refers to the forms of governance emerging from the internalization of shared communal senses as "aesthetic governmentality."[10] I illustrated in earlier chapters how eco-developmental aesthetics are a crucial mode through which governmental power operates in China. Aesthetic repertoires surrounding ecology, however, are not merely produced through the top-down state scientific planning gaze. Nor are aesthetic regimes simply internalized by state subjects. Instead within China's rural population (a heterogenous social group), symbols of rurality and ecology are differentially imagined, given meaning, and deployed—at times in ways that reinforce state logics of governance but often in ways that counter eco-developmental logics. Through individual and collective counter-conduct, that is, actions that counter state efforts to govern social conduct, rural people aesthetically emplace signifiers of social difference in landscapes of rural dispossession.

It is to difference within aesthetic imaginaries that I draw attention. Geographer Brandi Summers illustrates how forms of difference are reproduced through seemingly banal practices of neighborhood aesthetics. Summers, drawing on bell hooks, theorizes aesthetics as a "way of inhabiting space, a particular location, a way of looking and becoming."[11] With this conceptual grounding, Summers coins the term "Black aesthetic emplacement" to describe ways in which modes of representing Blackness are operationalized and accrue value within the built environment of Washington, DC.[12] Drawing on Summers's insistence that imaginations of authenticity are integral to landscape aesthetics and the uneven distribution of value, and Ghertner's insight that shared aesthetic senses are essential to the operation of power, I argue that rural people's differentiated spatial practices emplace aesthetic forms of difference in landscapes of rural dispossession.

I propose differentiated aesthetic emplacement as spatial practices that aesthetically express social difference, and reproduce inequality and uneven power relations. In this chapter, I consider differentiated aesthetic emplacement through two kinds of aesthetic forms. The first is built environments and infrastructures such as houses and factories. The second is cultural goods and services, such as cuisine, music, art objects, and embodied performances. The spatial production of aesthetic forms reflects social differences, class conflicts, and contradictions. Aesthetic forms become animating forces of power relations through sensorial experiences of representations (e.g., portraits, images), lived spaces (e.g., labor, houses, cuisine), and imagined spaces (e.g., futurist projections, nostalgic memories).[13] In my account, I emphasize how the production of space entails continuous aesthetic reproductions of difference. Highlighting how aesthetic forms reflect social inequalities, however, is insufficient. Instead, I aim to illustrate how differentiated aesthetic emplacement reflects uneven power relations, differentiated aesthetic sensibilities, and uneven socioeconomic trajectories.

Uneven social position figures centrally in how rural people access space in post–land acquisition villages. Bo and Wang's class differences, for instance, inform how each imagine and reproduce rural-ecological aesthetics. Socialist-era class positions, as I demonstrate below, shape reform-era labor relations and unequal access to rural spaces in transition.[14] Despite state efforts to urbanize the rural population, intrarural difference and multigenerational class legacies remain. These sedimented differences shape how rural people are able or unable to capitalize on so-called communal properties, such as rural land and infrastructure. Social inequalities permeate these spatial expressions.

Inequality in China is intimately tied to the social production of urban and rural difference. Because hegemonic discourses associate urban modernity with the Han Chinese majority, there are myriad conflations of rurality with backwardness and ethnic minorities. For instance, it is common, though inaccurate within popular discourse and academic scholarship, to associate ethnic minorities with poverty. Analogously, scholarship on urban-rural difference often revolves around the politics of hukou registration, a geographical control system that demarcates whether citizens have access to rural land use rights or urban social welfare benefits. While "urban" (nonagricultural) or "rural" (agricultural) hukou status has historically shaped socioeconomic differences, such as access to land, social services, and job opportunities, it doesn't fully account for the social production of difference between urban and rural people or socioeconomic differences within rural populations. In accounting for these dynamics, I consider relations between class, identity, place, and gender as always entangled with processes of social differentiation, which find material expression through aesthetic forms and practices.[15] The ways rural people produce rural-ecological aesthetics are indelibly shaped by and reflect their uneven subject positionalities. Moreover, uneven subject positionalities are significant to the ways memory, longing, and representation are evoked and aesthetically emplaced.

"This Land Is Mine Now"

Bo Ximing enjoyed boasting about his family. As we sat in the tearoom of Green Fields, he poured tea and began to talk about generations of family leadership with the booming confidence of one accustomed to public speaking. "My ancestors served as village representatives to the Qing state," he exclaimed proudly. "During the late Qing, my great-great grandfather (*gaozufu*) was a scholar and gentry in our village in Dali. This position helped make us relatively well off." During the Sino-Japanese war that bled into World War II, Bo's family moved from the nearby Bai ethnic minority capital of Dali to a village near Kunming, the provincial capital. Bo was the third generation of leaders in this village. Arriving in 1949, just after the formation of the People's Republic of China, his family was still relatively new to this village. They brought with them substantial family holdings and built political connections within the newly empowered Communist Party. Bo's father was part of the educated youth sent down to the countryside (*xiaxiangzhiqing*) during Mao's campaigns and the anti-right struggle of 1957 (*fanyoudouzheng*). Despite familial ties to landed gentry in Dali, Bo's parents were able to join the Chinese Communist Party early on. His mother fared well during the early socialist period, becoming a leading village cadre. She held leadership positions in the village production team for decades.

Bo, stout with greying hair, came of age as an educated Maoist youth, the name associated with a 1970s national social movement of young people who returned to the village to remake the countryside (*zhiqing huixiang*). Near the end of the Maoist era, Bo obtained a leadership role in the village collective. Immediately on graduating from high school in 1976, he returned to his village and took a position as general secretary of the village production unit. His high school education gave him skills and the political capital to stand out among his fellow villagers. The pedigree of an educated Maoist youth qualified him for village leadership. This background, accompanied by the fact that his mother was a party official, secured him a leading position on the village production team. As general secretary, he oversaw the village production team finances and public welfare. At nineteen years of age, in addition to his role as general secretary, he became the village headman, a position he served in for seventeen years.

By 1980, Bo became the local branch secretary of the communist youth league. In the mid-1980s, when reform-era pro-rural policies came into effect, he became the production team leader (*shengchan duizhang*) spearheading a new township-village enterprise (TVE) partnered with a state-owned enterprise (SOE) to produce agricultural products. Economic alliances between TVEs and SOEs became the backbone of rural industrialization from the 1980s to the mid-1990s.[16] Bo held that position for nearly twenty years, up until 1999. The TVE produced agricultural goods for domestic consumption and export. Fish from Lake Dian were the only product that the factory produced throughout Bo's tenure. Various products including rice, garlic shoots, and cucumber became popular in the late 1980s with the bulk of exports heading to Japan and South Korea. By the late 1990s, flowers became more profitable. September 1999 marked the end of rice production in this village. Instead, they produced flowers for Dounan Market, the "largest floral market in Asia" with exports to Japan and the Netherlands. The village TVE entered the global flower trade with Bo at the helm. It maintained consistent profits over this time and established a cooperative relationship with a state-owned enterprise for exporting products. However, by the late 1990s their SOE partner was on the verge of bankruptcy. In addition, the TVE's economic success brought political unrest in the village.

Bo noticed that by late 1999, in the wake of the TVE economic boom and growing economic inequality in the village, villagers were growing jealous of the profits he earned as the production leader. His fellow villagers pressured him to step down. The TVE had earned more than US$1 million in 1998 from the international flower market and exporting dehydrated vegetables to Taiwan, Japan, and Korea. "It was as if everyone's eyes were clouded with jealousy [*dajia yanjing youhongbing chulai*]," he recalled. At first, Bo resisted calls to step down. He eventually ceded under pressure from other members of the village council. Bo insisted that his assets were less than what other villagers assumed. Instead of gaining financial capital through his position, he insisted that he had accumulated "intangible assets" (*wuxing zichan*) that were larger than the financial holdings of the township-village enterprise. Bo was referring to the political connections (*guanxi*) between business and party-state necessary for state-directed capitalist business operations within reform-era China.[17] Without Bo's intangible assets, TVE production did not last long.

> They asked me to go, but I told them that they need me otherwise the company is going to be embarrassed. They didn't believe me . . . they even offered me 300,000 RMB to step down. But I said I don't want your money. I am staying. I will even stay here and be a door guard. But they didn't give me a chance. . . . They dug a hole and buried me in it. Within three years our company, which had 9.8 million in assets when I left, was bankrupt. The state-run enterprise relationship also fell apart, as it went bankrupt. Those villagers were like little wild pigs. They did not understand how to do anything.[18]

At that time, Bo wanted to stay in the village, but under political pressure from villagers to leave he moved to Dali temporarily. In his absence, the TVE went bankrupt and fell into ruin. The TVE leveraged its shares in the form of 26 mu (4.3 acres) of land contiguous with TVE production facilities. The debts from the SOE partner were absolved by the national bank, but private shareholder debt remained. The TVE mortgaged the land to the bank as collateral. As the collective enterprise went bankrupt, the bank possessed the village land held as collateral. But the land was not enough to absolve the village collective enterprise of the debt that remained. The bank withheld the village land and TVE infrastructure, including factory buildings and equipment. Over the next few years, the land remained unused, and the infrastructure fell into disrepair.

In 2004, Bo returned to the village. He leased the land and purchased the TVE infrastructure from the bank. He did so by leveraging his savings from decades of working as production team leader, village headman, and TVE director, in addition to a small bank loan. He signed a contract with the village collective that allowed the remainder of the debt owed to the TVE's private shareholders to be passed on to him. This facilitated the return of land to the village collective that was held as collateral by the bank. The land was immediately leased to Bo. He thereby acquired the TVE infrastructure and land previously held in debt. The village council agreed to this arrangement, in part, because it alleviated the TVE's debts. Bo discussed this process as bringing the money from the TVE back to the village (*gongsi de qian wo laihuan*). Through these means, Bo returned to the village and gained control of the dilapidated factory infrastructure, as well as the land surrounding it.

> This land is mine now. I own it because I took on the debt. If the state decides to appropriate this piece of land, I can claim personal interest on the asset [*lixi*], calculate the capital that I invested, and be compensated according to the current market prices of land. When I get compensated, I will consult with everybody [in the village]. If I am kind, I will take a portion and give the collective a portion. If I am not feeling kind, I will first take more for myself and give a smaller portion to the collective.[19]

As Bo recounted this to me, he was the only villager with licit access to rural land. All others had lost access to their agricultural land as it was zoned within an ecological protection area and transformed into a treatment wetland. Bo's class positionality facilitated his continued access to land and infrastructure. The economic and political capital he acquired through his leadership positions in the TVE and village government facilitated his territorialization of rural land and postindustrial infrastructure.

Despite this, Bo considered himself a relatively modest and benevolent village leader. He maintained that he did not earn much as a village headman even as he held the position through the 1990s. However, he is quick to critique the current village council, which he claimed, is leveraging their positions to amass wealth, multiple houses, and "wives." In highlighting what he characterized as an immoral trend in rural government leadership, Bo portrayed himself as a champion of village interests. As he recalled his own efforts as a village leader, he became nostalgic for rural life he felt to be gone. He bemoaned the Chinese state for rapidly urbanizing rural China:

> [China] has ran toward two things. First, we ran into communism and now we are running into urbanization. Our development has become all about privatization, where individuals take on all the responsibilities for themselves. Now we are running into the era of urbanization and I am hanging on to its back leg. . . . "Urbanize the village" [*nongcun chengshihua*] "urbanize the peasantry" [*nongmin shiminhua*]—what is this urbanizing of the village? It's the beginning of the second war on steel![20] Why are our state representatives so corrupt? It is connected to the decline of the peasant. Under Mao, through efforts to build socialism, and during the time of overturning class relations [*fanshen*], policies reflected the party's service to the people. This has all changed. Now they reflect money worship [*baijinzhuyi*].[21]

Bo was critical of what he considered to be new directions in state-led development and the shift from glorifying the peasantry to urbanizing the rural population. Embedded in his critique is nostalgia for how the village used to be and how he imagined it to be under his leadership. Critical of a nation "running into urbanization," Bo imaged the rural past as inseparable from his own. In his memory, Bo exhibited benevolent leadership that he associated with the socialist and early postsocialist government. His departure from village-level political leadership coincided with the moral deterioration of government.

The irony of Bo's critique was thick as we sat in the plush grounds of Green Fields. Bo established Green Fields in 2004. It since became his primary home. But he maintained his second home in Dali. His capacity to obtain the bankrupt TVE infrastructure and rural construction land where it stood was due to his class position and political contacts. His financial and "intangible" assets propelled an upward socioeconomic trajectory experienced by few rural people. Even after taking on the remainder of the village debt, Bo claimed he no longer needed to worry about making money. Aside from the sign in front of his *nongjiale*, Bo did not advertise. He hired a full-time staff to service customers. In the absence of customers, the staff cooked for Bo and his family. Bo claimed that he had enough wealth to be able to maintain Green Fields in his retirement from village affairs regardless of whether it ever became profitable.

Legacies of class difference and political position are central to rural elite territorialization and repurposing of rural spaces in transition. These legacies, in the aesthetic register of bell hooks, condition the possibilities for spatial practices and ways of inhabiting space. I continue to illustrate how histories of social difference matter to people navigating rural spaces in transition by juxtaposing Bo with Wang, a multigenerational peasant without party affiliation.

Fishing for Leisure Capital

Wang Jiaqiang's daily work is rhythmic. He wakes up well before sunrise and paddles out on a small boat to drop fishing nets. After returning for breakfast, he enters the treatment wetlands just outside his home to entice early morning tourists to come to his nongjiale.

The first time we met in the summer of 2015, he had already returned from fishing. Tall with dark black hair and a strong build, he spoke with a metered cadence. Wang had the ability to make immediate connections with total strangers—key to attracting customers. After making the rounds through the wetlands, Wang boarded his six-foot, army-green pontoon raft and paddled out to check and reposition his nets. He returned for an early lunch. After eating quickly, he returned to the ecological protection area to invite potential customers to his home. Wang approached tourists resting or walking along the artificial beach in the ecological site to tell them about his nongjiale. Lunchtime was crucial. The lunch hour usually had the largest number of tourists in the ecological protection zone. And many came intending to try local rural cuisine.

During our meetings over the years, I occasionally accompanied him as he talked with tourists. He showed them photos of his house and talked about the "rural" and "ecological" dishes that they could enjoy there. If he met people on the side of the beach close to his house, he would point to the nongjiale sign on his roof. Despite the proximity, it was a daily struggle to get people to come inside. When I was with Wang, he would be sure to assert that foreigners, like me, really enjoyed his food. Wang hyperbolized that I was a customer who came every week. He took out his phone to display photos he took of my daughter Akira and I eating in his nongjiale—representational proof to potential customers. Then he would scroll through pictures of us accompanying him on his fishing boat to check the nets. These were communicative tools in his repertoire of spatial practices to make a living without access to agricultural land.

It was a challenge for Wang to attract customers because of the intense competition from other service providers. Just outside of what remained of Wang's village was a line of store fronts and nongjiale restaurants. The land was now controlled by the proprietary owner of the ecological protection area (see chapter 3). The proprietary owner leased out commercial spaces in the protection area for restaurants and kiosks. The spatial agglomeration of service providers attracted tourists to stores and restaurants conveniently located together. Like Wang, these nongjiale advertised "rural specialties, ecological foods and authentic experiences." Wang employed multiple strategies to maintain a livelihood without access to land, including selling rural food and services through his home, selling fish to tourists on-site and at the local market, offering boat rides, as well as "traditional" fishing excursions on Lake Dian. Wang walked the beach to peddle his leisure services daily.

One stormy day, when the lake was too choppy for fishing and no tourists were in the wetlands, Wang drew a map that explained the challenge of attracting guests to his nongjiale. It displayed his house in the top left corner, below which was his neighbor's home. Between his neighbor's house and an entrance to the ecological protection area was a pop-up food stall. The map showed intravillage competition for leisure capital as individuals used their homes and the spaces surrounding them to serve tourists. Pointing to the map, Wang explained that in between his nongjiale and the ecological protection area, his neighbor built a kiosk to sell rural foods, such as bean noodles (fensi). The stand had a large tent that provided shade. Importantly for Wang, the stall was in front of his neighbor's house, between the treatment wetlands and Wang's house, such that one needed to walk directly through the food stall to arrive at his nongjiale. Many stopped there. Wang lamented that his neighbor's stall and tables were blocking customers who might otherwise patronize his nongjiale. The map highlighted competition between villagers to attract tourists along the interstices of the village and ecological protection area.

Akira and I joined tourists on several of Wang's fishing excursions. On one excursion, Wang hoisted his pontoon raft onto the port bow of a red six-meter metal boat, preparing to set out. The hull was shaped like a Rodney boat, high sided and flat bottomed. A green single-person raft lay against the port bow. Seats were fashioned from three wood planks running gunnel to gunnel. Akira sat next to another child in the middle. Standing and directing the boat with a long poll, Wang maneuvered from the shallows into deeper waters. Once in deeper waters, he started a handheld motor steering the broadside of the hull into crushing waves.

Algae-bloom-green water droplets shot into the boat, splashing our faces. We careened toward buoys that indicated the position of fishing nets a hundred yards offshore from an artificial beach in the treatment wetlands. Wang turned the motor off. He dropped anchor and walked to the front of the boat instructing the tourists to sit tight. Wang had already checked the nets at 7:00 a.m. This was the second time checking the nets that day and the tourists were eager to see how "traditional" fishing was done. After dropping anchor, he moved the dual pronged raft into the water. With waiters on, he dangled his feet over the center board and rowed the small boat to the floating buoys. Tourists looked on from the boat and the sands of the nearby beach. Wang pulled the net out slowly inspecting it for fish. Nothing. He dropped it and paddled slowly to the next. Occasionally, he would hold a fish up and smile triumphantly back at the boat before placing it in a bucket. He was sure to adopt the pose long enough for tourists to snap photographs of him in action. In embodied performances of labor, like these, Wang inhabited space in a starkly different way than Bo. Motivated by economic need, Wang adopted rural performativity to create moments of "authentic" experience for tourist consumption.

After inspecting the nets, he paddled back and repositioned the raft. With four fish in total, we motored toward shore. Docking back at the village, I lent a hand offloading the fishing vessel from the hull. On shore, tourists closed in on the landing, taking pictures of Wang and his boat. The tourists disembarked and paid Wang 20 RMB per person for the trip but declined to buy any of the fish. As soon as Wang brought the catch into his yard, another group of tourists walked through the narrow alleyway leading to Wang's house asking for a boat ride. They had seen him from the shore. Wang asked Akira and I to meet him at the beach later and gathered life jackets for the next set of tourists.

FIGURE 17. Peri-urban villager displays traditional fishing for tourists. Photo by author.

In the meantime, Akira and I went to visit other villagers. When we returned to the beach, Wang had already set up a small perimeter net to hold his newly caught fish. He placed some of the larger fish into the net and attached smaller fish to strings. A group of tourists formed around him. Wang posed for pictures, once again, as a triumphant fisher. Tourists watched the display and asked about the price of the fish. He sold three large fish to one patron and another, too small to fetch a good price, as a toy on a string. He gave another fish-on-a-rope to Akira and, to my chagrin, she walked the fish through the water like a dog on a leash. Tourists smiled at the spectacle and commented on how Wang was "such a clever peasant [*nongmin*]." As the fish began to sell, Wang told customers and those that looked on from a distance about his nongjiale. "I make food with rural tastes (*nongjiade weidao*), with special flavors that only come from a rural household. It's not like what you will find in other restaurants. Many urban people really like the taste!"

Two uniformed security guards with "special duty" (*teqin*) printed on their arm badges approached Wang slowly, clearing the crowd as they walked. "You again," one said, "you can't sell here. How many times do I have to tell you?" One of the security guards moved the crowd back, Akira and I included, while the other spoke to Wang at close-range. Later Wang told me that the guard threatened to fine him if he sold fish within the ecological protected area. Wang quickly picked up his nets and began rowing back toward his house. We walked back to ask him what happened. Wang explained that, initially, when tourists began to come in higher numbers, villagers lined the streets around the entrance selling fruit, noodles, fried fish, and other goods. Pop-up stalls were set up early in the morning and taken down at night. Some villagers reported making upward of 800 RMB in a single day. But in 2017, over the spring festival, this all changed.

Armed guards were brought in to stop villagers from selling goods along the perimeters of the ecological protection area. Some altercations between villagers and armed guards became violent. As surveillance and securitization of the ecological protection area increased, illicit sales were curbed. Most villagers gave up on the prospect of informal service provisioning. Wang was one of the few who continued to venture into the ecological protection area in search of leisure capital. But Wang's altercations with the guards were becoming more frequent. The presence of security guards made navigating the protected area challenging and economically risky. Wang had already faced numerous fines for violating conservation mandates.

As Wang navigated this risk, he could see high-rise resettlement apartment complexes being built several kilometers away. He sensed that his time in the village was limited. "Two more years. I can only do this for two more years,"

Wang reflected, estimating when he would move into a resettlement complex. "After two years I will be unemployed. If I am lucky, I could be hired as a security guard. I only studied through third grade." He lamented losing access to land and the impending loss of his nongjiale. "I rely on this territory [*dipan*]. I developed it myself, first as a farmer and now with rural characteristics." Wang went through a protracted process to obtain health and safety permits needed to transform his home into a nongjiale. He did not have guanxi like Bo that could expedite the process. It took two years for him to obtain his business certificate. After several other nongjiale opened in the ecological protection area, the township refused to renew his business license. Wang continued to operate without up-to-date permits. Without access to his farmland and with fishing increasingly regulated, operating a nongjiale became an essential component of Wang's livelihood.

> If you have land, how much could you make in your life? Who knows? 40,000 RMB is what we got for our land. If this land wasn't expropriated, I could grow vegetables and flowers. I could make this much within four years. And I could continue to grow in the future. . . . Just think about that other village where they killed six people [in an attempt to prevent land acquisition] and two of their own died.[22] Thirty villagers still have not come out [of prison]. They won't come out for their whole lives. Because the government won't discuss land acquisition, just criminality. . . . In the future if I go out and become a beggar just to eat, I guess they just don't care. That would be better than being in prison. But everyone has this thought, to protect their home and save the land for future generations.[23]

Even though he still had his house, living without access to land was a crucial blow for Wang. Not only did he have to compete with his neighbors and other nongjiale in the ecological protection area, but he also had to contend with security guards who watched out for illicit commerce. On top of these challenges, he knew that his time in the village was limited. Wang had already been fined multiple times for trying to sell fish and for soliciting customers in the ecological protection area. He did not have access to a tourist license to give boat rides. When he loses access to his home, he will lose his nongjiale and the material means of his livelihood.

Jesse Ribot and Nancy Peluso define resource access as a bundle of powers that shape the ability to derive benefits from something.[24] Contrasting Wang's bundle of powers with Bo's, exhibited in the preceding section, illustrates how class continuities, which carry over for generations, continue to shape differential access to land and resources. The spatialization of class difference is evident in the ways each person is able or unable to access rural space. Rural elites like Bo, for instance, acquired and repurposed TVE land and infrastructure, so-called communal properties. On the other side of the spectrum, multigenerational peasants such as Wang, struggle to navigate ecological protection area regulations to make ends meet. Juxtaposing how differently positioned rural people navigate rural spaces in transition illustrates the role of class in shaping access to land and resources and the spatialization of social differences.

Curating Rural Nostalgia

Bo drew on his own imaginaries of rural heritage to transform TVE infrastructure into a nongjiale and rural museum. For more than a decade Bo has collected rural artifacts and tools at antique markets. He undertook a long-term project of turning the TVE factory infrastructure into a rural museum featuring historical relics of agriculture and fishing. Bo envisioned the rural museum as an adjunct to his nongjiale restaurant. He emphasized that curating a museum with rural artifacts was a way to represent primitive ecology (*yuanshi shengtai*) and provide an experiential glimpse of the rural past.

Rural-ecological displays are a significant cultural industry nationwide.[25] Anthropologist Yu Luo illustrates how notions of primitive ecology circulate in relation to rural identity, indigeneity, and natural foods, essentially operating as a branding mechanism.[26] Luo argues that Chinese elites and government officials mobilize discourses of primitive ecology to promote local distinctiveness and identity, as well as authentic experiences in tourism and the arts. Additionally, Luo describes how there has been increasing popularity among urbanites for primitive ecological experiences since the early 2000s, evinced by national singing contests, public cultural performances, and national eco-tourism plans that draw explicitly on the language and aesthetics of primitive ecology. Alongside these popular cultural displays and national eco-tourism plan, early 2000s national-level state campaigns to forge a "new socialist countryside" and promote rural tourism in China (*zhongguo xiangcun you*) propelled rural nostalgia into the popular zeitgeist.[27] Within this context, rural people, such as Bo and Wang, strive to produce rural-ecological aesthetics for their own ends. They are both acutely aware of the widespread nostalgia for rural China and undertake practices, in competition with one another, to attract capital from leisure activities. But they are differentially positioned to produce rural-ecological aesthetic forms. Bo, for instance, undertook the project of remaking a derelict TVE infrastructure into a rural museum. When the project is complete, Bo hopes to have one of the premier regional museums dedicated to rural culture.

Whenever Bo found new rural artifacts at antique markets, he invited me to walk through the museum-in-progress to view the new additions. I came in the spring of 2017 to see some of his new findings. Before the tour, we had tea in the tearoom where a classic portrait of Mao Zedong graced the eastern wall. Hanging scrolls with a rhyming couplet on either side of Mao's portrait read: "The liberation came through the Communist Party; in your happiness don't forget Mao Zedong" (*fanshen doukao gongchandang, xingfu buwang Mao Zedong*). Bo hosted guests, drank tea, and practiced calligraphy under Mao's enduring gaze. Years earlier, I recalled, Bo took a phone call from the person who donated Mao's portrait to him. She was moving out of the village and no longer had space for the large portrait in her new apartment in the city. Bo happily took it in. But after moving, she called to ask for the portrait to be returned. It was a family heirloom and worth a lot of money, she claimed. Bo was furious. He refused. She called back an hour later and threatened to send someone for the painting who would take it by force if Bo refused to return it. He exploded. Cursing in a fury and holding the phone away from his face, he screamed into the receiver. "I will beat up anyone who comes to take this painting." He walked from the tearoom into the courtyard, his voice growing even more strident as he repeated the threat and slammed down the cell phone. Livid, he slurped two cups of tea, looked over at me and exclaimed, "Mao is a god [*shen*], once a god is hung on the wall it cannot be taken down."

Curating space entails both senses of aesthetics highlighted in his chapter—ways of inhabiting space and shared senses. To curate space, one must control space. For Bo, the capacity to inhabit space is inseparable from his differentiated access—the bundles of powers through which he took control of rural space in transition. The spatial practices through which Bo represented the rural illustrate how shared aesthetic senses are mediated by class positionality. Bo's spatial practices drew on aesthetic objects he associated with the rural and his own memories of a rural past.

In remaking the built environment of a TVE into a rural museum, Bo reproduced rural aesthetic forms in ways shaped by his class position. Bo came of age and into political power in village-level government in the transitional period between Mao and Deng. His class position, wealth, and memories of village life are the product of two socioeconomic eras melded through transitional reforms. Under Mao, Bo's family obtained political positions as communist cadre members, affording him the chance to receive a high school education and take on leadership roles in the communist youth league. His education gave him the skills to manage investments and the political capital to serve as village party secretary. The position also afforded him managerial expertise. As a former production team leader, he transitioned seamlessly into the role of

TVE manager. His political connections and assets allowed him to remake this TVE factory space into a hall of rural representations based on his imaginary of a rural past.

Unlike Wang who did not have guanxi, Bo's political connections served him well. He was able to quickly obtain health, sanitation, and business certifications needed to open his nongjiale. But in recent years with the opening of competing nongjiale within the ecological site he, like Wang, is struggling to renew his business licenses. Bo was concerned that the proprietary owner of the ecological protection area was blocking the renewal of his certificate. Bo wondered if he found a limit of his political power. He felt angry toward what he perceived to be municipal government officials' utilization of state environmental policy to profit from rural land:

> If the state calls on me to stop, I will stop. We should respect state policy. But they [the municipal government] have the power to say stop running your business! "Just stop your business." . . . And they won't allow you to continue to make money. . . . Ecological projects like this are all about money, they claim to be serving the people. But you can see for yourself, they have already taken people's land and forced people into temporary labor positions. When people leave the land, they no longer have energy [*qi*]. People no longer have spirit. People's thoughts begin to change. People are filled with sorrow. And they are susceptible to sicknesses of the heart.[28]

The rural nostalgia Bo referred to underlies his spatial practices of remaking the TVE factory into a rural museum. Bo's historical relation to land and rural production is key to shaping the bundle of power necessary for him to accumulate rural artifacts. It also shapes how he imagines the project of curation. As Bo articulated, psychological pain often accompanies the loss of land, which he referred to as a "sickness of the heart." Bo saw the project of building a rural museum as one way to curate rural nostalgia and reconnect to the land.

Nostalgia and class are inseparable. In Northern Europe, the term *nostalgia* emerged as a medical malady often associated with the pain of losing *homeland* or being away from one's country for long periods of time. Nostalgia was the result of class-oriented geographical displacement coined in relation to lower-class Swiss mercenaries fighting battles far from home.[29] It was characterized as a yearning for the past. Symptomatically, nostalgia crossed the physical and emotive. It was felt as pain, heartache, or even happiness. In Chinese, however, the word for nostalgia—*xiangchou*—consists of two characters. The first character *xiang* means the *village* or *countryside*. *Chou* is translatable as "to worry about," "to miss," or "to be filled with sorrow." Nostalgia, in Chinese, is linguistically oriented toward a longing for rural life and an anxiety about missing or losing access to the countryside. To experience nostalgia, in this context, is to miss the village. In other words, nostalgia encompasses the feelings associated with the absence of, or geographical displacement from, the countryside. For Bo and for Wang, missing rural life, worrying about the village, and differentially navigating displacement from rural land infused their daily lives. For them, creating non-gjiale was deeply emotional. The process entailed entanglements with anxieties about the future, memories of disappearing lifeways, and struggles over space. In this, their nostalgia is simultaneously past- and future-oriented.

Literary theorist Svetlana Boym categorizes "restorative nostalgia," as a postreform longing to fill or restore a sense of a lost time.[30] Bo aimed to restore the rural through spatial practices that simulate idealized aesthetic forms that he associated with a lost rural past. Bo's restorative nostalgic space-making practices drew on memories and nostalgic longing for particular versions of the rural. His spatial practices reified rural difference in relation to ecology. As noted above, the museumification of rural and ecological forms has become widespread across contemporary China, driving many cultural industries to represent the rural in relation to primitive ecology.

Bo was excited to show me what he called his latest primitive ecological findings. Leaving our teacups for Mao to look after, we walked toward the future rural museum. From the front gates, the factory infrastructure was hidden from view behind a row of palms. Inside the factory was a wide-open space with three-story-high ceilings and brick walls filled with an array of artifacts. Concrete floors had several gaping holes from equipment removal. Beams of light streamed through broken windows into the dusty factory air. The main factory floor, previously used for fish processing, was filled with accoutrements of agrarian production. We walked through rows of hoes, brooms, shovels, plows, doors, finely carved latticed window frames, sickles, and boats. A thin layer of dust coated the floor. Wooden boats lined the northern end of the cavernous brick room. Bo claimed that he has one of the largest collections of wooden boats once ubiquitous across Lake Dian. Long wooden vessels supported awnings that ran down the middle of the frame. On some boats the awning covered most of the vessel. On others they covered only the stern offering shelter from the elements for humans and animals. These boats were once homes. Boat dwellers kept chickens on board. The well-off kept pigs. Families and their animals slept on board anchored close to shore. Others anchored at docks managed by landlords. For centuries, whole clans lived on boats coupling fishing with agrarian labor.[31]

Several of these long boats rested perpendicular to the rectangular factory walls, framing the artifacts inside and around them (figure 18). A latticed windowpane with ornately carved swallows rested on a bed of branches. Woven containers for straining rice and drying fish were covered in dust. A plow designed to be carried by an ox rested in the center of the factory hall. Tan woven fishing baskets with holes on the top for reaching in a hand lined one wall. White carved millstones lined the opposite wall, testament to village rice processing. Bo said that he moved one of the millstones from the village temple to his property to keep it from being stolen. The temple laid abandoned and boarded up in the middle of the village square. During the Maoist period, after the campaign to be rid of old traditions (*posijiu*), the temple was turned into a public meeting area and rice processing center. Villagers brought grain there to be weighed, milled, and either immediately distributed or held for collective consumption. "When I was secretary, most of the temples were being demolished. As secretary I protected the temple."[32] Bo gathered the millstone and the baskets for drying fish from the temple remains. He stored them in the factory as he continued to collect rural artifacts.

I followed Bo into a room adjacent to the main factory hall. Previously, it was the refrigeration room for fish. Waist-high wooden tables formed rows of art objects. The walls supported three lines of shelves with more art objects. Wooden

FIGURE 18. A boat within a former TVE factory that is being turned into a rural museum. Photo by author.

statues, rocks of various shapes and sizes, anthropomorphic driftwood, unique stones, and wood carved into ornate landscapes, and other natural objects filled the room. In addition to finding artifacts of rural life, Bo collected and displayed what he described as "ecological art" (*shentai yishu*). As we talked about his eco-logical art collection, Bo exclaimed that the collections in these two halls show "rural people are closer to primitive ecology" (*yuanshi shengtai*). Through curating rural artifacts side by side with ecological art objects, Bo felt that he was preserving rural-ecological culture.

Alongside these art objects, the factory halls and nongjiale walls were deco-rated with images of Yunnan Province's ethnic minorities. Bo is Baizu, an ethnic minority common to the Dali region. He suggested that many of his customers associate rural experiences with ethnic minorities. To cater to them, he decorated the dining area and tea room with prominent displays of art featuring ethnic minority women with long hair, bare stomachs, and sizable silhouetted breasts carrying water containers. The images Bo displayed resemble what Dru Gladney described as the Yunnan School of painting, a style developed primarily by Han Chinese artists in the 1980s and 1990s that features brightly colored landscapes with eroticized depictions of ethnic minorities. Among the most common signi-fiers of difference associated with economic prosperity in China are tropes of the modern, civilized, urban Han male. Bo and others signify rural-ecological experiences through inverse representations of the traditional, primitive, rural, ethnic, and feminine. Gladney makes the point that the Yunnan School's artistic representation of ethnic minorities as feminized exoticized primitives is central to the homogenization of Han identity as civilized, modern, urban, and relatively conservative.[33]

Bo explained that he chose these images because his customers came to experience the countryside. And in Yunnan, he continued, rural life is synony-mous with primitive ecology and ethnic minorities who live in the most natu-ral areas across the province. In the collection and display of rural artifacts and ethnic minority arts, Bo created a space that invites associations between ecol-ogy and rural natures, primitivity and femininity, ethnicity and traditional life-ways. Anthropologist Louisa Schein details what she calls "internal orientalism" as practices that contribute to portraying minority cultures as different from their domineering counterparts.[34] Schein illustrates how internal orientalism is expressed via essentialized and often gendered forms. Bo's spatial compositions, in his nongjiale and future rural museum, invite the viewer to see feminine, rural, ethnic, and ecological tropes as integral aspects of an internal other—an essen-tialized figure marked by their difference.

These associations of difference exhibit similarities to internal othering practices in the West. For instance, bell hooks details how dark feminized bodies are commodified to cater to a white male gaze.[35] In China, dark ethnic bodies and primitive natures have become the counterpoint of a Han male gaze. To cater to this gaze, rural people actively create aesthetic forms that portray rural alterity and ecological primitivity. Bo's utilization of aesthetic symbols fosters an association between eroticized ethnic minorities, rural people, and primitive ecology. Through the display of preindustrial agricultural tools alongside ethnic minority art and natural art objects, rural natures are aesthetically inscribed as the antithesis of the modern Han urbanite. In aesthetic expressions of social difference such as these, the rural-ecological sublime reinforces codes of difference embedded within the eco-developmental sublime. For Bo, producing rural-ecological aesthetics also functions as a form of counter-conduct. His spatial practices are integral to processes through which he refuses state-led urbanization and strives to maintain connections to his rural past.

In curating rural space, Bo was only marginally interested in attracting customers to his nongjiale. Profiting from the enterprise was of little consequence to him. Instead, he claimed to be curating rural space to preserve his nostalgic memories of rural life, relive them in his daily life, and to share his memories with others. As we walked toward the exit of the future museum space, he reflected on how he tried to imbibe the themes of the museum within his own life. He tried to keep his pace of life slow and even, like he remembers the rural past. He strived to maintain an intimate relation to "primitive ecology," which he considered an animating force of nature. He reflected on the importance of sensing this animating force around him and how curating rural space allows him to appreciate the "traditions of his ancestors." Bo's nostalgic imaginary of the rural past not only informed his curation of rural space, but also his sense of self. His capacity to create this idealized space is inseparable from his own political-economic legacy. He came of age and into power late in Mao's reign. Reform-era rural privatization allowed him to profit from that power and control postindustrial rural space.

In contrast with Bo's attempts to crystalize a timeless rural past in a museum built on the dregs of rural reform, Wang was nostalgic for a much more recent rural past, one that he associated with the 1980s.

Remembering the 1980s

His face stern with purpose, Wang walked into the dining area on the second floor of his nongjiale and stood in the middle of the room. He turned on the stereo and took several steps to center himself on the floor. A heavy beat permeated the air followed by the unmistakable sound of 1980s pop-synth. As his body warmed up to the sound, Wang started gyrating and pulsing like a squid through water. He danced with an utterly serious countenance. His arms rose up and down. Then side to side. Legs followed the rhythms. A standing-in-place jog. Hand over hand to the rhythmic beat he slowly moved himself forward along an imaginary rope toward where I sat. Moonwalking backward he stepped back to the middle of the room and began rotating his shoulders backward in small circles rhythmically pulsing like a boxy David Bowie. I could tell he was really enjoying himself dancing alone in the serving area of his nongjiale. "This is how we used to dance on the beach before it became an ecological protection area," he huffed between motions. "This dance is called 'freestyle.' It isn't like dances these days, which are pretty rigid," he said. "It's how we all danced back then in the 1980s when times were freer." After several minutes of elated display, he took a break and sat down.

Dancing set Wang into a nostalgic mood for the 1980s. But we had been working toward that temporality for the last eight hours. His dance of remembrance came after a long day in which he accompanied me to conduct oral histories with village elders. As his breath slowed down, he got up and went back to his bedroom returning with an old photo album. He opened the pages, and we began looking at photos. Wang began to reminisce about how village life used to be. He showed me photos of his marriage and his wife's family. Both were multigenerational peasant farmers and fishers.

As Wang talked, he recounted what village elders had said earlier that day. In the early 1900s, Wang's ancestors lived on boats—the kind that Bo displayed in his rural museum project. A small handful of those boat dwellers rented slips from a landlord with the surname Jin. They parked their boats on the Jin-family docks. And they paid docking fees in the form of labor on Jin-family rice fields. Rent was charged per household in relation to the number of people living on the fishing boats. Boat dwellers also exchanged fish caught in Lake Dian for rice that they harvested from the Jin estate. During the late 1800s and early 1900s some boat dwellers began moving to land. These families, to which Wang traced his history, were eventually granted access to land for building small houses in exchange for labor on rice fields and monthly payments in fish. Elders recalled that five households began sleeping on the site of the current village in tents made with bamboo beams and old sails. After several years these families erected sturdier thatched homes (caofang) made from woven reeds. And, after another decade, they built mud brick homes (tufang). When "liberation" came during the early Maoist period, land was wrested from landlords and collectivized into newly formed village production teams.[36] With new access to land, households that remained living in boats moved onto land and a village formed.

Wang remembered starting to work when he was six years old. In the 1970s he helped his family obtain ration cards that could be exchanged for food. He worked from early morning to late night carrying lanterns to light the darkness. Wang labored from childhood to make his home. When we met, Wang lived in a concrete two-and-a-half story structure, built in the 1980s. With the end of the Maoist period and beginning of Deng's reforms, many were able to earn, save, and spend. For multigenerational peasants like Wang, it was not only for the first time in their lives, but also the first time in generations. New concrete and brick homes cropped up throughout the village. Other houses renovated dirt floors and mud brick walls into concrete floors and lime brick. Going from making one's home to buying the materials to renovate a home marked a socioeconomic leap. Of course, not all villagers jumped together or as far. Class remained. Some mud brick homes still remain.

During the 1980s, Wang's family worked the agricultural plots assigned to them as part of the household responsibility system. They saved enough for a new concrete house with a large kitchen. Wang had planned to expand the house with an additional floor when his son married but, since municipal conservation zoning, that future became a memory. Conservation moratoriums halted Wang and other villagers from adding additional floor space. Wang's family relied on land-based production for generations. His son was the first to enter wage labor relations outside of farming and fishing. He became a security guard at an apartment complex near the village. Wang realized that, with moratoriums on building extra floors and displacement from his home imminent, welcoming his son's family to live with him and passing on his home to them will not come to fruition.

It was, in part, this recognition that brought Wang into deep reflective nostalgia for rural life in the 1980s. "Reflective nostalgia," as Boym describes, thrives on longing itself. It entails a longing for a past, or imagined future, that may not have come to fruition but remains an integral and productive aspect of one's memory.[37] It is a form of individual cultural memory with simultaneous elements of mourning and melancholy. Here it is crucial to point, once again, to how forms of difference matter in producing a rural-ecological sublime. Wang's dance—a way of inhabiting space—revealed fissures in shared distributions of senses. What the rural meant to Wang, differed substantially from Bo. As did how Wang remembered the rural, how that memory found expression, and became associated with time.

When is the rural? Wang oscillated between nostalgia for his rural past and an imagined rural future. In playing his 1980s music and dancing the way that he remembered in his youth, he was nostalgically reflecting on a time of great hope and possibility he felt to be gone. The beach was severed from the village and securitized as part of an ecological protection area. Yet, he remembered it as a gathering place where village children would swim naked from the docks and adults would spend what little leisure time they had after farming. He played his favorite songs and reenacted how he used to dance on that beach with his friends. Through his dance, he remembered the 1980s as a golden age, a period where profits from newly redistributed rural land held promise of upward socioeconomic mobility and material improvement. Rural China in the 1980s was a place of hope and possibility for Wang. It was a time when Wang imagined possibilities for the future to be embodied in rural land and industry.

In visiting Wang's nongjiale, customers tapped into their own nostalgic impulses for rural experience. As we sat at one of the dining tables on the second floor looking through photos, a group of tourists walked in for lunch. They were repeat customers, the presence and patronage of which were key to Wang's livelihood. As they entered, Wang performed a cultural code switch. He stood up quickly, changing the music from 1980s pop-synth to *Sounds of the Southwest*—ethnic minority music. Ethnic minority music, he later insisted, sounds more rural and customers like it.

Wang's actions significantly refute Bourdieu's notion of the "em-peasanted" body. Bourdieu argues that peasants' techniques of the body involuntarily betray their class positionality. But unlike Bourdieu's French peasantry, Wang not only dances, he also DJs. Wang's dance and curation of sound illustrate his capacity to perform multiple modes of embodiment, including what could be considered urban dance styles. He is certainly more familiar with what he called "freestyle" dance than rural or ethnic minority styles, which as anthropologist Jenny Chio illustrates, are often learned for the purpose of display to tourists. Chio notes how rural tourist experiences are crafted through performative stages.[38] She refers to the "front stage" of tourism as the performative actions that tourists are meant to see. But this front stage is always produced through complex negotiations in backstage places where people learn how to act authentic. My observations of Wang's performance of front stages for tourists were revealing. Contrary to Bourdieu's conceptualization of the peasantry, Wang is not confined or betrayed by his bodily disposition. Instead, he actively shifts aesthetic modes of embodiment to express tropes of rural nature when it serves him. At different times, Wang performed various forms of embodied labor and corporeal representations of the rural for the tourist gaze.[39] He posed as the fisher with his net and boat, the clever peasant making a sale, and in this instance, the proprietor of a rural restaurant.

Consuming Rural, Eating Ecological

As Wang code switched to perform rurality, he proceeded to take an order for food. Wang made suggestions to the newly arrived customers, claiming the dishes served in his nongjiale were "more ecological" (*bijiao shengtai*) than foods served in the city. "Ecological," in this sense connotes a range of taste qualities and characteristics including freshness, organic cultivation, and being locally produced. In the wake of recent food-related public health scares, from contaminated baby formula to toxic levels of additives found in processed foods, there is growing social awareness of food safety in China. It is now common to seek out ecological and locally produce foods. Rural food is often considered more ecological than urban fare. Wang was aware of this association and actively drew on this shared sense in describing his nongjiale's cuisine as ecological food.

Customers, like the group that just arrived, assumed that Wang grew the produce himself. But without access to agricultural land, the only items that Wang produced were fish caught from Lake Dian and wild rice (*jiaobai*) that he cultivated by funneling rainwater into shallow paddies. The paddies blended in with the artificial wetlands landscape. Security guards failed to notice the crop growing in the interstitial spaces within the ecological protection area. Though, as if to assuage his customer, he quickly drew attention to the atmosphere of his house and ensured them that the cooking style was very rural and ecological. Wang suggested to his customers that growing wild rice is ecologically beneficial because freshwater shrimp come to feed on small organisms that live in the stalks. Cultivation creates a favorable environment for Wang to net shrimp and offer them as ecological dishes on his menu. This group of customers developed a relationship with him and trusted that his food was ecological, which they described as "not full of processed chemicals like food in the city." The fact that Lake Dian, where the fish were caught, is one of the most polluted lakes in China did not alter the conviction that these fish dishes were ecological and eating them was a rural-ecological experience. Wang affirmed this to each of his customers.

This monthly dining group began as a few friends who ate at Wang's nongjiale after he introduced himself in the ecological protection area. They decided to come back again the following month. Their numbers grew after they told their friends about the authentic nongjiale on the banks of Lake Dian. They eventually decided to come to Wang's nongjiale every month. On this occasion, they were ten. They invited me to join their table lined with dishes. Conversation oscillated between the beauty of Lake Dian and the authentic rural-ecological food. One patron talked about how this place reminded her of her grandma's village, which she frequented as a child. Pointing to the fish she said, "This one is just like how my grandma used to make it back in our village." Restorative nostalgia for a rural past informed customer experiences of nongjiale. Embodied spatial practices of consuming food and place in tandem linked the rural and ecological in the palettes and memories of patrons. Wang's culinary representations of these signifiers were central to maintaining his precarious livelihood.

After the lunch crowd left, he brought out family pictures again, as well as those he took as part of my photovoice research. He held up an image of the artificial beach that was once accessible to villagers, an image of the treatment wetland that used to be agricultural land, and several images of homes in the village. He laid the photos on the table and said:

> They have done a fine job of ecological construction here. . . . The ecology has been built beautifully. But our ability to continue to exist has been greatly affected. First our houses are going to be demolished. They labelled our village a slum area. Secondly, they have taken over our land and built a *beautiful ecological landscape*. Many common people [*laobaixing*] have had their ways of life [*shenghuo fangshi*] seized by their ecology. We have experienced a huge loss. The ecology of course is good. But do you know what is behind this positive ecology? It has already stripped us of our ability to subsist. Our loss is huge, and it's a question if we will be able to subsist in the future.[40]

Wang remembered what it used to be like when he wasn't being fined for selling fish. When he could play music and freestyle dance on the beach. The village felt like it was his own. He felt like he belonged. He remembered when his house was just a home and not a commodified space for rural experience. Yet despite his nostalgic impulse for the 1980s, Wang recognized the cultural importance of older, seemingly timeless forms of rural life that he represented in his nongjiale. Re-creating senses of rural pasts, through rural food and fishing expeditions, was key to attracting tourists.

Social difference and class position shaped how Wang remembered the past and remade his livelihood. How Wang and Bo remade the rural was not merely meaningful to their customers. It was also meaningful to themselves. Bo's and Wang's nongjiale served as regenerative specters that memorialized rural imaginaries, albeit different ones. Wang continued to fish and farm in the margins of the ecological protection area. Bo continued to curate a rural museum from the dregs of a TVE factory. Each strived to keep alive the memories of once daily agrarian realities by generating simulacrum of rural life within representational spaces of rural consumption. Each did so by tapping into their class-mediated nostalgic memories of rural pasts in aesthetic forms: the labor of tilling, sewing, and harvesting inscribed for some in bodily memory, and others in forms of sensorial representation—literary, televisual, infrastructural, and gastronomical.

Drawing on Gastón Gordillo's insight that affect and memory are embodied in the material remaking of ruins,[41] I consider Bo and Wang's spatial practices as relational navigations of memory and class position. They re-created rural pasts in ways shaped by their histories of social difference. In catering to bourgeoning urban tastes for rural experience, Wang and Bo performed difference and accrued value unevenly. The spatial practices through which they do so are indelibly shaped by differing class positions, memories and longing, and the bundles of powers their divergent positionalities afford.

* * *

Wang and Bo's agricultural land was transformed into treatment wetlands within a year of being zoned for ecological protection. The land within and surrounding the protected area witnessed a surge in commodified spaces. Large parking lots hosted hundreds of cars a day. 15 RMB to park for three hours. On weekends the parking lot filled by noon. A pick-it-yourself vegetable garden abutted the main parking lot. A team of gardeners tended vegetables for tourists to pick. Tourists paid by weight for the experience. They either took them home or ate them at a nongjiale partnered with the garden.

A plastic roof, etched in the shape of a giant whitebait, covered an open-air market lined with kiosks adjacent to the parking lot. Kiosks rented for 500 RMB per month. Most sellers were villagers from the region, as well as ecological migrants who already moved into nearby high-rise resettlement complexes. Many rural food stalls were run collectively by extended family. Near the main parking lot was a row of nongjiale. One was named "ecological hot pot" (*shengtai huoguo*). The restaurant leasers were originally from this village but had moved to a high-rise resettlement complex. They utilized the capital from their land sale to lease the restaurant for one-year. They could renew for a second. But, surrounded by options for rural foods, they were struggling to attract customers.

Much like opportunistic municipal bureaucrats and proprietary owners (see chapter 3), villagers operated under market conditions to profit from ecological protection land with whatever means they have. Entrepreneurs aesthetically emplaced rural-ecological motifs into the built environment. They performed rurality for photos. They curated the rural. They served rural cuisine. In undertaking these spatial practices, villagers became active agents of differentiated aesthetic emplacement in the landscapes of their own displacement.

Accounting for how social differences matter within the production of rural-ecological aesthetics deepens and extends theories of aesthetic governance. My theorization of difference-within circumvents a tendency to imagine aesthetic power affecting a given social group uniformly. Rural people in China are not homogenous. Neither are the aesthetic forms they produce, nor the effects of aesthetic emplacement. They draw on and reproduce a rural-ecological sublime differently based on legacies of social differentiation, which continue to shape access to land and resources in the present. Social inequalities shape how villagers navigate commodified rural spaces and transitional livelihood practices.

For both Bo and Wang, the rural lives they remember have changed dramatically. Each navigated rural remains in competition with others vying to capitalize on the production of rural difference. Wang surreptitiously entered the ecological protection site to lure guests to his nongjiale and traditional boating excursions. Wang's reflective nostalgia shaped the aesthetic contours of his nongjiale, his fishing practices, and his longing to return to a freer rural past. Bo's elite class positionality set him on a starkly different socioeconomic trajectory, one that allowed him to purchase TVE infrastructure and rural land. His project to turn a bankrupt TVE into a nongjiale and rural museum embodied his restorative nostalgic impulse for a timeless rural past. These differentiated aesthetic emplacements reinforce social difference between urban and rural people while obfuscating processes of rural displacement in plain sight. In ways such as these, Bo and Wang's active production of a rural-ecological sublime reifies forms of rural difference, which also find expression within the eco-developmental sublime. In other ways, however, their spatial practices counter state logics of socio-natural optimization and techniques aimed at urbanizing rural people. The contrapuntal tensions between these aesthetic expressions are particularly thick in Wang's efforts to perform rurality while circumventing ecological protection area mandates and Bo's attempts to resist urbanization by territorializing rural space and transforming it into a rural museum. These tensions are visible not only through rural people's spatial practices, but in others' attempts to represent the rural within ecological protection areas.

When Bo finishes his museum, he will be competing with a rural museum in the ecological protection area leased to a proprietary owner. The three-story glass museum housed bronze statues of peasants working the land with hoes, oxen, plows, and sickles. Lifeless casts were surrounded by living agricultural produce. The museum memorializes agrarian labor and production, which animated this locale for generations. Silent effigies to agrarian labor stood frozen on highly fertile soil, much of which has been dredged and filled in as wetlands. The rest of the ecological protection land supported seasonally changing flower installations. Flowers, grown in this area since the early 2000s, remain one of the main attractions in the ecological protection site. But their organization now reflects logics of optimization. Seasonally curated for visual and experiential consumption of nature, the "sea of flowers" (*huahai*) exhibit displayed neatly aligned violets, chrysanthemums, and roses in intricate color-coordinated spectral patterns. The trees lining the walkways harbored chemical pollutants from the water in their trunks. Such optics of socio-natural optimization permeated the site's

WeChat handle. Advertisements and photo essays entreated the viewer to travel to this site and "enjoy the ecology of this place where families can experience traditional rural culture and an ecological environment" (*shengtai huanjing*). The popularization of rural tourism and visual signification of rural life as something of the past, embodied in both the physical landscape and digital representations, contributes to naturalizing processes of rural displacement. Indeed for many it not only seemed natural, but highly enjoyable.

Inside the treatment wetlands, children played carnival games. They rolled around in spinning plastic inflatables. Motorboats filled with tourists cruised through canals carved into the treatment wetland. Filled beyond capacity, they toured the shores of the lake, making waves as they sped past the places where Wang laid his fishing nets. In contrast, the high walls of Bo's TVE compound shielded the carnival-like scene. He drank tea and practiced calligraphy in relative peace. From their respective positions, they differentially sensed and inhabited space. The contrast in their embodied spatial practices is a banal marker of differentiated aesthetic emplacement. While Wang hustled for his own subsistence, Bo rested leisurely. Secure in his wealth and access, Bo no longer needed to turn a profit from rural space or rise from his chair to enter the fray in the ecological protection area.

Uneven power relations underlie these spatial practices and banal landscapes of dispossession across China. Although common, displacement is often experienced as a solitary crucible. Isolation amid displacement, however, is no accident. The final chapter analyzes the operation of power through infrastructural techniques that diffuse collective counter-conduct, thereby stifling social organization and isolating individuals.

INFRASTRUCTURAL DIFFUSION

Reaching the final stop on Kunming's subway, I disembarked expecting to find a row of cars waiting for a fare. Entrepreneurial drivers usually lined the exits to give rides across the outskirts of the city. I had taken this line frequently over the years and was habituated to a bustling scene. Walking out of the subway exit into the sunlight revealed an unfamiliar sight. There were no line of cars or motorbikes. The streets were empty.

I reentered the subway to check the south entrance. A block away, three people stood next to their cars. Recognizing a driver, I approached asking for a lift. He explained that, since the civilized city campaign started, transport hubs were under high surveillance. He pointed to a grey car several blocks away and said "That car is undercover police watching us." Police officers and "volunteers"—untrained and low-paid temporary laborers hired to police traffic—warned unlicensed drivers to stop offering transportation services. Those that did not heed the warning faced vehicle impoundment and heavy fines. I waited at the bus stop for the line that would take me to the ecological protection area. Up to this point, I regularly made use of informal transportation. But on April 1, 2017, within a week of hiring volunteers to police traffic and street-level transportation, informal transportation providers disappeared from the streets.

Kunming had just entered the final stage of assessment to qualify as a "civilized city," the culmination of a three-year evaluation process. The city was being rigorously tested through scientific methods for levels of civilization by a group of anonymous surveyors from Beijing. Surveyors were tasked with tabulating a score worth 60 percent of the city's three-year assessment rating. In 2005, the Central Spiritual Civilization Steering Committee (CSPCP) created a set of criteria for assessing urban civility called the National Civilized City Assessment System (*quanguo wenming chengshi ceping tixi*). The first honorary titles were distributed in 2008 after three years of individual city assessments by expert judges. In 2008, there were 111 indicators to measure urban civilization. The number of indicators expanded after the 2011 announcement of an enhanced indicator system. The assessment team is formed from members of the Propaganda Department and the City Investigation Team of the National Bureau of Statistics (*guojia tongjiju chengshi diaocha dui*). A team of state representatives drew on field visits, observations, material reviews, survey questionnaires, and online surveys that queried sanitation, public transport, infrastructure, economic development, moral behavior of citizens and elected officials, as well as citywide levels of "sustainable ecological environment."[1]

What exactly was being assessed and how was known only to the Propaganda Department team of surveyors and central government officials. Geographer Carolyn Cartier details how secrecy is maintained throughout the civilized city evaluation process, even between government agencies.[2] In order to avoid potential intergovernmental conflicts of interest, Cartier writes, evaluators are given a confidential envelope on their way to the airport to board their flight. Within the envelope is a plane ticket and directions specifying the location where they are going to make their assessments. The assessment team works incognito, disguised as ordinary people, and uses public transportation infrastructure. These plain-clothes assessors could be anyone, anywhere, at any time. Visits are supposed to be unannounced. But in the case of Kunming's third assessment, newspapers ran stories announcing the presence of state investigators. Even without reading the newspaper, everyone in the city became aware they were being surveilled due to the actions of the municipal government.

The municipal government hired five thousand volunteers to police street-level traffic civility.[3] Reminiscent of Maoist-era propaganda campaigns, so-called volunteers wore a red sash over their shoulder that read "civilized city volunteer." These were, in fact, not volunteers in the sense of someone freely offering up their labor, but hourly wage workers who stood at nearly every street corner of the city. Many I spoke with were villagers from the surrounding area. Stopping at busier intersections, I counted fifteen traffic volunteers on a single street crossing. They directed traffic, handed out tickets for traffic violations, and exhorted people to move within lines painted on asphalt. Coupled with these volunteers was an additional five thousand army reserve guards who were put into active duty to control traffic. Ten thousand street volunteers were impossible to avoid.

They constituted a veritable army of surveyors shaping street-level movement through urban infrastructure.

Like a roving panopticon, the third wave of civilized city assessment took hold of the city. Informal transportation services common for day-to-day urban mobility disappeared. Despite the demand for informal transportation and the inadequacies of public transportation services to access peri-urban locales, informal transport was deemed uncivilized and traffic police undertook extensive efforts to curtail these services. After the influx of volunteers immobilized informal transportation, I began riding my electric motorbike to peri-urban ecological protection areas.

Returning to the streets on e-bike revealed how the street-level mobilities were changing under the surveillance of an army of traffic volunteers. A week after the volunteers appeared, I stopped at a red light and was immediately struck across the head by a baton wielded by a volunteer surveilling a three-meter bike lane. As my retinas flashed, the traffic volunteer exhorted me to "back up the motorbike. You are violating the law." I looked down to see my front tire on top of the white stop line. My eyes refocused on a traffic volunteer displaying a baton with a red banner in front of the line of bikes forming behind me. As the light turned green, the baton and banner raised letting all pass. The influx of these volunteers and police presence transformed the ways people moved throughout urban space. Conducting street-level mobilities through thousands of traffic volunteers is a highly visible governance technique.

There are, in contrast, techniques that make highly visible forms of counter-conduct invisible. The following is an excerpt from a message shared in an active WeChat group that recounts an assault by traffic police during the civilized city campaign's third assessment in Kunming. WeChat is one of the most widely used digital platforms in China. Like other forms of social media, it is heavily surveilled.[4] An excerpt from a message, sent to a chat group of more than two hundred people reads:

> This Kunming traffic volunteer beat me up as I was on my e-bike over a 20 RMB [US$3] fine. Yesterday afternoon I was on my way back home from picking up my child from school and riding my e-bike. . . . 10th battalion constable traffic policemen Bing Lei (Police Number 504187) stopped me to issue a fine for riding on a part of the road where bikes were not allowed.[5] Then he wanted to confiscate my e-bike. . . . I continued to sit on my bike and said, "You want to put me to death over a 20 RMB fine . . ." Soon afterwards officer Bing Lei yelled at me, pushed me off my e-bike and started to beat me.
>
> I begged for mercy, but he just continued to beat me. He finally stopped, but then came back to beat me again. Afterward, he called out

for another officer to bring a rope to tie up my e-bike. . . . Five or six people then beat me until I had to be taken to the hospital. Last night I was throwing up blood. I was diagnosed with a concussion and stayed in the hospital for monitoring. My child was so scared he cried all night without sleeping. And up till now, nobody cares [*wuren wenjin*]. I took pictures of my injured face and neck to have proof of the beating I got from Bing Lei (Police Number 504187), but the police station said that it didn't matter if I took pictures or not. I needed the pictures to be taken by the forensics unit.

Is it alright to beat people over a 20 RMB traffic violation? Aren't these volunteer traffic police supposed to enforce the law through education, with fines as a secondary method? I thought that going to the police station would result in a just handling of this altercation, but in the end what I saw was partialness and one-sidedness [*tanhu*] with favor toward the traffic police. This causes me to doubt whether their enforcement is fair. Is this really what a national civilized city is supposed to be like? Is this person really the people's servant? Where is the law? Where is the justice?

This excerpt illustrates how state-sanctioned values and meanings associated with political campaigns are not simply internalized but become discursive terrain through which citizens operationalize political contestation. In this instance, a WeChat user drew on the discourse of ecological civilization building to counter municipal state methods of policing traffic and a police officers' abuse of power. Their message indexes countervailing interpretations of morality, civility, and justice than those articulated by the state. This was an incredibly active WeChat group with people posting throughout the day on a range of topics. I was accustomed to timely quips in quick succession in reply to every message. What struck me after reading the lengthy account was the silence of the WeChat group. Not a single response came from any of the two hundred people in the group chat. No solace, sympathy, or support. No suggestions regarding venues to seek legal redress. No expression of any kind. Within the day, WeChat erased the message from the group chat—a reminder that we were not only surveilled on the streets but in our digital worlds.

Authoritarian Power through Infrastructural Diffusion

Authoritarian power is often depicted, by scholars and pundits alike, through violent events, displays of force, or inner struggles of ruling parties and autocrats.

Considering authoritarian power in the context of China, many recall the 1989 Tiananmen massacre. The event entailed the violent repression of a youth-led public protest and multiweek occupation of public space. Protestors organized in Beijing's Tiananmen Square around calls for greater democratic governance and public participation.[6] The occupation was met with brutal state violence, portions of which were recorded by media outlets. Scholars tend to analyze expressions of organized violence that are either explicitly or tacitly endorsed by state apparatuses.[7] They also analyze authoritarian power through political ideology,[8] repertoires of contention,[9] norm-bound institutional continuity, and mass mobilization.[10] Public displays of monopoly power over the use of force, political ideology, and exchanges between political regimes, civil society, and media, while integral to authoritarian governance, are part of a wide array of techniques through which authoritarian power operates.

Scholars of authoritarian governance in China have recently turned their attention to ways that state power operates through social organizations and everyday practices. Sociologists Ching-Kwan Lee and Yonghong Zhang detail the microfoundations of Chinese authoritarianism, including protest bargaining, legal-bureaucratic absorption, and patron-clientelism. These grassroots practices facilitate state rule by limiting citizen behaviors, motivations, and interests.[11] In their account, grassroots state-society relations are a marketplace where bargains take place between protestors, civil society, and local officials. They refer to the processes of maintaining sociopolitical stability as "bargained authoritarianism." Street-level officials negotiate with protestors case-by-case to alleviate political contention. This bargaining among social groups is central to the maintenance of authoritarian power. Similarly, sociologist Julia Chuang details how local government officials deliberately use deception and misinformation regarding hukou transfer, compensation, and relocation to effectively displace rural people from their land and bureaucratically absorb objections to becoming urban citizens.[12] Luigi Tomba, in contrast, focuses on governance inside urban residential compounds. These neighborhood spaces, Tomba contends, are central for citizens to elaborate grievances and discuss residential policies. Community participation in these shared living spaces, he demonstrates, reinforces government legitimacy.[13] The production of consensus to be governed in urban neighborhoods, for Tomba, entails "the existence of a space where bargaining between state and society and within society is made possible through formalized institutions, routinized practices, and discursive boundaries."[14] These works illustrate the varied ways that state apparatuses bureaucratically preempt and absorb contention.

While a vast number of stability-maintainers strive to channel contestation into bureaucratic procedures and patrimonial bargaining, there are many situations in which these techniques fail to contain contention. In instances where bargained authoritarianism and political absorption fall short, authoritarian power finds expression through infrastructural forms. In this chapter, I depart from the conceptualizations noted above by drawing attention to how authoritarian power is constituted through nested infrastructural relations. Subjects are active in ontologizing state power in everyday practices and navigating power relations within infrastructural spaces. In this vein, geographer Emily Yeh conceives of state-society relations and authoritarian governance through their everyday production.[15] Yeh demonstrates that state power operates through formal institutional channels, social interactions in everyday life, and physical interventions in the built environment.

Authoritarian power in China entails not only complex state-society interplays that maintain stability and produce consent, but nested relations embedded within the dismantling of everyday physical and social infrastructures. Writing in the context of urban redevelopment in China, anthropologist Julie Chu discusses how state power manifests through distributed forms of agency lodged in infrastructural disrepair. Chu brings attention to how the mundane effects of infrastructural disrepair serve state interests and shape political sensibilities of villagers living amid ruinous landscapes. The material effects of disrepair are substantial. Not least of which are the partitioning of everyday social life and the disintegration of village political unity. Chu refers to the intentional disrepair of infrastructure as the embodiment of the state's "spectral forces."[16] State power, for Chu, operates through the dematerialization of infrastructure and the effects of infrastructural disrepair on the aesthetic sensibilities of residents. Analogously, architect Keller Easterling, writing in the context of urban redevelopment in the West, details how techniques of infrastructural removal shape urban governance.[17] This chapter builds on Chu and Easterling's insights that power operates through physical infrastructural forms of demolition and infrastructural disrepair. AbdouMaliq Simone, on the other hand, makes the case for considering collective organization as "social infrastructure," thereby extending theories of infrastructure to people's social activities, interpersonal relationships, and mobilizations.[18] The forms of counter-conduct I highlight in this chapter contrast with the flexible social organizations discussed by Simone and differ from the collective forms of protests described by Lee and Zhang.[19] This chapter emphasizes, instead, how infrastructural techniques diffuse social cohesion and isolate individuals.

The two examples in the introduction of this chapter, the immobilization of unlicensed drivers and a WeChat user whose personal account of police violence was digitally erased, are instances in which infrastructural techniques diffused forms of counter-conduct. As discussed in the introduction of the book, counter-conduct refers to the ways people struggle with and against governmental techniques to conduct society.[20] In this chapter, I argue that infrastructural techniques and their effects are integral to authoritarian power. To support this argument, I demonstrate how infrastructural techniques and their effects diffuse counter-conduct. I point to the role of infrastructure in weakening social cohesion, thwarting contestation, and containing politically sensitive scenarios. Infrastructural techniques and their effects are crucial to maintaining authoritarian power.

By *infrastructural diffusion* I refer to the processes by which physical and social infrastructures are removed, which has the effect of diffusing forms of counter-conduct. Infrastructural diffusion operates across built environments, state actors, and hybrid organizations such as demolition bureaus (*chaiqianban*); apparatuses of surveillance; as well as forms of corporeal, coercive, and symbolic violence. Infrastructural diffusion produces what I call archipelagos of isolation, the isolation of places from the surrounding environment, communities from communities, and individuals from their community. Here I am using the term *archipelago* in a metaphorical sense. An archipelago generally refers to strings of islands forged from a shared heat source, subduction zone, or continental shelf that gives rise to their spatially proximate landforms. Islands within an archipelago share common origins and, because of these shared properties, are considered interconnected geographical bodies. Archipelagos of isolation are the outcome of effective subjugation and the individuation of collective resistance. They are produced through infrastructural diffusion and their effects, which delimit counter-conduct and thwart collective political actions.[21]

Infrastructural diffusion spatially and socially disconnects people and places. This has the effect of neutralizing political solidarities. The effects are cumulative. Over time the effects of infrastructural diffusion hinder prospects of collective mobilization and contribute to social isolation. In instances in which forms of collective counter-conduct are strong, infrastructural diffusion has the effect of atomizing communities. In cases where individual counter-conduct is strong, infrastructural diffusion has the effect of isolating individuals.

In what follows, I detail examples of infrastructural diffusion, first through an example of how demolition bureaus *disintegrate* rural infrastructure and villagers' political solidarity through partial demolitions, violent repression of collective counter-conduct, and coercive violence. Demolition bureaus and their hired hands, in another example, *disassemble* utilities infrastructure to make villages less habitable. Village councils, thereafter, are disassembled in the wake of rural-to-urban resettlement. Without utilities infrastructure or formal representation at the village level, residents that remain living in the village are further isolated. Coercive threats of infrastructural damage and physical violence not only have the effects of silencing the afflicted, but also *blind* society from their experiences, thereby preventing greater solidarity. In the final example, village cadres and military personnel physically *uproot* subsistence agriculture. Doing so ruptures the biological relation to land necessary for sustaining life on the margins. In these examples, infrastructural diffusion transforms places, communities, and individual people into archipelagos of isolation.

Disintegrating

As the municipal government zoned Xiaoxi village for ecological protection, villagers experienced violent struggle with a demolition bureau over control of their housing.[22] Like cases discussed in previous chapters, their agricultural land was swiftly enrolled in conservation-oriented development. This section is based on interviews with ex-village council members and residents who were present during violent altercations with the demolition bureau, as well as observations during village residential meetings. This account illustrates how infrastructural techniques diffused villagers' political unity and collective will to resist displacement. The Xiaoxi demolition bureau figures centrally in this process.

A demolition bureau is not strictly a state institution. Instead, demolition bureaus are ad hoc hybrid organizations consisting of local government officials including municipal and township-level government representatives, villagers, as well as representatives from private companies and development institutions.[23] Demolition bureaus are formed to manage the purchasing and dismantling of housing and other infrastructures. They manage contracts with individual households, as well as leases with developers. After ecological protection area zoning, the municipal government purchased Xiaoxi's agricultural land and allocated it to a proprietary owner, which I will call the Jinlin development company (see chapter 3).[24] Jinlin began building conservation-oriented infrastructure and a sports club on Xiaoxi village's former land.

While construction was underway, a group of Xiaoxi villagers, with the support of the village council, invested compensation capital from their land sales into new high-rise apartments built on rural construction land. They built six-story apartments, which they called New Xiaoxi. Many of the original buildings and the village temple were in Old Xiaoxi. Some villagers continued to live in Old Xiaoxi while others moved to New Xiaoxi. Most families in New Xiaoxi lived in apartment units on the second floor and opened commercial enterprises on the first floor. They rented out the additional floors, predominantly to migratory laborers.

Xiaoxi demolition bureau formed while New Xiaoxi was still under construction. After forming, the demolition bureau had a continual presence in the village. The demolition bureau rented a building, which previously hosted village council meetings and served as the village council office.[25] Representatives from the demolition bureau notified villagers that they sought to purchase their high-rise apartments in New Xiaoxi in addition to housing in Old Xiaoxi. The proximity of new commercial developments built on former agricultural land increased the value of Xiaoxi's rural housing and construction land. Despite this, the Xiaoxi demolition bureau offered prices lower than what villagers had just invested into their new apartments. Villagers balked at the prospect of selling their new housing infrastructures for so little. The economic losses of selling newly built apartment housing would have been substantial. But demolition bureau representatives insisted.

Representatives from the demolition bureau began going door-to-door taking housing measurements. They then devised and presented housing sale contracts to residents. Bureau representatives claimed that, ultimately, residents didn't have a choice in the matter. But if they signed a housing contract early, residents may be eligible for compensatory gifts or priority choice for resettlement housing. Instead of public discussion or negotiation with village government representatives, demolition bureau representatives individually approached each village household with a contract. Despite making strong claims that they had "no choice" in the matter, the demolition bureau initially struggled to convince residents to sign housing contracts.

After completing housing measures, drawing up contracts, and meeting with a glut of refusals, the demolition bureau began making threats to contact the employers of residents who held government and public service positions. Demolition bureau representatives took their threats door-to-door. Teachers, for instance, began to fear that the superintendents of their schools would be informed that they were not cooperating with the government. This threat proved tangible. Some teachers who refused to sell their housing were dismissed from their jobs. Other residents who worked in the public sector ceded, selling their housing to the demolition bureau. Slowly, more residents began to sign contracts to sell their housing. After residents signed housing contracts and moved out, a wave of infrastructural demolition ensued.

The demolition bureau began partially demolishing the houses of those who signed contracts. They demolished parts of the physical infrastructure, but left debris, sharp wires, concrete, and pipes littered across the village. In the process of partial demolition, the demolition crew damaged nearby vehicles, adjacent housing, and utilities infrastructure. There were no attempts to compensate villagers for the damages. The demolition crew left a trail of ruins in their wake. The village landscape began to appear like a patchwork of infrastructural hazards.

Partial demolition, the intentional piecemeal disintegration of infrastructure, is a key technique of infrastructural diffusion, the effects of which amplify over

Housing Area Survey

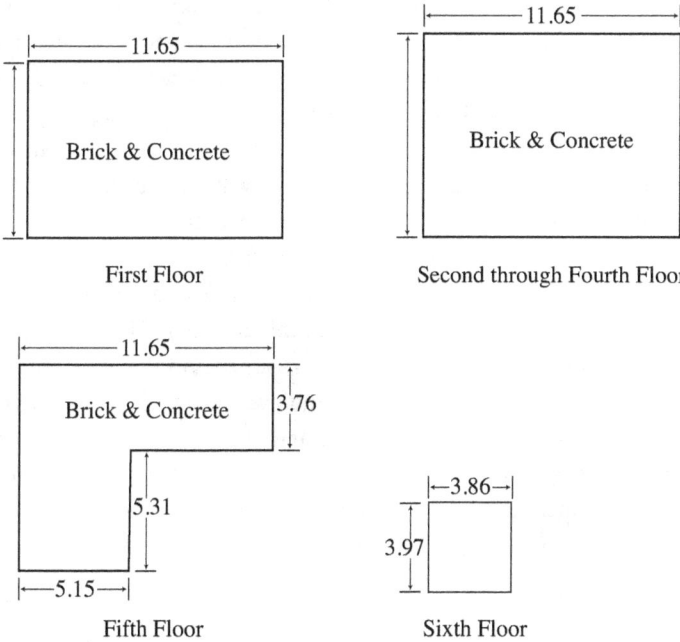

First Floor — Brick & Concrete (11.65)

Second through Fourth Floor — Brick & Concrete (11.65)

Fifth Floor — Brick & Concrete (11.65, 3.76, 5.31, 5.15)

Sixth Floor (3.86, 3.97)

Structure	Floor	Calculation Method						
Brick & Concrete	First Floor	S=11.65*7. 70=89. 71 m²						
Brick & Concrete	Second Floor	S=11.65*9. 01=104. 97 m²						
Brick & Concrete	Third Floor	S=11.65*9. 01=104. 97 m²						
Brick & Concrete	Fourth Floor	S=11.65*9. 01=104. 97 m²						
Brick & Concrete	Fifth Floor	S=11.65*3. 76+5.31*5. 15=71. 15 m²						
Brick & Concrete	Sixth Floor	S=3. 86*3. 97=15. 32 m²						
Structure Type	Frame	Brick & Concrete	Earth & Wood	Simple Construction	Steel Frame	Patio	Total Area
Area		491.09					491.09

FIGURE 19. A model housing contract. This contract values six floors based on area and infrastructural materials. Original contracts on file with author.

time. Partial demolition produces a landscape of strategic blight and a shared sense of imminent threat. The remaining infrastructural ruins were physically dangerous, which from the standpoint of residents, diminished senses of safety and habitability. Doors, walls, and windows, once damaged, created a shared sense of unsightliness. Broken water and sewage pipes caused not only a loss of access to water and sanitation services for sections of the village, but unsightly and odorously foul streets. Living among infrastructural ruin transformed senses of place and caused significant disruption to daily life. The diffuse effects of partial demolition influenced many to sign housing sale contracts and leave the village. Many other residents remained, at least initially.

As most residents continued to resist relocation, the demolition bureau employed increasingly confrontational techniques. Zhao Huangyong, a member of the village council during this time, explained how the demolition bureau hired "strongmen" (dashou) to break windows, smash water pipes, cut electricity lines, and damage cars at night. These illicit attacks on infrastructure, including housing, utilities, and sources of mobility, amplified disruptions to everyday life. Water and electricity services stopped for many, fomenting fears that they would not return. Residents became wary of people they perceived

FIGURE 20. A partially demolished house. Photo by author.

FIGURE 21. Partially demolished housing and cars damaged by a demolition bureau. Photo by author.

as strangers walking through the village. Infrastructural attacks foreshadowed bodily violence to come.

Village council members organized means of collective counter-conduct to resist attacks on property by the demolition bureau. In China, large group meetings in public spaces are forbidden. Villagers couldn't meet in their normal meeting place because the demolition bureau had rented the building for their office. Despite this setback, village council members devised a way to gather while avoiding the appearance of coming together in public spaces. They initiated, what they called, "bridge meetings" (*qiaotouhui*)—fluid meetings that involved walking and standing in small groups of people, usually five to six people at a time, in which they exchanged information about villagers' rights and experiences. They called these bridge meetings because they occurred near public news boards, a place villagers considered to be a bridge between New and Old Xiaoxi. So as not to appear as a group gathering in a public space, they stood in front of the news board as if reading and chatting. A cohort of professionals, familiar with the hardships the village was facing, contributed information about legal rights. Village council members relayed their messages to residents. During bridge meetings, residents also discussed their experiences with the demolition bureau. This form of collective counter-conduct cultivated a shared knowledge base. It also helped forge political solidarity in the face of infrastructural threats from the demolition bureau.

Members of the Xiaoxi demolition bureau became aware that Zhao was organizing bridge meetings. This placed him in their crosshairs. One evening, while walking home, Zhao noticed three people following him. Concerned, he quickened his pace. They quickened their pace. He turned down a side street. They turned down the same street. When Zhao looked over his shoulder and saw they followed him around a second corner he ran. They sprinted after him and began to gain ground. Zhao scrambled for his keys as he arrived at his front door, and quickly slammed the door behind him. Tensions between villagers and the demolition bureau heightened in the wake of attempted attacks, such as this one.

After this failed attack, the demolition bureau began partially demolishing the houses of residents who had not yet signed housing sale contracts. The demolition crew used excavators, bulldozers, and sledgehammers to smash in doorways and walls, leaving the rest of the infrastructure intact. Residents were shocked to return to their homes and find them damaged. Structural damage left many houses unsafe to inhabit. Open walls and doorways exposed belongings increasing vulnerability to theft. For some, the infrastructural damage to their house had the effect of sowing seeds of distrust as personal items and human bodies lie exposed day and night. But this was not the end of villagers' collective counter-conduct.

Villagers responded swiftly with new forms of collective counter-conduct. They surrounded the industrial demolition machinery to block access to demolition bureau crewmen. Skirmishes with demolition crewmen broke out when crew members tried to enter excavator cabs or approach demolition equipment surrounded by villagers. Days of guarding heavy demolition equipment turned into weeks. With the heavy machinery blocked in the village center, the demolition bureau sent crewmen to houses and stores on the outer perimeters of the village. There they continued the infrastructural onslaught manually. Partial demolition and property defacement ensued with shovels, sticks, and farming tools, whatever the demolition crew could get their hands on. These attacks on infrastructure lasted days. Zhao recalled how the bureau went so far as to send the crew out in the heavy rains with umbrellas to knock over market stalls, shatter windows, and commit petty robberies.

Frustrated by the lack of police response to these illegal activities, villagers protested outside government offices. Their pleas were ignored. They turned to the media, contacting multiple outlets in effort to gain wider attention. A CCTV news team came to cover the standoff between villagers and the demolition bureau. The crew began filming interviews for Focus (*jiaodian fangtan*), a popular news series. On the third day of interviews, half a dozen cars surrounded the CCTV journalists and their van. Hired hands emerged and stood around the reporter and camera operator menacingly. One snatched the camera and smashed it on the ground yelling, "Don't air any of this and don't come back to the village." The news team jumped into their car and drove off. The crew proceeded to chase the news van down the street. When other reporters came to the village in the following days, some from as far as Hong Kong, hired hands began barricading and guarding entrances to the village effectively blocking reporters from entering. Barricades at each intersection cut off traffic arteries. No cars could come in or out. The village was isolated. This infrastructural barrier geographically disintegrated the village from surrounding communities and media outlets.

Without wider public support that media coverage may have generated, villagers tried a more direct form of counter-conduct. A group of five representatives went to appeal to higher government authorities (*shangfang*). In their meetings, municipal government officials promised to investigate the matter. Ultimately, they did nothing to intervene. And no formal response ever came. Police did not respond to calls regarding partial demolition or petty thefts that followed. Villagers were on their own. And to many, it seemed that no end was in sight. As attacks on housing infrastructure escalated, a shared sense of desperation spread like wildfire.

After the failed attempt to seek municipal government intervention, roughly two hundred men dressed in black security guard attire appeared in the village. They surrounded the residents who were surrounding the demolition machinery. Both were armed. Villagers with sticks, farming tools, and bricks. Hired hands held clubs. It was unclear who dropped the brick from the top of a nearby building into the concentric assembly below. But, when that brick hit the pavement, violence erupted. A rush of bodies and farm tools, clubs and bricks, hammers and fists. Bodies fell to the ground bruised and bloodied. Some people ran from the skirmish. Others ran in headlong. Some broke off to fight away from the chaotic center.

A blur of bodies and movement filled the screen as Zhao and I watched the footage of the violent altercation on his living room television set. It was surreal to see the encounter unfold. Supporters had come to the village and smuggled camera equipment past the barriers, which they used to document the violent encounter. After this incident, they absconded with the footage and a handful of recorded interviews, thereby avoiding confiscation. During the altercation, a friend of Zhao's was seriously injured after a hired hand bludgeoned his head with a club. Two migratory laborers renting rooms in New Xiaoxi were killed in the altercation. Villagers pitched in for their coffins. As the violence illuminated the screen, we fell silent. Zhao smoked a cigarette while his wife Ran Hong cut up an apple and offered me slices. I wasn't hungry.

After watching the violence, Zhao continued to recount the events that followed. Roughly eighty villagers were detained. They were taken to police cars waiting outside village perimeter blockades. There they were arrested and charged with assaulting security guards. Some spent several months in jail. Some are still in prison. The whereabouts of others remain unknown. Zhao and others in the village felt like the demolition bureau set them up for the altercation and that the arrests were part of their efforts to acquire village housing.

The day after the altercation residents countered with their own infrastructurally destructive conduct. Residents doused heavy demolition equipment with gasoline and lit it ablaze. Then they proceeded to the demolition bureau office and set it on fire. The blaze in the demolition bureau office destroyed the computers and most of the documents. After the fire dissipated, villagers recovered several filing cabinets and ledgers from the building's remains. These contained documents about the internal operations of the demolition bureau, including names of bureau members, demolition bureau employees, financial transactions, village infrastructural layouts, as well as proposed and completed housing contracts. Zhao shared copies of these documents with me. One of the recovered spending ledgers held financial information regarding demolition bureau transactions. The spending ledger and other documents, on file with the author, indicate that the demolition bureau hired thugs to attack Zhao months prior.

After Xiaoxi villagers set the demolition bureau office and the demolition equipment on fire, attacks on infrastructure ceased. But the damage was done. Houses and other infrastructure across the village were partially demolished. There was no place where residents were not confronted with piles of rubble and crumbling walls. Partial infrastructural demolition created a palpable sense of blight. Before these incidents, residents were proud of their houses in New Xiaoxi and their traditional homes in Old Xiaoxi.

The demolition bureau's infrastructural techniques were designed to be divisive. In their aftermath, deep divisions took root among residents. Many were concerned with the way the village looked. Buildings were in disarray. Crumbling infrastructure symbolized, for many, painful memories of violence and loss. Infrastructural ruins were reminders of the violence they experienced, which induced fear that the demolition bureau would resume partial demolitions and physical violence. Moreover, many perceived the landscape as unsightly.

I listened to debates between residents. Some argued for rebuilding and holding on to village traditions. Others condemned rebuilding noting the difficulties of "living in shambles" in a place that "looks so poor."

Members of the original village council who initially galvanized support to resist housing sales tried to garner support for remaking Xiaoxi into an "historical cultural heritage village." They hosted a weekly Chinese opera troupe that performed in the village temple. Additionally, they began raising finances for renovating housing in the old village. But their influence within the village continued to wane, and with it political solidarity. Residents were not only feeling the effects of living in a landscape of strategic blight, but a competing faction consisting of new village representatives who were incorporated in the demolition bureau were becoming influential. New village representatives began meeting individually with households to try to convince them to sell their housing. Their stance conflicted with previous members of the village council. These two political factions espoused competing visions for the village's future. Political unity, once strong, began to disintegrate as time passed living in a landscape of strategic blight.

In the context of living in an infrastructurally disintegrating and politically divided village, residents weighed the costs of staying and rebuilding against the benefits of moving into resettlement housing. Water pipes remained in disrepair after demolition bureau crewmen broke them. Garbage collection services in the village ceased. Sewage ran through the streets. The village landscape, as many villagers described, became unpleasant to see (*tai nankan*). Architectural ruins reflected village political unity. Like the material infrastructure, a singular galvanizing vision from village leaders disintegrated. With it, collective counter-conduct in Xiaoxi also disintegrated. Bridge meetings ceased. As did embodied collective efforts to surround demolition machinery and confront the demolition bureau. Instead, infrastructural diffusion took effect shaping trajectories of flight from the village. Residents struggled to live within quotidian landscapes of ruin. They struggled to hold together a disintegrating community. They felt isolated and afraid for their families. Ensconced in an aesthetic of detritus, residents began to approach the demolition bureau independently at their new office, further away from the village, to sign housing contracts.

The aesthetic effects of partial infrastructural demolition shaped the sensibilities of residents. As daily exposure to potentially harmful infrastructural remains became commonplace, newly built resettlement apartments appeared ever more desirable. Over time, more Xiaoxi residents moved into resettlement housing. Techniques of infrastructural diffusion and their effects disintegrated not only material infrastructure, but also forms of collective counter-conduct, political solidarity, and ultimately, a residential community.

When negotiations over contracts failed, infrastructural techniques, supported by the inaction of police and government officials, contributed to disintegrating physical and social infrastructures. Partial demolition of infrastructure had the effect of creating a landscape of strategic blight. Coercion and violence at the hands of demolition bureau crewman had the effect of disintegrating a sense of security from daily life. Municipal government inaction disintegrated trust in sovereign powers to take effective action and made the prospect of lawful recourse implausible. Governmental inaction and lack of legal accountability revealed the impunity with which demolition bureaus are allowed to act. Direct threats to media had the effect of shielding Xiaoxi's struggles from a wider public.[26]

Infrastructural diffusion and its effects produced archipelagos of isolation in Xiaoxi village. With each house the demolition bureau acquires, their crew leaves demolished remains in place as hazard, aesthetic eyesore, and omen. As residents move out, infrastructural disrepair widens compounding its effects and contributing to the slow disintegration of residents' collective will to remain in place.

Blinding

As Wang Bairui, a grey-haired village resident, talked about how his village's agricultural land was zoned for ecological protection his countenance slowly changed. His smile faded and he suggested we talk at his home instead of the public square. We entered his home and sat down on low stools in the kitchen. In hushed tones, Wang recounted a violent assault he experienced at the hands of village council members after he contested inaccurate farmland measurements. After the agricultural land was assessed, Wang found his household farm plots to be significantly undermeasured. Concerned about being undercompensated, Wang went to the village council to dispute the matter.

> My land was going to be taken by the government. I went to the village office in [place redacted] to meet about the village land measurements. At that time, villagers thought that the land would be paid for based on the amount of land assigned to each household. I realized that my plots were under-measured and went to take this up with the village council. The discussion quickly turned bad. The village headman and other members of the village council started cursing at me. I felt offended and delivered harsh words in return. Out of nowhere, in the middle of this argument, the son of the village council accountant punched me in the eye. He punched me with his knuckle extended to make an impact, causing blood to spill out of my eye socket.

As he spoke, Wang stuck out his middle knuckle to simulate the fist that landed in his eye. After being punched, the conversation was over. Wang's eye bled profusely. He called the police. Police officers arrived shortly thereafter and took testimony from Wang and the village councilmen. The police left without writing anything down or explaining how they would deal with the matter. They never filed a case or followed up with Wang.

The village headman gave Wang 300 RMB (US$50) and told him to go to the hospital for treatment. Wang ended up with six stiches in his left eye and 10,000 RMB (US$1,500) in medical bills. After the incident Wang hired a lawyer and filed a civil case against the village council accountant's son. A court-appointed doctor ruled Wang totally blind in one eye. The court awarded the expenses of his medical fees but did not pursue criminal prosecution—a slap on the wrist. Wang was visibly upset while he recounted the events to me. Tearing up, he lamented his lost eye and ability to perceive depth.

Halfway through our discussion he stopped talking and closed the kitchen door. Returning to his seat, he said he was worried that someone might hear him and file a report against him or use his words against him somehow. Without the door fully closed, Wang felt unnerved discussing the assault he experienced, even within the confines of his own home. "Those people [other villagers] will stab you in the back, even though you are just sharing information. These petty people [xiaoren] will do something behind your back," he said.

Land compensation in Wang's village was eventually awarded according to registered hukous not agricultural plot sizes. Each registered hukou received 190,000 RMB in compensation capital. His attempt to counter land measurements with the village council was a moot venture. Nonetheless, Wang was partially blinded by disputing land measurements with the village council. And the personal violence against his body had tangible effects, particularly regarding how Wang interacted with fellow villagers. After his violent meeting with the village council, Wang avoided group meetings and social interactions with government representatives. He also felt leery discussing government-led initiatives for environmental protection with his fellow villagers.

The village council most closely engages and represents village interests.[27] Bodily violence and unjust legal redress put Wang at odds with them. Since the dispute happened at the village level and courts did not provide punitive justice, Wang felt apprehensive to take the case to higher levels. The violent and juridical squelching of his individual counter-conduct had the effect of isolating him from social infrastructures. This left Wang in an isolated state. His fears extended from government officials to his own neighbors. Unsure of who might be an ally, Wang became an island unto himself.

The isolation of Wang's experience masks the violence undergirding land and housing displacement from the wider public. Wang became a visible example to his fellow villagers of what can happen to citizens who counter local state efforts to acquire land. Additionally, Wang's account sheds light on the impunity with which village council members, the closest link between villagers and higher levels of government, can enact violence and the effects such violence has in isolating villagers from one another. In this sense, the partial blinding of Wang prevented him from seeking community support. Mutual informing on one another is an ever-present danger. This imminent threat cautioned Wang against discussing his experiences with his rural community or sharing it with a wider public. Keeping such experiences unseen and unheard contributes to the maintenance of authoritarian power. I heard numerous stories, such as Wang's, throughout fieldwork. The prevalence of such accounts indexes how "blinding," or violently and juridically diffusing individual counter-conduct, undergirds authoritarian power.

Disassembling

"Refugee district" migrants, discussed in chapter 4 as poorly compensated ecological migrants resettled in low-quality, high-rise housing, spoke about fellow villagers who refused to relocate. Refugee district ecological migrants told me the location of their village, which I refer to in this section as Wailong. And I visited Wailong to learn more about how the few village residents there remained in place.

Arriving in Wailong, I could see a few houses standing at the main intersection of what appeared to be a ghost village amid an industrial tree planation. I stopped at a house with a front door converted into a general store. Beverages, cigarettes, snacks, and household items were on display. I asked the middle-aged store attendant what happened to all the other houses. "They became trees," she said pointing to the young saplings growing across from her house. "These all used to be houses, but they tore them down and planted fields of trees." After being zoned as an ecological protection area, Wailong's farmland was transformed into a plantation. Individual household plots were incorporated into a commercial fruit orchard. "A greening company (*lühua gongsi*) came and planted trees on the land that used to be ours," she continued. I later learned through interviews, that the proprietary owner of the fruit orchard was a private company. "Afforestation" was the function assigned to the ecological protection area in the urban-rural coordinated plan. Ecological construction for this company entailed planting and managing a commercial forest.[28]

Amid the forest and crumbled remains of houses, I met Huang Jiafu. Huang was among a handful of people still living in the village. More than two hundred others relocated to the refugee district resettlement complex. Huang's garage door was open. A sign on the doorway advertised "Huang's Special Sauce." Huang greeted me through the open garage door. Born in 1948, at the cusp of the PRC, Huang's balding middle brow shined as he walked into the sunlight in a red-collared, long-sleeve shirt. He told me about the history of the village, how it hollowed out, and the plantation that surrounded us. "This village was established six hundred years ago," Huang said. He retrieved a copy of the Huang Clan family record (*pujikao*), which catalogued nineteen generations.[29] Huang was the nineteenth generation to live in this village and was determined not to be the last.

In the 1980s, Huang was a production team leader in his village. He was also an elected member of the village council, but never became a communist party cadre. After two years in that position, he was forced to step down because, in his words: "I refused to lie about how things really were. I told the truth about what happened in the village and would not just say everything was alright. I tried to serve the people and wouldn't bow to the higher authorities [*pai mapi*]. So, they made me step down." Huang became familiar with rural policies through his service. So, when demolition bureau representatives presented an environmental survey to justify the purchase of Wailong's village land and housing, he did not sign their contract.

In Wailong, environmental surveys were used to rationalize village resettlement. Demolition bureau representatives distributed a document summarizing a scientific environmental survey to villagers titled, *Tier One Protection Area Core Area Pamphlet*.[30] The document was made by the Office of Immigration and Relocation Leading Group. Representatives from the demolition bureau delivered copies of the nearly fifty-page document to each household and told residents they were living in a "core ecological protection area" (*hexin shengtai baohuqu*). Demolition bureau representatives, noting the environmental survey, said villagers had to move out of their house. There were no formal notifications (*tongzhi*) outside the distribution of the document.

The introductory pages explain that a scientific survey of the area was conducted two years prior. Then, in question-and-answer format, the document states that since water quality measures in a nearby water source were first recorded by scientists, pollution levels have risen significantly. The document claims that villagers' agricultural activities were responsible for the increase in pollution. It then states that the municipality is implementing a "tier one ecological protection area migration project. Farmer's agricultural practices must cease immediately, and farmers must leave the land and their houses in accordance with state directed urbanization and resettlement."[31] The document contains tables illustrating data from a "material survey" (*wuzhibiao diaocha*) of households and land use types. Tables present the average household income for Wailong based on market prices of commonly grown crops. The document also details standards for land compensation based on these estimates and includes compensation figures for housing based on housing materials and square space. It states that this standardized amount will be distributed to each household after migration (*yimin*) into resettlement housing.

There could be two kinds of migration processes, the document states. One form of migration is to a different village located far from the ecological protection area; the second is in urban resettlement housing. The document does not specify which will occur or how that decision will be made. Tables within the document detail economic sums for compensation. The actual compensation for residents in the refugee district, however, was less than a tenth of the amount presented in the environmental survey. If each person was compensated according to the prices quoted in this document, each villager would have received approximately 1,200,000 RMB (US$170,000). Each household had 16.3 mu (2.7 acres) of mountainous farmland, and 3.5 mu (0.6 acres) of level-ground farmland. Instead, refugee district ecological migrants were being compensated at a rate of 7,200 RMB a year for a period of twenty years, which amounts to a mere 140,000 RMB (US$20,000). By the scientific survey's own measures, ecological migrants are being grossly undercompensated. These compensation payments recur monthly unless an ecological migrant passes away, at which point compensation goes to next of kin and the amount is half of what it would be if they were still alive (see chapter 4).

The environmental survey represents state efforts to create a shared understanding with villagers regarding their culpability for pollution. Assembling and distributing these materials was part of the process of justifying ecological migration to village residents. For some villagers, this document and demolition bureau representatives' insistence that all villagers must relocate was sufficient to convince them that there was no alternative to resettlement. But others, such as Huang, were unconvinced and had no intention of moving.

After the demolition bureau offered signing bonuses, representatives began daily visits to village residents who refused to sign housing contracts. In their initial visits, demolition bureau representatives discussed how much better life was going to be in resettlement housing and emphasized how their migration was predetermined by higher levels of government. In subsequent visits, discussions veered to how villagers were "uncivilized" polluters causing environmental degradation. Demolition bureau representatives pointed to the environmental survey as supporting evidence for such claims. As some village residents resisted ecological migration, the demolition bureau undertook more coercive techniques.

Demolition bureau representatives began telling villagers that bad things would happen to them or their families if they refused to sign the housing contract. Huang and others discussed these techniques as "ideological work" (*sixiang gongzuo*), an allusion to Maoist-era propaganda campaigns, where the object was to convince someone of campaign logics. In this case, demolition bureau representatives tried to convince village residents that moving into resettlement units was necessary for environmental protection and civilized behavior—both key logics underlying state efforts to build an ecological civilization. After several weeks of intensive ideological work by demolition bureau representatives many residents still refused to sign housing contracts.

At that point, the demolition bureau began to disassemble utilities infrastructure. The pipes funneling water into the village were broken. With the pipes broken, running water was inaccessible. Next, the demolition bureau disassembled electricity infrastructure. Residents discovered that a central conducting unit used to transfer electricity to the village had been removed. The electricity stayed off for weeks before villagers repaired the unit themselves. But the village remained without running water for more than a year.

After disassembling physical infrastructure, which had diffuse effects of disrupting villagers' daily life, the demolition bureau's crewmen adopted techniques that targeted Huang. They viewed Huang as a key figure holding together those that remained in the village. As such, they saw him as a linchpin in their efforts to disassemble social infrastructure. The demolition bureau went to great lengths to force Huang to resettle.

Huang recounted how, on one occasion, twenty strongmen (*dashou*) entered his home and used "heavy-handed methods" (*qiangzhi fangshi*) to try to force him to sign a housing contract. They surrounded him in his own house and yelled at him to sign the contract. Huang refused. After several hours of verbal threats, they departed warning that something bad would happen to him if he did not sign the contract and relocate. A week after this visit, an excavator tore a hole in the roof of his family's house, where he lived during his youth. Although he desperately tried to stop the demolition crew, they ignored him. Huang watched helplessly as the demolition crew broke through the roof and tore it to the ground. "It was illegal for them [the demolition bureau] to destroy my house and try to make us sell our land and housing. The whole thing was illegal, unfair, and irrational."

We walked through scattered remains, farming tools, debris, and dust. Thick mud brick walls, wooden beams, and a stone base were still intact, but the roof and second floor laid on the ground in tatters. Huang showed me the room where he was born. Then where the room he was married used to be. Huang explained that since the demolition bureau first started to, in his words, "make the village disappear," they enacted an infrastructural moratorium on building new housing additions, renovations, or repairs. Because he lived in an ecological protection area, Huang was prohibited from repairing his partially demolished house.

In Wailong, an assemblage of infrastructural techniques, including environmental surveys, infrastructural disassembly, moratoriums on infrastructural repair, and coercive threats, operationalized authoritarian power. Geographer Michael Watts, writing on resource governance, defines assemblages as "coordinated but dispersed set[s] of regulations, calculative arrangements, infrastructural and technical procedures . . . [that] render certain objects or flows governable."[32] Calculative infrastructural disassembly stopped the flow of water and electricity to Wailong village. And an infrastructural moratorium stopped residents from repairing damaged housing. When villagers tried to bring tools and construction materials into the village, demolition bureau representatives confiscated them and blocked entrances to the village—further isolating Wailong. For those who needed housing repairs, this assemblage of infrastructural techniques not only stopped the flow of infrastructural material for repair, but also disassembled social infrastructures. Much like Xiaoxi village, the removal of infrastructure had the effect, over time, of provoking many in Wailong to accept ecological migration. Most villagers relocated. Those that remained were barred from assisting one another with infrastructural repairs. For most residents, this assemblage of infrastructural techniques marked a final chapter on life in Wailong. For those that remained, like Huang, more coercive techniques were still to come.

One day, a hundred strongmen forced their way into Huang's house and began removing his furniture and other belongings. They took approximately 30,000 RMB worth of items, including farming tools and cooking equipment he used to make Huang's Special Sauce. He recalled thinking that there was nothing he could do. There were so many of them. Huang felt alone. The police did not respond to his phone calls. Few other village residents remained. Isolated, without support, there was no way to stop them from taking his possessions.

Despite the loss, Huang was determined to remain in his home. In addition to land, his house had been key to his livelihood. In the late 1990s, Huang turned his home into a *nongjiale*, a rural-themed restaurant (see chapter 5). He forged relationships with restaurants in the city to sell food products. But since his village was zoned for ecological protection, he was unable to renew his restaurant license. He kept his old license to prove that his establishment was once officially registered. By disassembling his culinary infrastructure, however, the demolition bureau had removed the material means to operate his rural-themed restaurant. Huang was forced to close. Huang lived, increasingly, in isolation.

The disassembling of rural infrastructure mirrored the village's social infrastructure. After most village residents relocated to urban high-rise resettlement housing, Huang submitted documents and petitions to different levels of govern-ment pleading to take account of the inconsistencies between the compensation capital promised in the *Tier One Protection Area Core Area Pamphlet* and the amount actually meted out to ecological migrants. His efforts have been to no avail. As villagers became urbanites, their hukou were officially changed from rural to urban. When they became urban hukou holders, they were no longer entitled to agricultural land use rights or rural housing land. Of crucial impor-tance is that after changing hukou status from rural to urban, the village council disassembled. The few who remained in Wailong no longer had village council representation. "The village has disappeared [*xiaoshi*]," one resident explained. "There is no longer even a village council that governs us. Now we self-govern [*ziji zhili*]." Without a village council, those that remained in Wailong lost their representational body for communicating with the local state, further isolating residents. Those who refused resettlement continued growing produce in the interstitial land between commercial orchards. For the time being, they labored without oversight from a village council.

The small number of Wailong villagers who remained were isolated in their counter-conduct. Petitions for higher-level governmental support went unanswered. Damaged houses cannot be repaired due to the infrastructural mortarium. No media coverage amplified their story. Under the veil of threat, they remained separated from their former village community as islands unto themselves.

Uprooting

The ethnographic accounts in this chapter reveal how infrastructural diffusion is sewn into the fabric of authoritarian governance. Infrastructural diffusion has the effect of dividing communities and isolating individuals, thereby producing archipelagos of isolation. Although isolated from one another, the accounts in this chapter share common features. In each case, infrastructural techniques dif-fused collective or individual counter-conduct. My aim in presenting them is to draw attention to a lexicon of infrastructural techniques that contribute to the maintenance of authoritarian rule.

Archipelagos of isolation, the geographical products of infrastructural dif-fusion, are integral to the spatial constitution and everyday expressions of authoritarian power. As such, they point to the limits of counter-conduct under authoritarian rule. Those who counter state efforts to build an ecological civiliza-tion face techniques of infrastructural diffusion the effects of which are isolat-ing. Infrastructural diffusion transformed once vibrant places into landscapes of disrepair. Once unified communities divided. Collective counter-conduct morphed into a babel of dissenting politics. Demolition bureaus disassembled and disintegrated physical and social infrastructures. Individuals' counter-conduct was met with violence, coercive threats, and ultimately social isolation. Others who sought justice and legal redress for police violence encountered digital erasure. Infrastructural diffusion turned shared crises into solitary crucibles. The effects of these infrastructural techniques forced the few who remained in villages into a fundamentally ambiguous realm of citizenship, at odds with the state-sanctioned contract to become part of the urban citizenry.

These vast archipelagos of isolation are veiled geographies of an urbanizing citizenry under authoritarian rule. Forms of counter-conduct are diffused through infrastructural techniques that appear as banal aesthetic features of demolition, redevelopment, or conservation. Partially demolished housing and construction projects are ubiquitous across China. In this sense, infrastructural diffusion operates on a grand scale of visibility. The banality of infrastructural disrepair contributes to normalizing displacement and expressions of authoritarian power in action. Infrastructural diffusion, therefore, is crucial to reorienting the subject positionalities of China's citizenry and bringing the state's eco-developmental vision to fruition.

Although those who counter prescribed eco-developmental trajectories find themselves uprooted from familiar moorings, disaggregated nodes of contention harbor alternative ways of imagining governance and more equitably provisioning for a society transforming in the name of ecological civilization. As people navigate becoming part of ecological civilization's urban citizenry, they articulate through word and deed alternative desires for inclusion and, at times, needs.

* * *

I met Cui Liang, an elderly villager outside her home as she fed chickens. She spoke loudly to match the diminishing range of her ears. She farmed her whole life. And after her village agricultural land was incorporated into an ecological protection area, Cui refused to stop growing produce in the interstitial spaces that were, in her view, "not being used." Her children had moved out long ago and provided minimal support. Growing vegetables and raising chickens in between newly planted trees were key sources of sustenance. Farming, for her, wasn't merely a pastime; it was a survival strategy.

The village headman warned Cui to stop growing on land that no longer belonged to the village. But she was desperate. Low-income state subsidies (*dibao*) were not enough. Nearly a year into growing on ecological protection land, a group of uniformed military personnel arrived in trucks at one of her guerrilla garden plots as she was picking weeds. Filing off, they marched into the plot and tore her vegetables out of the ground. The troop leader loomed above her and yelled "stop growing here." The soldiers filed back onto their truck and drove off. Cui was scared by this extraordinary military display and stopped growing for a time. But her hunger did not abate.

After several months, and with what little savings she had diminished, she started a new plot in the interstitial spaces of the ecological protection area. She, once again, tilled the soil and planted vegetables. Half a year later, a member of the village council came to her new plot with a handheld weeding device and destroyed her crops in moments. Dejected, Cui returned home. Her eyes began to tear up as she recounted these events to me in her house. It took months to cultivate a plot that provides sustenance. And, like the last plot, it was destroyed in moments. Despite the physical uprooting of her produce, she continued growing vegetables in the in-between places of the ecological protection area.

Cui's individual counter-conduct was her refusal to stop growing. She refused, out of necessity, to abide by the ecological protection area moratoriums placed on agricultural production and animal rearing. She collected food scraps from rural-themed restaurants (*nongjiale*) that catered to tourists within the ecological protection area. Cui dried the scraps, then she ground them into powder to feed chickens. She hid the chickens in her house to avoid potential confrontations with those enforcing environmental policy. Cui reconstituted subsistence strategies in relation to the waste products from the conservation site and continued growing.

This brief closing account, detailing the uprooting of Cui's guerrilla agricultural plots, illustrates how state efforts to bring a particular eco-developmental vision to fruition omits the needs of those most intimately effected. Cui's experience points to not only the inadequacies of the social welfare system, but also the effects of forfeiting land for conservation and urbanization on the well-being of those most vulnerable. The process of being incorporated into the state's eco-developmental vision entails myriad uneven social trajectories. Villagers like Cui face a trajectory steeped in precarity and isolation.

Cui's counter-conduct, as well as other examples of counter-conduct detailed above, index deep fissures between eco-developmental logics, totalizing techniques of socio-environmental management, and more equitable sustainable development trajectories. Cui is one among many who inhabit China's vast archipelagos of isolation. She felt alone as she struggled to survive the transitions underway. But her experiences are not uncommon. Millions of people are experiencing uneven incorporation into state projects of green urbanization and ecological civilization building. And many, like Cui, are resilient, capable, and hungry.

GLOBAL ECOLOGICAL FUTURES

During 2021, the city of Kunming hosted part one of the Fifteenth United Nations Biodiversity Conference titled "Ecological Civilization: Building a Shared Future for All Life on Earth." The director of the UN Environment World Conservation Monitoring Center, speaking after the initial announcement of the conference theme, said, "Ecological civilization not only reflects the essential role that nature plays in underpinning people's lives but also the need to improve our relationship with nature. . . . We are working to help the world re-establish a balance in our relationships with other life on earth and we look forward to continuing to support the development of the future plan for nature."[1] The conference outlined a global conservation plan for the next thirty years. The timeline for the plan aligns with the 2049 centennial of the People's Republic of China, such that the PRC's 100th year will mark ecological civilization becoming a shared reality for "all life on earth." Vice Premier Han Zheng, in the inaugural speech, proclaimed, "Ecological civilization building a shared future for all life on earth captures the international communities wishes for recalibrating relationships between humans and nature, the harmonious co-existence between humans and nature, and a collective effort to safeguard the common homeland of planet earth." In international conservation venues such as this, ecological civilization building is mobilized to project a *global* sustainable development trajectory.

As this book goes to press, the UN post-2020 global biodiversity framework calls for the entirety of earth's land and water to be brought under spatial planning for land use change and 30 percent of the planet to be set aside as protected conservation areas.[2] The latter target is circulating within global discourse as "30 by 30," shorthand for zoning 30 percent of the earth for conservation by the year 2030. How will such large-scale interventions transform nature, society, and space the world over? What do global articulations and celebrations of ecological civilization building have in store for the future of planetary environmental governance? To consider these questions, I examine how the Chinese state's approaches to environmental governance are shaping global ecologies, geopolitics, and sustainable development trajectories.

First, there are important lessons to be garnered from China's ecological protection zoning efforts. Opportunistic municipal government officials implement conservation zoning for multiple political-economic and governmental ends. Generating local revenues from land, urbanizing rural people, and beautifying landscapes are some examples. Techniques of ecological optimization facilitate the extension of municipal state power over rural land, thereby contributing to the rescaling of local state power. Ecological protection zoning policies pave the way for conservation-oriented development and population control mechanisms. In these ways, state power has come to be expressed and constituted in relation to ecology territorially and through institutionalized bureaucratic state formations.

As large-scale ecological protection zoning goes global, it is crucial to be attentive to how efforts to conserve vast stretches of the world's lands and seas, such as those detailed in the post-2020 global biodiversity framework, serve governmental ends and effect societies. Researchers who modeled the effects of the post-2020 biodiversity conservation framework argue that protecting half of the earth would effect upward of one billion people.[3] This scale of conservation efforts would disproportionately effect marginalized populations living within or in the vicinity of protected areas, as well as those whose access to resources would be constrained.[4] It is clear from estimates on the social effects of global conservation planning that planetary-scale conservation efforts require substantial safeguards against marginalization and displacement if they are to align with the sustainable development goal of alleviating poverty.

The uneven socioeconomic outcomes of incorporating rural land and housing into state conservation projects in China, for instance, point to a pressing need for more robust social welfare mechanisms that attend to the needs of those displaced, as well as greater attention to land use and housing security. Although the Chinese state aims to alleviate poverty, ecological migration contributes to reorienting and deepening social inequalities. Uncritical celebrations of large-scale conservation zoning portend a future wherein global inequality could deepen if inadequate attention is given to the social effects of conservation efforts.

On a fundamental level, uneven displacement and resettlement processes beg the question of why urbanization retains its iron-clad grip on state science and policy in China. Indeed, many argue that there are alternative ways to foster sustainability, which celebrate and maintain rural lifeways.[5] Maintaining small-holder land use rights and advancing redistributional policies aimed at mitigating urban-rural inequality are among the alternative development platforms that remain on the fringe. The disjuncture between state scientific planning projections and social outcomes points to the importance of situating ecology and sustainable development within historical and political conditions that give meaning and shape practices.

Over a century of global engagements, China's natural and social scientists came to articulate ecology in relation to state-led developmental progress toward a sustainable future. Ecological civilization, in this techno-scientific imaginary, is a future state of being and attainment wherein socio-natural relations exist in optimized balance—a balance produced through state intervention. This articulation of ecological states contrasts with assessments of modernist states as relatively rigid simplifiers of socio-natural complexity.[6] Instead of simplifications, ecological states operate through logics and techniques that harness complexity to govern nature, society, and space. State-led efforts to urbanize rural people through resettlement in spatially optimized environments reify the malleable nature and value (*suzhi*) of the rural citizenry. Historicizing the emergence of eco-developmental logics and techniques illuminates the role of ecological thought in naturalizing uneven subject positionalities within China's citizenry. Shedding light on the historical contingency of such logics lays a foundation for reorienting socio-environmental governance and state policies toward less socially stratified platforms.

Counterintuitive as it may seem, shared aesthetic sensibilities are embedded within eco-developmental logics and shape scientific techniques. Aesthetics shape the content of scientific theories and practices, how values are ascribed to nature, and how societies are defined within scientific paradigms. And yet, in most contexts, scientists deemphasize the aesthetic registers that animate their work. The case of ecological restoration in the Lake Dian basin, for instance, illustrates how shared aesthetic sensibilities inform scientific practices. Beauty is embedded in scientific practices such as ecological restoration, as well as techniques of quantifying the beautiful at a national scale. President Xi Jinping articulated the Beautiful China Initiative (BCI) as an explicitly aesthetic component of ecological civilization building. In 2020, the Chinese Academy of Sciences created the Beauty Index to quantify the level of beauty attained nationally in effort "to realize the BCI timetable and roadmap to a high quality and high standard."[7] Scientists proposed the BCI index to be used in yet another layer of comprehensive zoning to optimize beauty. The BCI index introduces a new era of eco-developmental quantifiability wherein metrics of beauty can be measured, quantified, and mapped.

Citizens navigate ecological expressions and constitutions of state power in highly uneven ways. Unequal subject positionalities shape how rural citizens are able or unable to access spaces in transition, as well as the differentiated spatial practices through which they counter and capitalize on state attempts to govern society and nature. In effort to accrue value from representing rural experiences in and near ecological protection areas, rural citizens emplace shared aesthetic senses within landscapes of displacement. Their efforts resignify ecology through a rural-ecological sublime. In detailing this aesthetic, I draw attention to the limits of eco-developmental signification and the fact that societies imbue ecology with alternative meanings. As ecological civilization building resonates across global contexts, it is imperative to examine how different states, societies, and scientific communities ascribe their own meanings.

Ecological civilization building animates dialogues on socio-environmental processes and sustainable futures across global contexts. For example, the California-based nonprofit Institute for Ecological Civilization (EcoCiv), an organization with close ties to the Claremont School of Theology, promotes discussions on ecological civilization at the nexus of theology, Whiteheadian process-oriented philosophy, and relational ontology.[8] EcoCiv organizes public lectures and conferences. One of their flagship programs, EcoCiv Korea, involves partnerships with South Korean organizations to promote dialogue on ecological civilization. Their conferences in Seoul featured speakers from academic, civil service, and ecclesiastic backgrounds who articulated a range of ideas on ecological civilization. The meanings they associate with ecological civilization, however, differ substantially from materialist conceptualizations developed by China's scientific communities, which aim to synthesize ecology with socialist thought and state efforts toward green modernization.

The alignment of ecology and state power in China provides a cautionary tale, one that is not merely relevant to my research sites but to state projects that mechanize nature across the nation and beyond. For instance, China is undertaking a series of large-scale water- and weather-oriented environmental engineering projects. These include the south-north water diversion project aimed at preventing water shortages in comparatively dry northern regions. The south-north water diversion project will redirect nearly forty-five billion cubic meters of water from the Yangtze northward through a system of pipes to service water-starved cities like Beijing and Tianjin. Analogous to the peri-urban villagers unevenly incorporated into municipal conservation projects, the water diversion project has already displaced and resettled hundreds of thousands of people.[9] The south-north water diversion project entails myriad power struggles between the state and citizenry for control over resources, as well as intrastate struggles for territorial control over nature.[10] China's mechanistic approaches to governing nature, however, are not limited to the domestic sphere. This is particularly evident when considering China's role in geoengineering.

China is taking a leading role among the world's authoritative voices on climate change, particularly through climate geoengineering. In recent years, China developed the largest state-funded geoengineering research program in the world. This, among other efforts, places China in a prime position among the world's leaders in researching and assessing technologies for altering climactic conditions. While recently on the fringes of science, geoengineering has exploded into mainstream scientific discourse over the last decades. Frequently discussed geoengineering strategies include displacing sunlight in the stratosphere and changing the reflective character of clouds to block the sun's rays. During the 2008 and 2022 Olympics, geoengineering techniques were used to alter Beijing's weather to ensure a "blue sky" day for the opening events. Since the 2008 games, these techniques have already become a commonplace feature of state bureaucratic performance. Creating blue sky days is a process—both technical and aesthetic—through which government officials are evaluated and seek promotion.[11] Such mechanistic approaches to governing nature have become part of the metrics through which bureaucrats advance within the party-state. As such, geoengineering blue sky days is yet another way ecological expressions of state power are institutionalized.[12] The effects of these expressions are not limited to China. Mechanistic approaches to alter the atmosphere can fundamentally alter global climactic relations.

In 2018, as part of a cloud-seeding effort directed by a state-owned enterprise (SOE), China launched the world's largest weather-control program. The program, in 2018, had the capabilities to alter weather patterns over an earth surface the size of Alaska. The geoengineering project produces artificial rain by emitting thousands of iodide particles via machines placed within earthen chambers across the Tibetan Plateau. These machines, coupled with aircraft, mechanize nature by lacing clouds with silver iodide that thickens water molecules to fall as precipitation. A state declaration claims that the project will produce ten billion cubic meters of artificial rain each year to replenish rapidly depleting water reserves. These waters flow from the Tibetan Plateau to the Yangtze River en route to major rivers in Southeast Asia, including the Brahmaputra, Mekong, and Salween rivers.[13] In 2020, the central state announced a fivefold expansion of this program to cover an area more than one and a half times the size of India.[14] This large-scale project to mechanize nature and optimize ecology is but one among many.

The Tianhe Project (Sky River), currently being developed by Chinese scientists, aims to use weather modification techniques to divert water vapors toward dry regions of the Yellow River basin.[15] Across China's desert landscapes, the state, in cooperation with private enterprise, is seeding the desert with draught resistant plants in effort to control sandstorms and mitigate desertification. These efforts to engineer water, wind, and sand effect not only ecological migrants displaced in the name of ecological security, but also the particulate quality of air in Japan and the western United States.[16] Large-scale weather modification projects exist alongside regional-scale efforts, such as the those directed by the Beijing Weather Modification Office, tasked with controlling weather in Beijing, Hebei, and Inner Mongolia. In ways such as these, climate engineering is well underway, and techniques of mechanizing nature are already institutionalized within the Chinese state.

The Chinese state, therefore, is firmly at the forefront of the technological fix paradigm. The state portrays technical fixes as a panacea for myriad environmental problems and a means to bring about ecologically civilized relationships between humans and nature. The myriad problems of climate change, according to this mechanistic logic, can be solved through proper science and engineering. It is increasingly clear that such mechanistic techniques also extend the reach of the state. China extends state power not only through aerial volumes and atmospheres but also through mechanizing ocean ecologies.

In 2014, Chinese vessels dredged underwater coral reefs to engineer more than 3,200 acres of terra-formed islands in the South China Sea. The state proceeded to lay sovereign claims to the newly terra-formed islands, the air above them, and ocean surrounding them, in volumetric ecological expressions of power.[17] Terraforming artificial islands transformed underwater ecologies into military outposts with surface-to-air missiles and runways long enough to launch and land fighter jets. Underwater reef ecologies became the infrastructure on which the state expressed and materialized sovereign claims. Bolstered by the nine-dash line—a dotted line on Chinese maps that extends from Hainan, China's southernmost province, to Taiwan encompassing the bulk of the South China Sea— China maintains sovereign claims despite repudiation by the UN Convention on the Law of the Sea.

Terraforming artificial islands is a global ecological expression of China's sovereign imaginary, one that is already reshaping geopolitical futures. The party-state and national media refer to these areas as part of "blue state territory" (lanse guotu). Official figures giving the extent of blue state territory weigh in just shy of three million square kilometers—roughly one-third of China's entire mainland territory. Since the creation and militarization of these geo-infrastructures, military techniques to support sovereign claims over water, land, and air have become routine. Military boats patrol fishing vessels and trade across the ocean's surface. Routine flyovers in international airspace near these islands are met with radio warnings not to violate China's sovereignty.[18] Hanging in the balance is one-third of global maritime trade that traverses the South China Sea in cargo tankers and sovereign control over natural resources below the ocean's surface. These ecological expressions and constitutions of state power mark a new era of maritime geopolitical order.

The present moment wherein ecology and state power align for China echoes the US maritime colonial project of the nineteenth and twentieth centuries, which extended the reach of the American military far into the Pacific Ocean. The United States, like China, operationalized state power in relation to ecology. From the 1940s to 1970, research on ecology in the United States was funded predominantly by the US Atomic Energy Commision. The US government was interested in establishing a baseline regarding the effects of atomic radiation on aquatic animal populations and biophysical conditions. More than one hundred nuclear detonations in the island Pacific Proving Grounds were instrumental to developing concepts in ecological sciences, such as Howard and Eugene Odum's steady-state equilibrium theory, and to popularizing Arthur Tansley's term *ecosystems*. Ecology, as a disciplinary field, developed through efforts to determine how nuclear fallout effects biological organisms.[19] As such, ecological sciences became deeply connected with the US atomic military complex and global nuclear hegemony. So, too, in the present, engineered ecologies figure centrally in the reconstitution of global maritime sovereignty. China's maritime state power in the South China Sea materializes through engineered infrastructures, which reconfigure ocean ecologies and global power geometries,[20] thereby marking a new era of ecological state formation. Ecology and state power are intimately interconnected all the way down: past, present, and future.

Xi Jinping, in 2017, announced that the future of global sustainable development would be shaped by China's Green Belt and Road Initiative (BRI). Although the BRI was first announced in 2013 as the Silk Road Economic Belt and Twenty-First Century Maritime Silk Road, Chinese officials shifted discourse to the Green Belt and Road in 2017. That year, China's Ministry of Ecology and Environment published *Guidelines on Promoting the Green Belt and Road*, which explains the aim of the green BRI is to "share the ecological civilization philosophy with the world and achieve sustainable development." The guidelines state that the green BRI is key in China's efforts to "participate in global governance and . . . forge communities of shared interest, shared responsibility, and a common destiny."[21]

The Ministry of Ecology and Environment highlights green finance, energy, and cooperation as main facets of the green BRI's global outreach agenda.[22] China already stands as a global leader in green bonds and green finance. Yet, the majority of green BRI projects are funded through traditional debt and equity finance channels regulated by green credit guidelines. Green BRI financing, to date, manifests predominantly in green bond financing for low carbon infrastructure in wealthier countries. China, currently boasting more than 15 percent of renewable energy capacity worldwide, aims to transfer green energy knowledge and sell renewable energy products abroad. Like green finance, alternative energy investments are taking place primarily in middle- and high-income countries. In contrast, low-income countries are receiving Chinese energy investment almost exclusively in hydropower, a form of energy generation that is socially and environmentally disruptive.[23] The third facet of green BRI, intergovernmental cooperation, entails science and technology exchange and policy cooperation. Given the fraught politics of mechanizing nature, as well as the targets detailed in the post-2020 global biodiversity framework, grounded studies are needed to examine how these international science, technology, and policy exchanges manifest across global contexts.

In 2019, the United Nations Environment Program welcomed the Belt and Road Initiative International Green Development Coalition to advance the 2030 Agenda for Sustainable Development. With its numerous leadership roles in global environmental governance, China is poised to shape global articulations of sustainable development. How will green BRI efforts transform global sustainable development trajectories? Will global North-South inequalities, currently being reproduced through green BRI efforts, continue to deepen? How will mechanistic techniques aimed at optimizing ecologies transform society and space across international contexts? The answers to these questions are of paramount importance to sustainable development in the twenty-first century.

The Chinese state's approaches to ecology are contributing to the reconfiguration of environmental governance globally. Perhaps this reconfiguration will be remembered as part of a global expansion of technocratic approaches to sustainability. Or perhaps, it will contribute to divorcing sustainable development further from efforts to foster social equality. The impetus of sustainable development is to be ongoing and unending. So too, it seems, are the horizons of geographical inclusion within global visions of building ecological civilization.

Appendix

RESEARCH METHODS

In 2014, China's central state assigned new ecological zoning mandates for municipalities. This book emerged from efforts to understand municipal ecological protection zoning processes. What were its aims? How was ecological land zoned? Once zoned, how was it managed and by whom? What did ecological protection mean for state scientists and urban planners? How did new conservation zones affect people living in these areas? These were some of the questions with which I began.

I started interviewing within my network of urban planners, which I had developed through previous work in China. This took me through Beijing, Chengdu, and Kunming. Through these early interviews, it became clear that peri-urban village land and what municipal government officials called ecological migration were central to processes of making ecological protection areas in municipal regions. At that time, there were no publicly available maps that showed where ecological protection zoning was taking place. So I came to find villages being incorporated into ecological protection areas through government officials who told me of their whereabouts. Over time, I found more sites by talking with villagers. I started conducting interviews in these villages and continued expert interviews with ecologists and urban planners in Beijing. But from 2015 onward I focused primarily on sites in China's southwest in the cities of Kunming, Chengdu, and Dali.

That year I began visiting resettlement complexes and establishing relationships with ecological migrants. These resettlement complexes became key research sites. Locating resettlement complexes was a challenge. In most cases, resettlement complexes resemble banal high-rise apartment complexes (*xiaoqu*) ubiquitous across China. I located resettlement complexes through four sources: villagers who knew where they were to be resettled, villagers who refused resettlement but knew where other residents were resettled, government officials who told me the location of resettlement sites, and protests at resettlement sites that attracted my attention.

Conducting interviews in resettlement complexes had its own set of challenges as residents moved through the rhythms of their daily lives. In some cases, many visits were necessary for participants to feel comfortable sitting for an interview. In other cases, residents were immediately interested in participating in interviews. At one site, which residents called the refugee district because of inadequate compensation for rural land and housing, ecological migrants crowded around to tell their stories of transition into what they described as high-rise poverty.

Multiple research affiliations shaped place-based connections and facilitated introductions, which broadened the number of participants.[1] The network of government officials, planners, and scientists with whom I conducted interviews expanded. This allowed me, for instance, to conduct interviews with scientists about the historical ecological record for the Lake Dian basin. Research affiliations also brought me in contact with new villages being incorporated into ecological protection areas.

Ultimately, I drew on multiple methods including interviews, participant observation, oral histories, photovoice focus group discussions, and archival work. I carried out fieldwork over a fifteen-month period spanning 2014 to 2017, with additional archival work during 2018–19. Research included 15 villages and 4 resettlement complexes. In total, I interviewed 223 peri-urban villagers, 130 resettlement complex migrants, 90 government officials and urban planners, 15 representatives from organizations involved in financing and managing ecological protection sites, and 23 ecologists. These figures include focus group discussions, in which I interviewed up to five people at the same time. I use pseudonyms throughout to ensure the anonymity of people, places, organizations, and government bureaus. For the same reason, I do not include the exact date of interviews or tabulate an index of interviewees.

It should be clear by now that I did not randomly sample. I asked villagers to introduce me to other villagers, urban planners to introduce me to other urban planners, ecological migrants to introduce me to other ecological migrants, and so on.[2] This form of sampling inherently limits the fields of interlocutors. For instance, my sample does not include ecological migrants who moved out of resettlement housing or work as migratory laborers in cities, although, I learned about these experiences through interviews. Similarly, I spoke with many people who were in-between employment or balanced multiple forms of labor across locales. Naturally, my sample includes only those who were willing to speak with me. Some were not interested. Others simply did not have time.

For scientists, planners, and government officials my sample tended toward those who were well-networked and interested in international or comparative perspectives. Regarding government officials, I sampled predominantly from middle-aged men, not because of my sampling procedure, but because the vast majority of government officials in China are middle-aged men. My sample of villagers and resettlement complex migrants is close to gender parity, with a higher number of middle-aged people (fifty and older). I offer two explanations for near gender parity and the age-orientation of the sample. I am a cis-gender male who conducted fieldwork as a single parent with full-time care-giving responsibilities for my daughter Akira (who appears in chapters 4 and 5). While men were comfortable speaking with me when I appeared to be a solo researcher, women were curious to learn about my daughter. When Akira was not in school, she was with me conducting fieldwork in villages, resettlement complexes, and (occasionally) in scientific labs and government offices. I noticed that when Akira was with me some women in villages and resettlement complexes in particular were curious to hear our story. After she accompanied me to research sites, I was often recognized on subsequent visits as the foreign researcher with a child.

The reason that the sample of villagers and ecological migrants is skewed slightly toward middle-age and older participants is due, in part, to the challenges this demographic faces in obtaining employment. China's laborers have been disenfranchised from the job stability once common during the socialist and early reform periods.[3] Significantly, for most jobs in China retirement is mandated at certain ages. Men are often forced to retire at sixty, and women at fifty. The retirement age for female civil servants is fifty-five. When people approach these ages, it becomes harder for them to find jobs. Companies are less willing to hire employees who will retire within a decade. This leaves many people in this demographic struggling to find work, particularly those who would otherwise be engaged in agricultural production but no longer have access to land.

I frequently conducted multiple interviews with participants. This proved particularly valuable for learning about ecological protection zoning practices. Over multiple interviews with government officials and urban planners, contradictory claims and inconsistencies pointed to key ambiguities surrounding urban-rural planning processes and ecological protection zoning. Interviews with government officials and urban planners provided situated views within a complex nexus of governance relations. In the text, I indicate a relative position so as not to reveal identities. My interviews included representatives from urban planning bureaus, environmental monitoring bureaus, environmental planning bureaus, forestry bureaus, land bureaus, and others.

The number of research participants from peri-urban villages and resettlement complexes grew as I spent extended amounts of time in each as a participant observer.[4] This method involves extended interaction with individuals and social groups, observing everyday activities, and writing field notes as a reflexive exercise for examining everyday life. In practice, I chose places based on how welcome I was. My appearance as a foreigner made it clear that I was not local, but few had ever met a white person with whom they could converse in Mandarin. In many cases, this generated curiosity, opening a vein for conversation. In most cases, I fielded many questions about myself and my daughter before asking my own. After multiple visits to a site, I became a more familiar face to some. When I received invitations to people's homes, I accepted them gratefully. I returned to visit those who welcomed me over the years.

In sites where I came to know villagers well, I not only conducted interviews and observations, but also organized photovoice focus group interviews. Photovoice is a visual participatory method. I adapted the method, however, from a set of rote procedures to a process-oriented method. Photovoice was initially conceptualized as a research method for carrying out public needs assessment with emancipatory and empowering potential.[5] Through the process of taking photos and discussing them collectively in focus groups, participants identify mutual needs and experiences. Three core principles underlie the method—give voice to communities, especially those underprivileged and without representational apparatuses to communicate needs; utilize photographs and focus group discussions to promote critical dialogue on community issues; and connect communities with those that have a direct role in governance. I conducted photovoice in two villages with representatives from an environmental bureau. It became clear during the focus group discussions, however, that many felt constrained voicing their thoughts in the presence of researchers from the environmental bureau. In response to this observation, I conducted follow-up open-ended interviews with and without photos.[6]

My approach to archival work was iterative. Identifying key scientists and texts across the natural and social sciences unfolded alongside twenty-three interviews with ecologists. I determined which scientists and texts to focus on by triangulating between interviews and close readings of works from the early 1900s to the present. I considered the relevance of the texts in historical context and in relation to contemporary scientific practices. The materials I focus on, particularly in chapters 1 and 2, took shape through this process. With this epistemological orientation, I aim for what Amartya Sen calls positional objectivity, where the objectivity of knowledge is necessarily dependent on the position of the observer.[7]

Finally, a word on the presentation of the findings. I write in a peripatetic ethnographic style to emphasize my process-oriented approach to research. This style of exposition integrates data, collected through multiple research methods, into an intersubjective narrative through which the argument unfolds. This parallels what Michael Burawoy calls the "extended case method."[8] The extended case method examines the in-depth workings of social processes through a single location or site. Like the extended case method, I draw out relational processes and outcomes over time. In contrast with the extended case method, I query multiple sites and triangulate across reflexive methods to identify key processes and relations. In writing, I emphasize the interactive component of field research, as well as the fact that I am representing people's ways of knowing, acting, and experiencing, which I learned about through extensive social interactions. My approach emphasizes commonalities shared across research sites, while holding in tension the indeterminate nature of processes and outcomes.

In sum, this work is the product of multiple methods grounded in interpersonal engagements. I encountered far more people and heard far more stories than I could include in these pages. I aim to present the findings in a way that situates myself as a researcher and reflects the affective character of social interactions during fieldwork.

Notes

INTRODUCTION

1. Xi 2017.

2. Xinhua 2017.

3. Hansen et al. 2018; Byrnes 2018; Rodenbiker 2021.

4. Bray 2013; Zhang 2015; Chen, and Zinda, and Yeh 2017; Zinda et al. 2017; Wilczak 2017; Zhang and Wu 2017; Rodenbiker 2019; 2020.

5. Shapiro 2001.

6. Liebman 2019.

7. For discussions of the Dazhai campaign as model and venue for politics see Meisner 1978 and Zhao and Woudstra 2007. For an account of how agricultural campaigns advanced state and military interests see Yeh 2013a.

8. Lü et al. 2013.

9. See Zhou and Grumbine 2011; Zinda 2012; Yeh and Coggins 2014; Wu et al. 2014 Zinda et al. 2017; Coggins 2017.

10. Xinhua 2021.

11. Ecological protection sites, of course, are not without historical precedent, but their scale and numbers have changed dramatically. China established its first nature reserve in 1956, and by 1965 there were 19 conservation sites. In 2008, there were over 2,500 conservation sites covering 15 percent of the entire country's land mass (Yeh 2013b), and by 2010, there were 2,541 nature reserves, 280 national scenic areas, and 660 national forest parks (Zinda 2012; Wu et al. 2014; Jiang et al 2019).

12. For a discussion on the political economy of conservations zones as "tourism dynamos," see Zinda et al. 2017.

13. Hsing 2010; Cartier 2015a.

14. Oakes (2019) argues that the "urban" is a significant ideological apparatus in contemporary China.

15. Selden 1993.

16. Chan and Li 1999.

17. Violent altercations over land are not uncommon. In October 2014, two months after my initial fieldwork visit to Zhang's village, protests over peri-urban land in Kunming left eight police officers and several construction workers dead (Ramzy 2014).

18. Liu and Wang 2017, 222–25.

19. The Hu-Wen administrations' (2002–12) modernization policies, in contrast, emphasized "building a new socialist countryside." For an historical account of how this discourse emerged in postsocialist China and its contested meanings, see Day 2013. On the effectiveness of policy implementation and local agency, see Ahlers 2014. And on how rural reform policies effect village modernization practices, see Looney 2015.

20. Urban-rural coordinated planning was introduced during the Third Plenum of the Sixteenth Party Congress of 2003. See Smith (2021) for an account of early urban-rural coordinated planning processes and local experimentation in Chongqing.

21. I use the term *comprehensive urban-rural planning* because the government officials and municipal planners I interviewed most commonly used "comprehensive" (*zonghe* or

zongti) to describe their practices of consolidating urban and rural planning. They less often used terms such as urban-rural "coordination" (*tongchou* or *xietiao*) or "integration" (*jiehe*), which appear in official state discourse and national planning policies.

22. Hsing 2010, 26.

23. Over the last decade, China's national and private companies are increasingly moving capital investments offshore as double-digit domestic GDP growth slowed to single digits. From extractive industries to soy to manufacturing to foreign aid—Chinese capital is increasingly global in scope (Lee 2017). Many of China's most polluting manufacturing industries moved out of country, largely to Southeast Asian locales such as Vietnam and Indonesia. In a similar shift, China stopped accepting foreign recyclables, such as plastics, forcing a scramble to reorient recycling industries in the Americas (Liebman 2021). These political-economic and environmental shifts mark the beginning of a long-term process of moving heavily polluting manufacturing industries offshore and transitioning to a service-oriented economy focused on domestic consumption.

24. Chio 2014.

25. Shapiro 2001.

26. Schmalzer (2016) details how "improved" (*liangzhong*) agricultural strains of the Green Revolution–era responded well to chemical fertilizer and were therefore considered improvements insofar as they grew well under chemically enhanced conditions.

27. Li and Shapiro (2020) draw on case studies and secondary literature to characterize a coercive form of governance that uses the "environment" to justify authoritarian rule. The present work differs in its focus on ecology as object of governance.

28. As Williams (1997) has argued, casting blame on previous political regimes for environmental degradation is a feature common to each political era since the founding of the PRC. Mao's regime blamed the Qing and Republican-era rulers. Reform-era rulers cast blame toward Mao's regime.

29. In dynastic China geomancy, the cosmological science of organizing the material world, justified the emperor's right to rule. During imperial times, state power was materially expressed in relation to geomantic prescriptions within built environments (Gaubatz 1996).

30. Forsyth 2003; Robbins 2011.

31. See Morgan 1877.

32. Spence 1999; Palmer 2020.

33. Bramwell 1989.

34. Foucault (2005), in *The Order of Things*, delineates epistemes, or forms of knowing, that determine particular truths in given historical periods. He considers scientific knowledge in particular places and times to order ways of knowing and acting.

35. The term *ecosystem* was coined by Tansley 1935.

36. Scott 1998.

37. Williams 1980.

38. Haraway 1988, 592–94.

39. Bramwell 1989.

40. Stepan 1991.

41. Kosek 2006.

42. Forsyth 2003; Robbins 2011.

43. Greenberg 2013; Rodenbiker 2017; Sze 2018; Rodenbiker 2021.

44. Williams 1995.

45. Among the most prominent voices offering alternative logics of ecological civilization is Wen Tiejun (Wen 2001; 2008; 2021; Wen et al. 2012). For a history of Wen's thought see Day 2013.

46. The insight that science serves governmental power is not novel. Lindeman (1940) lamented the role of ecology in technologies of warfare, a topic that retains relevance today (Martin 2022).

47. Foucault introduces biopower as an historical shift in the operation of sovereign power, from the power to put to death under monarchical rule, toward diffuse disciplinary powers over the body and the "biological existence of the population" (Foucault 1990, 137–45). Examples Foucault puts forward to characterize biopower include forms of population control, environmental management, classification, and regulatory controls that support the exercise of sovereign power (Foucault 2003, 28–30). For engagement with regimes of knowledge and power see Foucault 1995; 2003; 2009.

48. Foucault 2003.

49. Foucault 2003, 137.

50. My focus on disciplinary expressions of power and knowledge, and their effects on subject formation, differs from Agrawal's (2005) account of how environmental subjects are shaped through institutional relationships between actors and strategies of government. Agrawal deploys the term *environmentality* to detail the "knowledges, politics, institutions, and subjectivities that come to be linked together with the emergence of the environment as a domain that requires regulations and protection" (ibid., 226). In contrast, I am concerned with processes through which regimes of knowledge and power emerge in relation to ecology, as well as processes of subject formation and forms of counterconduct.

51. Hsing 2010.

52. Foucault 2003, 201–2. In the context of discussing "pastoral power," Foucault highlighted five elements: counter-conduct, asceticism, communities, mysticism problems of scripture, and eschatological beliefs. For an account on counter-conduct, see Davidson 2011.

53. Schmitt (2018), drawing on surveys, demonstrates that citizens tend to respond positively to state articulations of ecological civilizational, which suggests strong ideological resonance and, therefore, reinforcement of state power.

54. On the politics of quality (*suzhi*) and social difference, see Anagnost 2004. For work on cultural politics of nature and social difference see Moore, Kosek, and Pandian 2003.

55. Li 2002; Johnson 2013; Smith 2021.

56. Rancière 2013, 10–15.

57. Ghertner 2015.

58. Schiller 2016 [1795].

59. For a discussion of Zhang Jingsheng's thought on the aesthetic state and connections with Kang Youwei's notion of aesthetic education, see Zhou 1998, Lee 2006, and Rodenbiker 2022b.

60. Summers 2019.

61. Simone 2004.

CHAPTER 1. MAKING ECOLOGY DEVELOPMENTAL

1. Hu 2012.

2. Ecological modernity is widely debated globally with variants stemming from northern and eastern Europe. See for instance Hajer 1995 and Buttel 2000. Muldavin (2007) characterizes two variants of ecological modernity: the cornucopian and the Keynsian. The cornucopian variant holds that technological advances, which accompany industrialization, will remedy the environmentally degrading aspects of transition. In contrast, the Keynsian variant, common in China, holds that it is necessary to have a strong interventionist state with regulatory power to intervene.

3. Ma 2007.

4. Zhang and Wang 2013.

5. *China Daily* 2007.

6. Zhang et al. 2007; Pan 2013a; Junren 2013; Weng et al. 2015.

7. Zhang and Wang 2013.

8. Genealogical method is concerned with historical processes through which truths and categories are established, which become normalized as common-sense truths. Genealogy as method challenges dominant narratives surrounding ontologies of the present allowing instead for alternative understandings of subjects and power to emerge. For examples of works that draw on genealogical method, see Foucault 1990; 1995; 2003. For a discussion of power relations and subject formation see *The Subject and Power* in Foucault, Rabinow, and Rose (2003, 126–44).

9. Haraway 1988.

10. Odum 1959.

11. Kingsland 1985 and Hutchinson 1978. Although ecology emerged in the West as a critique of modernity, ecological sciences are often mobilized in support of development projects.

12. Williams 1980.

13. Needham (1954) laid foundational work in the study of science and technology in China, initiating the multivolume series *Science and Civilization in China*. For work on how global exchanges shape knowledge production, see Culp, U, and Yeh 2016.

14. Hathaway 2013.

15. Shen (2014) illustrates how belief systems and the Chinese nation evolved with geological science during the twentieth century. Analogously, Jiang (2016) details how scientific ideas travel across different cultural milieus through the work of China's early twentieth-century biologists.

16. Lewis 2004.

17. Lowe 2013.

18. Sze and Greenburg, for instance, draw attention to the multiple meanings underlying sustainability and the need for grounding divergent and often competing values within historical and political contexts. See Sze 2018; Greenberg 2013; 2018.

19. Stafleu and Cowan 1981, 528.

20. For an aestheticized compendium of botany and plant ecology see Miyoshi 1912. For a discussion of early usages of ecology in Japan and subsequent shifts see Ueda 2015.

21. See McIntosh 1986.

22. Miyoshi 1905.

23. Matsumura and Miyoshi 1900.

24. Miyoshi 1890.

25. Miyoshi's work differs from other premier botanists of his time, such as Tomitaro Makino, by his training, methods, and taxonomical styles (Makino 1949).

26. Shen 2014.

27. For a discussion of how eighteenth-century intellectuals deployed the method of drawing on classical texts in their scientific practice, see Elman 1984.

28. Jiang 2016, 168.

29. For example, see Hu 1922.

30. This quote derives from Hu 1927, 4. Cited in Jiang 2016, 176.

31. Hu's scientific expeditions across China and the United States were nearly contemporaneous with aesthetic depictions from plant ecologists in Japan, the United States, and elsewhere. For examples of how ecology is embedded in aesthetics in Euro-American contexts, see Gobster 1999 and Sayre 2010.

32. Rodenbiker 2022b.

33. For a discussion of these movements see Moise 2013.

34. See Condorcet 1955 [1795].

35. Li 1919; 1924. See also Meisner 1970, 158–61.

36. Morgan's (1877) stage-oriented social evolution entailed the movement from "primitive" society toward "civilized" society, expressed in relations between Native Americans and white colonial settlers.

37. Trotsky's (2008 [1930]; 2010 [1931]) "permanent revolution" held that progress toward global revolution depended on continual revolutions across countries. This idea was later reinterpreted by Mao Zedong during the Cultural Revolution as continual internal revolution—a notion mobilized by Red Guard youth. See Yang 2016.

38. Marx (1976 [1867]) is often discussed as a Eurocentric unilinear thinker who advocated for sociopolitical revolution through the urban proletariat. In contrast with this common reading, Anderson (2002; 2016) engages Marx's 1872 French edition of *Das Kapital* (as opposed to the 1867 version), the 1882 Russian edition of the *Communist Manifesto*, *Gundrisse* 2005 [1939], journalistic writings, and unpublished notebooks to make the case that Marx was an adroit global thinker on varieties of human social and historical development that include race, ethnicity, and nationalism. It is particularly relevant that within the 1882 Russian edition of the *Communist Manifesto* and personal correspondences Marx highlighted communal villages of Russia as a potential source of socialist development, which Li Dazhao parallels in his writing on China.

39. Li 1918. The translation of *yuli* as "surplus energy" noted in this text aligns with the translation undertaken by Meisner (1970, 65). Although, the term also connotes the "power," "ability," or "capacity" for social development. In other parts of Li's text when discussing social transformation Li uses the term *shili*, which could be rendered as "force" or "power."

40. For a firsthand account of class leveling in a village setting, see Hinton 1971.

41. For an historical account of the struggle over political ideology and territory during the Republican period, see Bianco 1971.

42. Interviews CXM001 Kunming October 2016; CXM003 Kunming May 2017.

43. Animal ecology in China developed in the 1970s. This mirrors much of the world where plant ecology preceded animal ecology. For an account of the development of ecological sciences in Western contexts, see McIntosh 1986.

44. Interviews with ecologists: BJ002 Beijing July 2014; BJ007 Beijing June 2015; KM 010 Kunming November 2016; CD 017 Chengdu February 2017; KM 019 Kunming March 2017; KM021 Kunming May 2017.

45. The term *ecosystem* was introduced by Arthur Tansley (1935).

46. Brundtland 1987.

47. Ma 1981, 97–99.

48. Ma 1981.

49. Ma 1981, 95–96.

50. Ma 1981, 96.

51. When reform-era earth systems scientists discuss "energy," they primarily use the term *nengliang,* which connotes energy in the sense of the power derived from the utilization of a resource, a byproduct of a relational biochemical or biophysical action or reaction, or stored potential.

52. Ma 1981, 97–98.

53. For Ma's diagrams and discussion of functional zones see Ma 1981, 97–99.

54. Ma and Wang, 1984.

55. These contradictions mirror those found in concepts of sustainable development since it became popular in development circles. For an account of these contradictions, see Lélé 1991.

56. Ma and Wang 1984, 7.

57. Ouyang et al. 2016.

58. Wang and Ouyang 2012, 341.

59. Wang and Ouyang 2012, 338.

60. For an account of the relation between five-phase cosmology and the political power in imperial China, see Wang 2006.

61. For a discussion of their models, see Wang and Ouyang 2012.

62. For a detailed description of the irony of historical claims to longstanding sustainable environmental stewardship in China, see Tong 2019.

63. Wang and Ouyang 2012, 344.

64. Wang 1999.

65. Fan and Li 2009.

66. Wang and Ouyang 2012, 342.

67. Zhao 2011; Lü et al. 2013; CCICED 2014.

68. Wang 1999, 53. Rodenbiker 2021.

69. National New Type Urbanization Plan 2014. See also Pan 2013a, 125.

70. Mao 1927; 1956.

71. Walder 2015.

72. Selden 1993.

73. Zhang 1985.

74. Writings on ecological civilization building began to emerge during the mid-1980s. They have grown exponentially since. Wang (2012) enumerates the voluminous writings on ecological Marxism in China, which increased significantly during the 2000s. He notes that during the decade of 1991–2000 there were forty-five academic peer-reviewed journal articles on the topic of ecological Marxism, from 2000 to 2010 the number was nearly six hundred.

75. Wang 1986.

76. Boulding 1953; Schumacher 1975; Agger 1979; Leiss 1976.

77. Wang 1986, 41.

78. Wang 1986, 39–40.

79. Wang Jin attributed steady-state economics to John Stuart Mill (1806–73), Adam Smith's *Wealth of Nations*, as well as other political economists. Wang interpreted steady-state economy as the stabilizing of national economic production, such that there is a balance between national resource extraction and production. This contrasts with neo-classical economists' readings of Smith that suggest national economies are endless growth machines. See Arrighi 2007.

80. Wang 1986, 44.

81. Contrary to claims that ecological economics originated in Sweden in 1982 (Røpke 2004), scholars such as Shi (2002) argue that ecological economics originated from a Beijing conference in September 1980. For accounts regarding the circular economy and connections with industrial ecology and socio-environmental modeling, see Geng and Doberstein 2008; Yuan et al. 2006; Su et al. 2013.

82. Cf. Gregson et al. 2015.

83. Ye 1988.

84. Ye 1987; 1988.

85. Ye 1988, 163–66.

86. Ye 1988, 191–93, 205–8; Ye 1987, 1–8.

87. Ye 1987, 4–5.

88. Ye 1987; 1988, 150. Rodenbiker 2021.

89. Ye 1987, 5.

90. See Anagnost 2006 and Schneider 2015. For work on the historical roles of the peasantry, see Day 2013.

91. Wen 2001.

92. Wen 2021.

93. For a discussion of Wen's articulation of "three rural problems" (*sannong wenti*) and its relation to state policy, see Day 2013. For an account of peasant organizations, the new rural reconstruction movement, and alternative formulations of sustainable development in China, see Hale 2013.

94. Wen et al. 2012.

95. The circular economy is conceptualized as a managerial relationship that closes the loop between economic and natural systems to maximize energy and material production. It has become popular as part of China's "scientific development strategy" since the third plenary of the Sixteenth CCP conference of October 2003. Circular economy concepts, however, differ across national contexts. See Geng and Doberstein 2008; Su 2013; Yuan et. al. 2006.

96. Pan 2013a, 159.

97. Pan 2013a, 159.

98. Carrying capacity has been critiqued for being idealistic and immeasurable at all scales, for the assumption of static qualities that in fact are highly dynamic, as well as for difficulties in determining veracity of data across scales of land management given changing environmental conditions and in-patch dynamics. For accounts detailing these critiques, see Sayre 2008; 2010.

99. See Central Committee of the Communist Party of China 2016.

100. Muldavin 2015.

101. Pan 2013a, 40 (my emphases).

102. Pan 2013a, 34–42.

103. Pan 2013a, 37–38.

104. Oakes 2019, 405.

105. Pan 2013a, 160.

106. For an account of scientific field studies in China see Yeh 2009.

107. Pan 2013a, 90.

108. Day 2013, 14–15.

109. CCP Third Plenary Meeting of 2013.

110. This argument parallels Li's (2007, 7, 123–26) assertion that "the will to improve," relies on identifying deficiencies in populations and environments and then rendering technical the solutions to these deficiencies.

111. Guldin 2016; Zhang and Donaldson 2010.

CHAPTER 2. BOTANY, BEAUTY, PURIFICATION

1. Ecological protection zoning is discussed in the Introduction, UNDP 2013, and the National New-Type Urbanization Plan 2014.

2. Li and Wang 2009.

3. The Kunming municipal government built the first water treatment plant in 1985. From the 1990s, the municipal government accepted World Bank financing to build water treatment plants. Before 1985, urban wastewater flowed through runoff systems into Lake Dian. Interview KM076 Kunming June 2017.

4. In addition to interviews, this figure is detailed in the Kunming Master Plan 2016. Portions of the plan are on file with the author.

5. For an historical account of ideas of "wilderness" in Western context, see Cronon 1996.

6. WL001 Kunming July 2015, reiterated in WL003 Kunming November 2016. Italicized emphasis added by the author.

7. Pu 2012.

8. Included within the policy shorthand "four removals, three returns, for one protection" (*situi sanhuan yihu*) are efforts toward agricultural pollution control that entail moratoriums on livestock and poultry breeding. These efforts involve requisitioning and redistributing rural land to various enterprises, which I discuss in chapter 3. For media accounts of these policies, see Liu 2013; Jiang Zhaohui 2016.

9. WL001 July 2015.

10. Lave 2012.

11. Lave et al. (2013) use the term *critical physical geography* to refer to approaches that bridge scientific practice, knowledge production, and cultural politics of nature. In their discussion, they illustrate how social and physical geography are interlinked with strong potential for intellectual synergy. This intervention crystalizes what were previously a set of dispersed debates. These include Castree and Braun's (2001) discussions on socio-natures that demonstrate how the social and the natural are intimately connected and inseparable, Forsyth's (2003) work on how environmental science is always political, as well as Latour's (1987; 1993) work that demonstrates how science is inseparable from human concerns.

12. The Society for Ecological Restoration refers to restoration as "the process of assisting the recovery of an ecosystem that has been degraded, damaged, or destroyed" (Wortley et al. 2013). The National Research Council alternatively defines restoration, as the "return of an ecosystem to a close approximation of its condition prior to disturbance" (NRC 1992). Ecological engineering refers to the "design of sustainable ecosystems that integrate human society with its natural environment for the benefit of both." Ecological engineering includes techniques of restoration ecology and designing novel ecosystems (Mitsch 2012).

13. Egan and Howell 2005.

14. The phrase "seeing like a state" was popularized by Scott 1998 and has since been deployed to discuss the lenses through which the state "sees," or in other words, how the state acts and makes legible that which it governs. For analogous uses, see Schmalzer 2016 who discusses "seeing like a state agent."

15. Rancière 2013, 4.

16. Ghertner 2015.

17. Scientific discourses that blame the peasantry for environmental degradation can be found across reform-era scientific works (Williams 1997).

18. Qu and Li 1983.

19. For an account of "three wastes" (*sanfei*) in Kunming, see Liebman 2019.

20. Qu and Li 1983, 7–8.

21. Qu and Li 1983, 13.

22. Qu and Li 1983, 13.

23. Qu and Li 1983, 14.

24. Song et al. 1947, 21.

25. Lacustrine deposits are common in lake beds with stream channels and tributaries that carry sediment.

26. Analogous processes of lake transformation have been catalogued in the work of Perdue 1987. His work on Hunan Province shows how peasant farming practices and state governance are intimately tied to lake water management from 1500–1850 CE.

27. Dong and Wu 2013, 126–30.

28. Dandy 1935, 134.

29. Qu and Li 1983; Lu et al. 2012; Yang et al. 2013. Lu et al. 2012 argues that *Ottelia* once covered large portions of Lake Dian.

30. Cook and Urmi-König 1984.

31. Higgs et al. 2014. Ecological restoration 1.0 approaches remain prevalent despite theories of disequilibrium ecology that hold equilibrium as an abstraction that never exists in nature. For a discussion of disequilibrium ecology, see Zimmerer 1994.

32. Lowenthal 2015 [1985].

33. Alagona et al. 2012.

34. Shapiro 2001.

35. Yang et al. 2013.

36. KM016 Kunming December 2016.

37. While aesthetic senses feature prominently in this case of ecological restoration, it is important to note that emphases on aesthetic functions can be found in ecological restoration projects across regional and national contexts (Higgs 2017).

38. Analogous to cases of environmental injustice discussed by Pulido (2000), the politics of determining environmental remediation sites are inseparable from processes that reproduce inequality in the built environment.

39. Elliot 2008.

40. This investment facilitated the "six great engineering projects" (*liu da gongcheng*), including a pollution interception barrier, a ring road built around the lake, underground sewage treatment centers, and a 3,500-kilometer underground drainage network with a capacity of treating 1,105,000 cubic meters of urban wastewater. In addition, sewage interception infrastructure was constructed along each of the thirty-five major river channels flowing into Lake Dian. Interviews KM023 September 2016; KM058 Kunming, June 2017.

41. Interview YB002 Kunming November 2016.

42. Interview BL003 Kunming October 2016.

43. Interview YL001 Kunming October 2016.

44. See Hsing 2010.

45. YH001 Kunming April 2017.

46. Tanaka et al. 2013; Li et al. 2019.

47. *Penghuqu* can be translated as a "slum," "shanty town," or an area with poor infrastructure. *Penghuqu*, in Chinese, differs from slums in other contexts, which largely refer to informal settlements with poorly built infrastructure within urban areas. The term *penghuqu* can be applied to infrastructure in urban or rural areas. As Document 535 indicates, local governments determine the definitional parameters of a slum.

48. Document 535.

49. This definition comes from interviews with municipal government officials: KM018 Kunming October 2016; KM023 November 2016; KM045 December 2016; KM 073 February 2017, as well as documents government officials shared with me. The following government website also provides a definition of slums for the Kunming municipality: http://www.km.gov.cn/zfxxgkml/zdlyxx/phqgz/ (accessed November 2, 2016).

50. Chengdu Municipal Government 2014.

51. Interview ZJL002 Kunming February 2017.

52. Interview ZJL002 Kunming February 2017.

53. Interview ZJ003 Kunming October 2016.

54. I discuss photovoice and participatory method in the appendix and in Rodenbiker 2022a.

55. Interview WJ005 Kunming January 2017. Italics for emphasis in the following quote Wang's. Part of this quote appears in Rodenbiker 2022a.

56. Pow (2018) illustrates how, in other regions within China, shared aesthetic senses are crucial to the operation of governance and material expressions of state power.

57. State policies mandate that 20 percent of municipal areas be zoned for ecological protection. In addition, since the 2014 Environmental Protection Law, the central state began holding local officials accountable for environmental governance within their jurisdiction (He 2019).

CHAPTER 3. ECOLOGICAL TERRITORIALIZATION

1. I use the term *organization*, like Ostrom (1999), to refer to groups of people organized around coordinated activities and shared interests. This contrasts with "institutions" as rules, norms, and shared strategies.

2. Elden 2010, 804.

3. There are extensive efforts to delineate differences between ecological protection areas and ecological red lines, particularly within Chinese-language scholarship (Li et al. 2014; Li et al. 2015; Wan et al. 2015; Wang et al. 2017).

4. Deng et al. 2016.

5. Lieberthal and Oksenberg 1988.

6. Mertha 2009.

7. For a discussion of the tiao-kuai system, see Mertha 2005; and Hsing 2010, 34.

8. Hsing 2010, 8, 12.

9. Scholarship on postsocialist transitions show how land exhibits elastic properties as actors struggle to lay claims on land as it is newly monetized and takes on exchange value (Hsing 2010; Verdery 2003, 20–23).

10. See CCP Constitutional Amendment Article 2, section 10.

11. State-owned enterprises are business enterprises whose supervisory structure is made up of state government employees and were originally established by government bodies. Under this heading there are multiple types. In the fully state-owned form, state-owned enterprises are entities with assets that are fully state owned, such as the State-owned Assets and Supervision Administrative Commission (SASAC), state-owned financial institutions that are part of China Banking Regulatory Commission (CBRC) and other entities, which are managed at the level of the central state. There are also state-owned enterprises operated by regional governments.

12. Naughton 1995, 68.

13. Ho 2001, 405.

14. Naughton 1995, 82.

15. McGee 2015.

16. Prior to this law, illegal leasing of village land was not uncommon. The 1988 valued use system that legalized land use transfer was codified in response to the recognition that this practice was already widespread in some areas of China and that land transfers could be taxed (Lin 2009).

17. Hsing 2006; Shue 1988.

18. Shue 1988.

19. Shue 1988, 104; Hsing 2010.

20. Ma 2005, 478.

21. Ma 2005.

22. Chung and Lam 2004.

23. Hsing 2006, 173–74.

24. Lin 2009.

25. Chuang 2020, 17–20.

26. Liu 2019.

27. Chuang 2020.

28. Chung and Lam 2004, 957.

29. Cartier 2015a.

30. Lin 2009.

31. For a detailed account of development zones (*kaifaqu*), see Hsing 2010.

32. Chu 2020.

33. SOEs have been under various stages of reform, corporatization, and privatization since the 1990s, with many larger enterprises introducing private assets through mixed ownership restructuring (Zhang 2008, 29–34). This entailed transitions in the 1990s and 2000s from wholly state owned to joint stock companies. The government is generally the majority stockholder of joint stock companies, colloquially referred to as semiprivatized state-owned enterprises (Imai 2003). There are semiprivatized SOEs that are partially, or majority owned by state-owned enterprise subsidiaries in and outside of China (Szamosszegi and Cole 2011). These are entities that have significant state holdings because a portion of the capital structure is private, and a portion of the assets are controlled by state-owned enterprises or their subsidiaries. They are not officially recognized as state-owned enterprises, but at least partial ownership is held by state entities (Deng et al. 2011).

34. Brenner (2004) details the rescaling of the neoliberal state through cities in the West. China's green urbanization processes, in contrast, facilitate the rescaling of the local state in the context of postsocialist political-economic transitions.

35. Ho 2001, 400.

36. Interviews KM068 Kunming April 2017; KM072 Kunming May 2017.

37. Diao 2021.

38. Wilczak 2017.

39. Interview ZJ002 Kunming, November 2016.

40. Interviews KM034 Kunming October 2016; KM058 Kunming March 2017; KM061 Kunming May 2017.

41. This shift mirrors central government bureaucratic reconfigurations since 2018 as the powers of multiple ministries have been reallocated to the Ministry of Ecology and Environment (MEE).

42. Interview KM025 Kunming October 2016.

43. For a detailed account of these shifts in policy and rural land types see Zhang and Wu 2017.

44. Xiao 2014.

45. Interviews KM027 Kunming November 2016; CD005 February Chengdu 2017; CD006 Chengdu Feb 2017; DL007 Dali February 2017; KM042 Kunming March 2017; KM043 Kunming March 2017.

46. Interviews KM025 Kunming October 2016; CD005 Chengdu February 2017; CD008 February Chengdu 2017.

47. Interview KM 027 Kunming March 2017.

48. Interviews KM025 Kunming October 2016; KM030 Kunming November 2016; KM035 Kunming December 2016; CD004 Chengdu February 2017; CB006 Chengdu February 2017; DL004 Dali February 2017. See also Xiao 2014.

49. CCP Constitutional Amendment 10, 1982; Ho 2017.

50. Administrative villages include multiple "natural" villages. Much of the decision-making power in villages rests with party cadres and the party secretary of village committees at the administrative village level. They are also key figures in protecting collective interests (Cai 2003).

51. Interview KM025 Kunming October 2016.

52. Interviews DL002 Dali January 2017; KM015 Kunming September 2016; KM032 Kunming December 2016; CD007 Chengdu Feb 2017.

53. Interview KM030 Kunming November 2016.

54. Interview KM025 Kunming October 2016.

55. Interview CD010 Chengdu March 2017.

56. Cao 2015, 56–58.

57. Interviews KM003 Kunming 2015; KM017 Kunming September 2016; KM025 Kunming October 2016; CD001 Chengdu July 2016; KM040 Kunming March 2017.

58. Interview KM047 Kunming April 2017.

59. Interview KM025 Kunming October 2016.

60. This is analogous to dual-function forests that serve both environmental and economic ends (Zinda et al. 2017).

61. Interview DL010 Dali April 2017.

62. Interview KM026 Kunming October 2016.

63. Interview CD012 Chengdu April 2017.

64. Interview KM029 Kunming October 2016.

65. Interviews CD015 June Chengdu 2017; KM070 Kunming May 2017.

66. Interview KM064 Kunming May 2017.

67. Interview KM057 Kunming March 2017.

68. Introduced more than twenty years ago, some of the most prominent cases of state-private partnerships are large infrastructural provisioning projects on China's East Coast. See De Jong et al. 2010.

69. Interview KM057 Kunming March 2017.

70. Interviews CD009 Chengdu March 2016; KM057 Kunming March 2017; KM063 Kunming April 2017.

71. Interview CD006 Chengdu February 2017.

72. Interview KM026 Kunming October 2016.

73. Interview KM053 Kunming March 2017.

74. Interview CD002 Chengdu October 2016.

75. Interview KM022 Kunming October 2016.

76. Interview KM022 Kunming October 2016.

77. Interviews KM022 Kunming October 2016; CD003 Chengdu September 2016; DL004 Dali January 2016.

78. Huang 2008.

79. Hsing 2010.

CHAPTER 4. ECOLOGICAL MIGRATIONS, VOLUMETRIC ASPIRATIONS

1. Xun and Bao 2007; Yeh 2009.

2. Stuart Elden notes that the term *volumetric* appeared as early as 1862 to denote something "of or pertaining, or noting measurement by volume" (2013, 15).

3. Weizman 2007, 12–20.

4. Elden 2013, 15.

5. Billé 2020.

6. See Graham 2016, 13. Other key works on vertical and volumetric relations in everyday life include Graham and Hewitt 2013; Harris 2015; Rodenbiker 2019; Marston 2020.

7. A growing body of scholarship examines process-oriented relations between the urban and the rural, not only problematizing the neat distinction between the two, but also illustrating how each are constituted in relation to the other (Brenner 2013; Zhang, Oya, and Ye 2015; Roy 2016; Caldeira 2017; Chuang 2020; Ghertner and Lake 2021; Smith 2021).

8. Cf. Brenner 2013; Angelo and Wachsmuth 2015.

9. For additional works in this vein, see Buck 2012; Chuang 2015; Schneider 2017a; 2017b; Walker 2009; Williams 1980; 2011.

10. Roy 2009; Robinson and Roy 2016.

11. Roy 2016.

12. Foucault 2003.

13. All conversions from renminbi to dollars are approximate and have been calculated from exchange rates in 2017.

14. A mu is a land measurement equivalent to 666.7 square meters.

15. Marx 1976 [1867] sarcastically refers to the separation from means of production as the "freeing" of people to sell their labor power on the market.

16. For an account on typologies of agrarian class position in rural China, see Zhang 2015.

17. For an account of the hollowing out of village spaces and how the process shapes gendered labor relations, see Wu and Ye 2016.

18. There are three kinds of village shareholding corporations, those that are self-funded, local-state-village shareholding groups, and corporate-village shareholding groups. Ecological migrants at this site formed a corporate-village shareholding group.

19. Marx (1976 [1867], 874–76) rejected the notion that primitive accumulation was nonviolent, instead theorizing it as an essentially violent process of displacement and general movement toward proletarianization.

20. See Harvey 2005, especially chapter 4. Harvey's work builds on Marx's theories of primitive accumulation. Marx (1976 [1867], 874–76; 2005 [1939], 459–516) discussed primitive accumulation as an historical moment involving the privatization of the commons, the proletarianization of labor, and global colonization.

21. Levien 2018.

22. In 2017, the highest average gross income was for white collar workers in Beijing who earned an average of 9,942 RMB per month.

23. On land and housing ownership in China, see Ho 2001; 2017.

24. The term *guodu* connotes the passing of one form, stage, or place, to another. *Fei* refers to payments or fees.

25. Temporary familial separation and fake divorces to maximize compensation have been catalogued in other contexts within China (Yeh 2013a).

CHAPTER 5. RURAL REDUX

1. "Green Fields" is a pseudonym for a nongjiale. Chio (2014) set a precedence in translating nongjiale as "peasant family happiness." In this chapter, I maintain the Chinese-language term throughout.

2. Yang (2007) claims that nongjiale first developed along the outskirts of Chengdu at Long Quan Feng. In addition to other sites, I conducted research at Nongkecun in Chengdu's Pixian County, where nongjiale proprietors claim that they started the first nongjiale. There are, however, earlier precedents than each of these. For an account on nongjiale historical origins, see Chio 2014, chapter 2.

3. Nostalgia for rural life is widespread in China. It is expressed in official state policies and speeches, popular sentiment, and through political economies of rural tourism (Qian 2017).

4. Zhang (2010) conceptualizes the spatialization of class in China through a Lefebvrian analysis (Lefebvre 1991) of the social production of urban high-rise spaces. Zhang argues that the production of commodity housing is a material instantiation of class difference.

5. Zhang (2015) identifies five types of agrarian class positions in rural China: capitalist employers, petty bourgeoisie commercial farmers, petty bourgeoisie dual-employment households, wage workers (semi-proletarianized and proletarianized), and subsistence peasants.

6. Bourdieu 2004 [1962].

7. Bourdieu 2004 [1962], 582.

8. Though I depart from Bourdieu in my account of village class aesthetics, my argument on the reproduction of social hierarchies within the village partially aligns with Bourdieu's work on the maintenance of class distinctions. Bourdieu (1984) illustrates how cultural capital factors into multigenerational class distinctions, arguing that symbolic systems play key roles in reproducing and naturalizing social hierarchies. My position differs in terms of the roles of and emphases on embodiment, spatial practices, and aesthetic differentiation.

9. Park (2014) refers to nongjiale as "contested spaces" where symbolic meaning over rural traditions and modernity, rural architecture, and eco-friendly ways of life are negotiated between urban consumers and nongjaile operators.

10. Ghertner 2015, 5–8.

11. Summers 2019, 21; hooks, 1990, 104.

12. Summers 2019, 3.

13. I derive these aesthetic categories, in part, through Lefebvre (1991, 8–10, 86) who argued that space is socially produced. In his theorization, Lefebvre advanced distinct yet overlapping spatial categories including spaces of representation, lived spaces, and spatial practices. Class struggles, for Lefebvre, occur within overlapping spaces of "hypercomplexity" in which people are always unevenly positioned.

14. For an account on how socialist-era class legacies continue in the reform era, see Chan, Marsden, and Unger 1992.

15. Massey 2013.

16. Early reforms of the 1980s included decollectivization and an inversion of the extractive taxation policies aimed at rural production. These spurred an influx of investment and entrepreneurial activity in the countryside (Oi 1992). Hundreds of millions of rural people rose out of poverty through postsocialist reforms. Many of the most enriched were local bureaucrats with transnational linkages to Taiwan and Hong Kong (Hsing 1998). Additionally, clientelist relationships with state bureaus were central to the functioning of TVEs (Huang 2008; Shue 1988), as were interinstitutional relationships between TVEs and SOEs (Buck 2012).

17. For an account on the relationship between the party-state and capitalist enterprises in China, see Huang 2008.

18. Interview BXM005 March 2017.

19. Interview BXM005 March 2017.

20. In using the phrase "war on steel," Bo is referring to makeshift 'backyard furnaces' built across China during the Great Leap Forward. At this time, in effort to increase national steel production, people melted household objects, such as silverware, tools, and pans to create steel. These efforts, however, proved disastrous as the metals they produced could not be used in industry. The war on steel foreshadowed the Great Leap Forward famine.

21. Interview BXM005 March 2017.

22. Wang is referring to a violent altercation over rural land on October 14, 2014. Eighteen people were reported injured and eight killed as villagers fought for their land (Ramzy 2014).

23. Interview WJQ009 November 2016.

24. Ribot and Peluso 2003.

25. Blumenfield and Silverman 2013; Chio 2014; Luo 2018.

26. Luo 2018.

27. See Ahlers (2014) for a detailed analysis of the new socialist countryside campaign and Chio (2014) for a discussion of the 2006 China National Tourism Administration campaign promoting rural tourism.

28. Interview BXM007, June 2017.

29. Boym 2001; Nadkarni and Shevchenko 2004.

30. Boym 2001, 41.

31. Oral histories in this village include: JM001 Kunming December 2016; JM002 Kunming January 2017; TD001 Kunming March 2017; CY001,002 Kunming March 2017; YJ001 Kunming March 2017; NR001 Kunming April 2017; ZL001,002 Kunming February 2017.

32. Interview BXM007 May 2017.

33. Gladney 1994, 109.

34. Schein 1997.

35. hooks 2012.

36. For a scholarly account of these transitional periods, see Bianco 1971. For an ethnographic account of early Maoist class-leveling projects, see Hinton 1997.

37. Boym 2001, xviii, 49, 55.

38. Chio 2014.

39. The term *tourist gaze* comes from Urry (2002) and has been developed in the context of rural China through the work of Oakes (2005).

40. Interview WJQ011 March 2017.

41. Gordillo 2014.

CHAPTER 6. INFRASTRUCTURAL DIFFUSION

1. Zhao 2011.

2. Cartier 2015b. For an account of civilized city programs in the context of spectacular "hyper-building" in western China, see Grant 2018.

3. Yunnan News 2017.

4. Rodenbiker 2022a.

5. China's law enforcement officers generally don't pursue individual vehicles for routine traffic violations. Instead, they rely on street surveillance technology to determine vehicle registration information and to identify drivers. Given this precedence, being pulled over by a police officer is a rare occurrence. Like elsewhere in the book, names are anonymized, as is the police number.

6. Gordon and Hinton 1996; Nathan 2001.

7. Balve 2020; Svolik 2016; Volkov 2016.

8. Arendt 1973 [1951].

9. Tilly 2010.

10. Nathan 2017.

11. Lee and Zhang 2013, 1477.

12. Chuang 2014.

13. An analogous approach to these works can be found in Mann (1984) who discusses "infrastructural power" as the ways state power punctuates civil society groups. For additional works on the exchanges between civil society groups, state actors, and state policy, see Mertha 2009; Teets 2014; Mattingly 2020. These works detail how authoritarian power operates through interactions between formal state powers and facets of society commonly considered to be "outside" of, or differentiated from, the state, particularly civil society.

14. Tomba 2014, 169.

15. Yeh 2013a.

16. Chu 2014, 352.

17. Easterling 2005, 178–79; 2014.

18. Simone 2004.

19. Simone 2004; Lee 2007; Lee and Zhang 2013.

20. See Foucault 2003; Davidson 2011, and the Introduction for discussions of counter-conduct.

21. For an account on techniques of isolation in the context of China's Northwest ethno-racialized minority communities, see Byler 2021; 2022.

22. Xiaoxi Village is a pseudonym for a peri-urban village.

23. Most demolition bureaus are made up of approximately twenty members derived from local government, development institutions, the private sector, and local residents.

24. Jinlin Development Company is a pseudonym for a proprietary owner.

25. It is not uncommon for demolition bureaus to make temporary offices in villages or residential areas that they are actively working to demolish. This spatial proximity can expedite the contract-signing process and resettlement.

26. See Rodgers and O'Neill (2012) for an account of how infrastructural violence operates through both active and passive modes.

27. Cai 2003.

28. For an account of the multiple functions and flexible deployment of turning farmland to forests, see Zinda et al. 2017.

29. The lineage record was compiled by a villager who worked in a regional records department. It was self-published as the *pukaoji puchuji*. The document, on file with the author, serves as a social history of the village. Other villagers in Wailong drawing on oral histories, however, suggest that the Huang family's presence dates to the Song dynasty.

30. A copy of the *Tier One Protection Area Core Area Pamphlet* is on file with the author.

31. Section of the *Tier One Protection Area Core Area Pamphlet* titled *Questions and Answers about Policies Related to the Resettlement of Migrants* [*Yimin banqian anzhi xiangguan zhengce zhishe wenda*].

32. Watts 2012, 443.

EPILOGUE

1. UNEP 2019.

2. See targets one, two, and three in UNEP 2020; 2021.

3. Schleicher et al. 2019.

4. West, Igoe, and Brockington 2006; Agrawal and Redford 2009.

5. Wen 2008; Wen et al. 2012; Day and Schneider 2018.

6. Scott 1998.

7. Fang, Wang, and Liu 2020. See also Pan et al. 2021.

8. Clayton and Schwartz 2019.

9. Duggan 2013.

10. Moore 2014; Crow-Miller and Webber 2017.

11. Shen and Ahlers 2019.

12. Rodenbiker 2022b.

13. Chen 2018.

14. Watts 2020.

15. Zheng 2016.

16. Zee 2020.

17. Rodenbiker 2019; Billé 2020; Marston 2021; Woon and Dodds 2021.

18. Beech 2018.

19. Martin 2018; 2022.

20. Massey 2009.

21. Ministry of Ecology and Environment 2017.

22. Zhou 2018.

23. AEI 2019; Harlan 2020.

APPENDIX

1. An affiliation with Sichuan University's Department of Land Resource Management and School of Public Administration facilitated research in Chengdu. A research affiliation with a government environmental bureau in Kunming facilitated research in Kunming and Dali.

2. Methodologically, this is referred to as snowball sampling and is commonly used to attend to situated knowledges, experiences, social networks, and power relations (Noy 2008).

3. Andreas 2019.

4. For works on participant observation, see Jorgensen 1989; Burawoy 1998; Walsh 2009.

5. Wang and Burris 1997; Wang 1999.

6. For an account of how I adapted photovoice research methods, see Rodenbiker 2022a.

7. Sen 1993. Similar points are made by feminist science studies scholars Donna Haraway (1988) and Sandra Harding (1995).

8. Burawoy 2009.

References

Abramson, Daniel B. 2016. "Periurbanization and the Politics of Development-as-City-Building in China." *Cities* 53 (Supplement C): 156–62.

AEI. 2019. "China Global Investment Data Tracker." American Enterprise Institute, Washington, DC. http://www.aei.org/china-global-investment-tracker/.

Agger, Ben. 1979. *Western Marxism, an Introduction: Classical and Contemporary Sources*. Santa Monica, CA: Goodyear Publishing.

Agrawal, Arun. 2005. *Environmentality: Technologies of Government and the Making of Subjects*. Durham, NC: Duke University Press.

Agrawal, Arun, and Kent Redford. 2009. "Conservation and Displacement: An Overview." *Conservation and Society* 7, no. 1: 1–10.

Ahlers, Anna. 2014. *Rural Policy Implementation in Contemporary China: New Socialist Countryside*. London: Routledge.

Alagona, Peter, John Sandlos, and Yolanda Wiersma. 2012. "Past Imperfect: Using Historical Ecology and Baseline Data for Conservation and Restoration Projects in North America." *Environmental Philosophy* 9, no. 1: 49–70.

Anagnost, Ann. 2004. "The Corporeal Politics of Quality (suzhi)." *Public Culture* 16, no. 2: 189–208.

Anderson, Kevin. 2002. "Marx's Late Writings on Non-Western and Precapitalist Societies and Gender." *Rethinking Marxism* 14, no. 4: 84–96.

Anderson, Kevin. 2016. *Marx at the Margins: On Nationalism, Ethnicity, and Non-Western Societies*. Chicago: University of Chicago Press.

Andreas, Joel. 2019. *Disenfranchised: The Rise and Fall of Industrial Citizenship in China*. Oxford: Oxford University Press.

Angelo, Hillary, and David Wachsmuth. 2015. "Urbanizing Urban Political Ecology: A Critique of Methodological Cityism." *International Journal of Urban and Regional Research* 39, no. 1: 16–27.

Arendt, Hannah. 1973 [1951]. *The Origins of Totalitarianism*. New York: World Publishing.

Arrighi, Giovanni. 2007. *Adam Smith in Beijing: Lineages of the Twenty-first Century*. London: Verso Trade.

Ballvé, Teo. 2020. *The Frontier Effect: State Formation and Violence in Colombia*. Ithaca, NY: Cornell University Press.

Bianco, Lucien. 1971. *Origins of the Chinese Revolution, 1915–1949*. Stanford, CA: Stanford University Press.

Beech, Hannah. 2018. "China's Sea Control Is a Done Deal, 'Short of War with the U.S.'" *New York Times,* September 20. https://www.nytimes.com/2018/09/20/world/asia/south-china-sea-navy.html.

Billé, Franck. 2020. *Voluminous States: Sovereignty, Materiality, and the Territorial Imagination*. Durham, NC: Duke University Press.

Blumenfield, Tami, and Helaine Silverman. 2013. *Cultural Heritage Politics in China*. New York: Springer.

Boulding, Kenneth. 1953. *The Organizational Revolution: A Study in the Ethics of Economic Organization*. New York: Harper.

Bourdieu, Pierre. 1984. *Distinction: A Social Critique of the Judgement of Taste*. Cambridge, MA: Harvard University Press.

Bourdieu, Pierre. 2004 [1962]. "The Peasant and His Body." *Ethnography* 5, no. 4: 579–99.

Boym, Svetlana. 2001. *The Future of Nostalgia*. New York: Basic Books.

Bramwell, Anna. 1989. *Ecology in the 20th Century: A History*. New Haven, CT: Yale University Press.

Bray, David. 2013. "Urban Planning Goes Rural: Conceptualising the New Village." *China Perspectives*, no. 3: 53–62.

Brenner, Neil. 2004. *New State Spaces: Urban Governance and the Rescaling of Statehood*. Oxford: Oxford University Press.

Brenner, Neil. 2013. "Theses on Urbanization." *Public Culture* 25, no. 1: 85–114.

Brundtland, Gro Harlem. 1987. *Our Common Future: World Commission on Environment and Development*. Oxford: Oxford University Press.

Buck, Daniel. 2012. *Constructing China's Capitalism: Shanghai and The Nexus of Urban-Rural Industries*. New York: Palgrave Macmillan.

Burawoy, Michael. 1998. "The Extended Case Method." *Sociological Theory* 16, no. 1: 4–33.

Burawoy, Michael. 2009. *The Extended Case Method*. Berkeley: University of California Press.

Buttel, Frederick. 2000. "Ecological Modernization as Social Theory." *Geoforum* 31, no 1: 57–65.

Byler, Darren. 2021. *In the Camps: China's High-Tech Penal Colony*. New York: Columbia Global Reports.

Byler, Darren. 2022. *Terror Capitalism: Uyghur Dispossession and Masculinity in a Chinese City*. Durham, NC: Duke University Press.

Byres, Terrence. 2008. "Political Economy, The Agrarian Question and the Comparative Method." *Journal of Peasant Studies* 22, no. 4: 561–80.

Byrnes, Corey. 2019. *Fixing Landscape: A Techno-Poetic History of China's Three Gorges*. New York: Columbia University Press.

Cai Yongshun. 2003. "Collective Ownership or Cadres' Ownership? The Non-Agricultural Use of Farmland in China." *China Quarterly* 175: 662–80.

Cao Junjian. 2015. *The Chinese Real Estate Market: Development, Regulation and Investment*. New York: Routledge.

Caldeira, Teresa. 2017. "Peripheral Urbanization: Autoconstruction, Transversal Logics, and Politics in Cities of the Global South." *Environment and Planning D: Society and Space* 35, no. 1: 3–20.

Cartier, Carolyn. 2015a. "Territorial Urbanization and the Party-State in China." *Territory, Politics, Governance* 3, no. 3: 294–320.

Cartier, C. 2015b. "Chapter 5: Building Civilised Cities." *The China Story*. https://www.thechinastory.org/yearbooks/yearbook-2013/chapter-5-building-civilised-cities/.

Castree, Noel, and Bruce Braun, eds. 2001. *Social Nature: Theory, Practice, and Politics*. Malden, MA: Blackwell Publishers.

CCICED. 2014. *Institutional Innovation of Eco-Environmental Redlining: Special Policy Study Report*. China Council for International Cooperation on Environment and Development. https://www.iisd.org/sites/default/files/publications/CCICED/conservation/2015/institutional-innovation-of-eco-environmetal-redlining.pdf.

Central Committee of the Communist Party of China. 2016. *The 13th Five-year Plan: For Economic and Social Development of the People's Republic of China.* Beijing, China.

Chan, Anita, Richard Madsen, and Jonathan Unger. 1992. *Chen Village under Mao and Deng: Expanded and Updated Edition.* Berkeley: University of California Press.

Chan Kam Wing and Zhang Li. 1999. "The Hukou System and Rural-Urban Migration in China: Processes and Changes." *China Quarterly* 160: 818–55.

Chen Jia-Ching, John Zinda, and Emily Yeh. 2017. "Recasting the Rural: State, Society, and Environment in Contemporary China." *Geoforum* 78: 83–88.

Chen, Stephen. 2018. "China Needs More Water. So It's Building a Rain-Making Network Three Times the Size of Spain." *South China Morning Post,* March 26, 2018. https://www.scmp.com/news/china/society/article/2138866/china-needs-more-water-so-its-building-rain-making-network-three.

Chengdu Municipal Government. 2014. "Chengdu Municipal People's Government Regarding Promoting Slum Reform in Five Districts *[Chengdushi renmin zhengfu bangongting guanyu jinyibu tuijin wuchengqu penghuqu gaizao gongzuode shishi yijian]*." http://gk.chengdu.gov.cn/govInfoPub/detail.action?id=63288&tn=6.

China Daily. 2007. "Ecological Civilization." http://www.chinadaily.com.cn/opinion/2007-10/24/content_6201964.htm.

China State Council. 2017. "Guidance on Promoting Green Belt and Road." Beijing: State Council. https://eng.yidaiyilu.gov.cn/zchj/qwfb/12479.htm.

Chio, Jenny. 2014. *A Landscape of Travel: The Work of Tourism in Rural Ethnic China.* Seattle: University of Washington Press.

Chu, Julie. 2014. "When Infrastructures Attack: The Workings of Disrepair in China." *American Ethnologist* 41, no. 2: 351–67.

Chu Yin-wah. 2020. "China's New Urbanization Plan: Progress and Structural Constraints." *Cities* 103: 102736.

Chuang, Julia. 2014. "China's Rural Land Politics: Bureaucratic Absorption and the Muting of Rightful Resistance." *China Quarterly* 219: 649–69.

Chuang, Julia. 2015. "Urbanization through Dispossession: Survival and Stratification in China's New Townships." *Journal of Peasant Studies* 42, no. 2: 275–94.

Chuang, Julia. 2020. *Beneath the China Boom: Labor, Citizenship, and the Making of a Rural Land Market.* Berkeley: University of California Press.

Chung Jae Ho, and Lam Tao-Chiu. 2004. "China's City System in Flux: Explaining Post-Mao Administrative Changes." *China Quarterly* 180: 945–64.

Clayton, Philip, and W. M. Schwartz. 2019. *What Is Ecological Civilization? Crisis, Hope, and the Future of the Planet.* Anoka, MN: Process Century Press.

Coggins, Christopher. 2017. "Conserving China's Biological Diversity: National Plans, Transnational Projects, Local and Regional Challenges." In *Routledge Handbook of Environmental Policy in China,* edited by Eva Sternfeld, 127–43. New York: Routledge.

Cook, Christopher, and Katharina Urmi-König. 1984. "A Revision of the Genus Ottelia (Hydrocharitaceae). 2. The Species of Eurasia, Australasia and America." *Aquatic Botany* 20, no. 1–2: 131–77.

Condorcet, Nicolas de Caritat. 1955 [1795]. *Sketch for a Historical Picture of the Progress of the Human Mind.* Translated by June Barraclough. London: Weidenfeld and Nicolson.

Cronon, William. 1992. *Nature's Metropolis: Chicago and the Great West.* New York: W. W. Norton.

Cronon, William. 1996. "The Trouble with Wilderness: Or, Getting Back to the Wrong Nature." *Environmental History* 1, no. 1: 7–28.

Crow-Miller, Britt, and Michael Webber. 2017. "Of Maps and Eating Bitterness: The Politics of Scaling in China's South-North Water Transfer Project." *Political Geography* 61: 19–30.

Culp, Robert, U Eddy, and Yeh Wen-Hsin, eds. 2016. *Knowledge Acts in Modern China: Ideas, Institutions, and Identities*. Berkeley: Institute of East Asian Studies, University of California.

Dai Quanyu. 1985. "Yunnan Fuxianhu, Erhai, Dianchi Shuisheng Zhibei de Shengtai Tezheng [Ecological Characteristics of Aquatic Vegetation in Fuxian Lake, Erhai Lake, and Lake Dian in Yunnan]." *Shengtai xuebao [Acta Ecologica Sinica]* 5, no. 4: 324–35.

Dandy, Edgar. 1934. "Ottelia acuminata (Gagnep.) Ottelia yunnanensis (Gagnep)." *Journal of Botany* 72: 137–38.

Dandy, Edgar. 1935. "Ottelia polygonifofia (Gagnep.) Ottelia cavaleriei." *Journal of Botany* 73: 214–15.

Davidson, Arnold. 2011. "In Praise of Counter-Conduct." *History of the Human Sciences* 24, no. 4: 25–41.

Davis, Deborah, David Kraus, Berry Naughton, and Elizabeth Perry, eds. 1995. *Urban Spaces in Contemporary China: The Potential for Autonomy and Community in Post-Mao China*. Cambridge: Cambridge University Press.

Day, Alexander. 2013. *The Peasant in Postsocialist China: History, Politics, and Capitalism*. Cambridge: Cambridge University Press.

Day, Alexander, and Mindi Schneider. 2018. "The End of Alternatives? Capitalist Transformation, Rural Activism, and the Politics of Possibility in China." *Journal of Peasant Studies* 45, no. 7: 1221–46.

De Jong, Martin, Rui Mu, Dominic Stead, Ma Yongchi, and Xi Bao. 2010. "Introducing Public–Private Partnerships for Metropolitan Subways in China: What Is the Evidence?" *Journal of Transport Geography* 18, no. 2: 301–13.

Deng Hongbing, Chen Chundi, Liu Xin, and Wu Gang. 2016. "Quyu shengtai yongdi de gainian ji fenlei [The Concept and Classification of Ecological Land]." *Shengtai xuebao [Acta Ecologica Sinica]* 29, no. 3: 1519–24.

Deng Yongheng, Randall Morck, Wu Jing, and Bernard Yeung. 2011. *Monetary and Fiscal Stimuli, Ownership Structure, and China's Housing Market*. Working Paper No. 16871. National Bureau of Economic Research. Cambridge, MA.

Diao Fangchao. 2021. "Yunnan Kunming 'huan hu kaifa' yu hu zhengdi, daliang fangchan xiangmu qinzhan Dianchi baohuqu [Development and Real Estate Projects Invade Lake Dian Reserve Land]." *The Paper*. https://www.thepaper.cn/newsDetail_forward_12539354.

Document 535. 2014. "Zhufang chengxiang jianshebu bangongtin guanyu penghuqu jieding biaozhun youguan wenti de tongzhi [Notice of the General Office of the Ministry of Housing and Urban-Rural Development on Issue Related to the Definition of Slums]." Jianban Baohan.

Dong Xuerong and Wu Ying. 2013. *Dianchi cangsang: Qiannian huangjingshi de shiye [The Vicissitudes of Lake Dian: A Thousand Years of Environmental History]*. Beijing: Zhishi chanpin chubanshe.

Duggan, Jennifer. 2013. "China's Mega Water Diversion Project Begins Testing." *The Guardian*. June 5. https://www.theguardian.com/environment/chinas-choice/2013/jun/05/chinas-water-diversion-project-south-north.

Easterling, Keller. 2005. *Enduring Innocence: Global Architecture and its Political Masquerades*. Cambridge, MA: MIT Press.

Easterling, Keller. 2014. *Subtraction*. Cambridge, MA: MIT Press.

Economy, Elizabeth. 2010. *The River Runs Black: The Environmental Challenge to China's Future*. Ithaca, NY: Cornell University Press.

Egan, Dave, and Evelyn Howell, eds. 2005. *The Historical Ecology Handbook: A Restorationist's Guide to Reference Ecosystems*. Washington, DC: Island Press.

Elden, Stuart. 2010. "Land, Terrain, Territory." *Progress in Human Geography* 34, no. 6: 799–817.

Elden, Stuart. 2013. "Secure the Volume: Vertical Geopolitics and the Depth of Power." *Political Geography* 34: 35–51.

Elliot, Robert. 2008. *Faking Nature: The Ethics of Environmental Restoration*. New York: Routledge.

Elman, Benjamin. 1984. *From Philosophy to Philology: Intellectual and Social Aspects of Change in Late Imperial China*. Cambridge, MA: Harvard University.

Fan Jie and Li Pingxing. 2009. "The Scientific Foundation of Major Function Oriented Zoning in China." *Journal of Geographical Sciences* 19, no. 5: 515.

Fang Chuanglin, Wang Zhenbao, and Liu Haimeng. 2020. "Beautiful China Initiative: Human-Nature Harmony Theory, Evaluation Index System and Application." *Journal of Geographical Sciences* 30, no. 5: 691–704.

Fiskesjö, Magnus. 2015. "Wa Grotesque: Headhunting Theme Parks and the Chinese Nostalgia for Primitive Contemporaries." *Ethnos* 80, no. 4: 497–523.

Forsyth, Tim. 2003. *Critical Political Ecology: The Politics of Environmental Science*. London: Routledge.

Foucault, Michel, 1990. *The History of Sexuality*. New York: Vintage Books.

Foucault, Michel. 1995. *Discipline and Punish: The Birth of the Prison*. New York: Vintage Books.

Foucault, Michel. 2003. *Society Must Be Defended: Lectures at the Collège de France, 1975–76*. New York: Picador.

Foucault, Michel. 2005. *The Order of Things*. New York: Routledge.

Foucault, Michel. 2009. *Security, Territory, Population: Lectures at the Collège de France, 1977–78*. New York: Picador/Palgrave Macmillan.

Foucault, Michel, Paul Rabinow, and Nikolas Rose. 2003. *The Essential Foucault: Selections from Essential Works of Foucault, 1954–1984*. New York: New Press.

Gaubatz, Piper. 1996. *Beyond the Great Wall: Urban Form and Transformation on the Chinese Frontiers*. Stanford, CA: Stanford University Press.

Geall, Sam, and Adrian Ely. 2018. "Narratives and Pathways towards an Ecological Civilization in Contemporary China." *China Quarterly* 236: 1175–96.

Geng Yong and Breet Doberstein. 2008. "Developing the Circular Economy in China: Challenges and Opportunities for Achieving "Leapfrog Development."" *International Journal of Sustainable Development and World Ecology* 15, no. 3: 231–39.

Ghertner, D. Asher. 2015. *Rule by Aesthetics: World-Class City Making in Delhi*. Oxford: Oxford University Press.

Ghertner, D. Asher, and Robert Lake. 2021. *Land Fictions: The Commodification of Land in Town and Country*. Ithaca, NY: Cornell University Press.

Gladney, Dru C. 1994. "Representing Nationality in China: Refiguring Majority/ Minority Identities." *Journal of Asian Studies* 53, no 1: 92–123.

Gobster, Paul. 1999. "An Ecological Aesthetic for Forest Landscape Management." *Landscape Journal* 18, no. 1: 54–64.

Goodman, David, and Michael Watts. 1997. *Globalising Food: Agrarian Questions and Global Restructuring*. London: Routledge.

Gordillo, Gastón. 2014. *Rubble: The Afterlife of Destruction*. Durham, NC: Duke University Press.

Gordon, Richard, and Carma Hinton. 1996. *The Gate of Heavenly Peace*. Roninfilms.

Graham, Stephen. 2016. *Vertical: The City from Satellites to Bunkers*. New York: Verso Books.

Graham, Stephen, and Lucy Hewitt. 2013. "Getting Off the Ground: On the Politics of Urban Verticality." *Progress in Human Geography* 37, no. 1: 72–92.

Graham, Steve, and Simon Marvin. 2001. *Splintering Urbanism: Networked Infrastructures, Technological Mobilities, and the Urban Condition*. London: Routledge.

Grant, Andrew. 2018. "Hyperbuilding the Civilized City: Ethnicity and Marginalization in Eastern Tibet." *Critical Asian Studies* 50, no. 4: 537–55.

Greenberg, Miriam. 2013. "What on Earth Is Sustainable? Toward Critical Sustainability Studies." *Boom: A Journal of California* 3, no. 4: 54–66.

Greenberg, Miriam. 2018. "Situating Sustainability in the Luxury City: Toward a Critical Urban Research Agenda." In *Sustainability: Approaches to Environmental Justice and Social Power*, edited by Julie Sze, 180–95. New York: New York University Press.

Gregson, Nicky, Mike Crang, Sara Fuller, and Helen Holmes. 2015. "Interrogating the Circular Economy: The Moral Economy of Resource Recovery in the EU." *Economy and Society* 44, no. 2: 218–43.

Guldin, Gregory. 2016. *Farewell to Peasant China: Rural Urbanization and Social Change in the Late Twentieth Century*. London: Routledge.

Hairong Yan and Chen Yijuan. 2015. "Agrarian Capitalization without Capitalism? Capitalist Dynamics from above and below in China." *Journal of Agrarian Change* 15, no. 3: 366–91.

Hajer, Maarten. 1995. *The Politics of Environmental Discourse: Ecological Modernization and the Policy Process*. Oxford University Press.

Hale, Matthew. 2013. "Reconstructing the Rural: Peasant Organizations in a Chinese Movement for Alternative Development." PhD diss., University of Washington.

Hansen, Mette, Li Hongtao, and Rune Svarverud. 2018. "Ecological Civilization: Interpreting the Chinese Past, Projecting the Global Future." *Global Environmental Change* 53: 195–203.

Haraway, Donna. 1988. "Situated Knowledges: The Science Question in Feminism and the Privilege of Partial Perspective." *Feminist Studies* 14, no. 3: 575–99.

Harding, Sandra. 1995. "Strong Objectivity": A Response to the New Objectivity Question." *Synthese* 104, no. 3: 331–49.

Harker, Christopher. 2014. "The Only Way Is Up? Ordinary Topologies of Ramallah." *International Journal of Urban and Regional Research* 38, no. 1: 318–35.

Harlan, Tyler. 2020. "Green Development or Greenwashing? A Political Ecology Perspective on China's Green Belt and Road." *Eurasian Geography and Economics* 62, no. 2: 1–25.

Harris, Andrew. 2015. "Vertical Urbanisms: Opening up Geographies of the Three-dimensional City." *Progress in Human Geography* 39, no. 5: 601–20.

Harvey, David. 2005. *The New Imperialism*. Oxford: Oxford University Press.

Hathaway, Michael. 2013. *Environmental Winds: Making the Global in Southwest China*. Berkeley: University of California Press.

He Xiangbin. 2019. "Chinese Local Governments to be Held Responsible for Their Local Environment: New Law, Old Problems." *China: An International Journal* 17, no. 3: 28–51.

Higgs, Eric. 2017. "Novel and Designed Ecosystems." *Restoration Ecology* 25, no. 1: 8–13.

Higgs, Eric, Donald Falk, Anita Guerrini, Marcus Hall, Jim Harris, Richard Hobbs, and William Throop. 2014. "The Changing Role of History in Restoration Ecology." *Frontiers in Ecology and the Environment* 12, no. 9: 499–506.

Hinton, William. 1997. *Fanshen: A Documentary of Revolution in a Chinese Village.* Berkeley: University of California Press.

Ho, Peter. 2001. "Who Owns China's Land? Policies, Property Rights and Deliberate Institutional Ambiguity." *China Quarterly* 166: 394–421.

Ho, Peter. 2017. "Who Owns China's Housing? Endogeneity as a Lens to Understand Ambiguities of Urban and Rural Property." *Cities* 65: 66–77.

hooks, bell. 1990. *Yearning: Race, Gender, and Cultural Politics.* Boston: South End Press.

hooks, bell. 2012. "Eating the Other: Desire and Resistance." In *Media and Cultural Studies: Keyworks*, edited by Meenakshi Durham and Douglas Kellner, 308–18. Oxford: Wiley-Blackwell.

Hsing You-tien. 1998. *Making Capitalism in China: The Taiwan Connection.* Oxford: University Press.

Hsing You-tien. 2006. "Foreign Capital and Local Real Estate in Chinese Cities." In *Globalization of Chinese Cities*, edited by Wu Fulong, 167–89. New York: Routledge.

Hsing You-tien. 2010. *The Great Urban Transformation: Politics of Land and Property in China.* Oxford: Oxford University Press.

Hu Jintao. 2012. Report to the Eighteenth National People's Congress. http://www.china.org.cn/china/18th_cpc_congress/201211/16/content_27137540.htm.

Hu Xiansu. 1922. "Xi tianmu [West Heaven's Eye Mountain]." *Xueheng* 1, no. 5: 4.

Hu Xiansu. 1927. "A Preliminary Survey of the Forest Flora of Southeastern China." CBLSSC 2, no. 5: 1–20.

Huan Qingzhi. 2016. "Socialist Eco-Civilization and Social-Ecological Transformation." *Capitalism Nature Socialism* 27, no. 2: 51–66.

Huang Yansheng. 2008. *Capitalism with Chinese Characteristics: Entrepreneurship and the State.* Cambridge: Cambridge University Press.

Hutchinson, G. Evelyn. 1978. *An Introduction to Population Ecology.* New Haven, CT: Yale University Press.

Imai, Ken-ichi, ed. 2003. "Beyond Market Socialism: Privatization of State-Owned and Collective Enterprises in China." Institute of Developing Economies. Chiba, Japan.

Jiang Bao, Bai Yang, Chistina Wong, Xu Xibao, and Juha Alatalo. 2019. "China's Ecological Civilization Program–Implementing Ecological Redline Policy." *Land Use Policy* 81: 111–14.

Jiang Lijing. 2016. "Retouching the Past with Living Things: Indigenous Species, Tradition, and Biological Research in Republican China, 1918–1937." *Historical Studies in the Natural Sciences* 46, no. 2: 154–206.

Jiang Zhaohui. 2016. "Kunming tuijin Dianchi zhili liudagongcheng [Kunming Promotes Six Major Engineering Projects to Treat Lake Dian]." *China Environmental News*, September 26. http://www.h2o-china.com/news/246775.html.

Johnson, Ian. 2013. "China's Great Uprooting: Moving 250 Million into Cities." *New York Times*, June 15. https://www.nytimes.com/2013/06/16/world/asia/chinas-great-uprooting-moving-250-million-into-cities.html.

Jorgensen, Danny. 1989. *Participant Observation: A Methodology for Human Studies.* London: Sage.

Junren Wan. 2013. "The Philosophical Wisdom and Action Implications of 'Beautiful China.'" *Social Sciences in China* 34, no. 4: 143–53.

Kingsland, Sharon. 1985. *Modelling Nature: Episodes in the History of Population Ecology.* Chicago: University of Chicago Press.

Kosek, Jake. 2006. *Understories: The Political Life of Forests in Northern New Mexico.* Durham, NC: Duke University Press.

Latour, Bruno. 1987. *Science in Action: How to Follow Scientists and Engineers through Society*. Cambridge, MA: Harvard University Press.

Latour, Bruno. 1993. *We Have Never Been Modern*. Cambridge, MA: Harvard University Press.

Lave, Rebecca. 2012. *Fields and Streams: Stream Restoration, Neoliberalism, and the Future of Environmental Science*. Athens: University of Georgia Press.

Lave, Rebecca, Matthew Wilson, Elizabeth Barron, Christine Biermann, Mark Carey, Chris Duvall, Leigh Johnson, K. Maria Lane, and Nathan McClintock et al. 2013. "Intervention: Critical Physical Geography." *The Canadian Geographer / Le Géographe Canadien* 58, no. 1: 1–10.

Lee Ching Kwan and Zhang Yonghong. 2013. "The Power of Instability: Unraveling the Microfoundations of Bargained Authoritarianism in China." *American Journal of Sociology* 118, no. 6: 1475–1508.

Lee Ching Kwan. 2007. *Against the Law: Labor Protests in China's Rustbelt and Sunbelt*. Berkeley: University of California Press.

Lee Ching Kwan. 2017. *The Specter of Global China: Politics, Labor, and Foreign Investment in Africa*. Chicago: University of Chicago Press.

Lee Haiyan. 2006. "Governmentality and the Aesthetic State: A Chinese Fantasia." *positions: east asia cultures critique* 14, no. 1: 99–129.

Lefebvre, Henri. 1991. *The Production of Space*. Oxford: Blackwell.

Leiss, William. 1976. *The Limits to Satisfaction: An Essay on the Problem of Needs and Commodities*. Toronto: University of Toronto Press.

Lélé, Sharachchandra. 1991. "Sustainable Development: A Critical Review." *World Development* 19, no. 6: 607–21.

Lemos, Carmen, and Arun Agrawal. 2006. "Environmental Governance." *Annual Review of Environment and Resources* 31, no. 1: 297–325.

Levien, Michael. 2012. "The Land Question: Special Economic Zones and the Political Economy of Dispossession in India." *Journal of Peasant Studies* 39, no. 3–4: 933–69.

Levien, Michael. 2018. *Dispossession without Development: Land Grabs in Neoliberal India*. Oxford: Oxford University Press.

Lewis, Michael. 2004. *Inventing Global Ecology: Tracking the Biodiversity Ideal in India 1947–1997*. Athens: Ohio University Press.

Li Dazhao. 1918. "Fa E gemingzhi bijiaoguan [A Comparison of French and Russian Revolutions]." *Yanzhi*. July 1. https://www.marxists.org/chinese/lidazhao/marxist.org-chinese-lee-19180701.htm.

Li Dazhao. 1919. "Wo de Makesi zhuyiguan [My Marxist Views]." *Xinqingnian* 6, no. 5 (May 1919): 521–37; and 6, no. 6 (November 1919): 612–24.

Li Dazhao. 1924. *Shi xue yaolun* [The Essentials of Historical Study]. Shanghai: Shangwu yinshu kuan.

Li Jie, ed. 2007. *Renxingwei yu hubo shengming* [Human Behavior and the Lake's Life]. Beijing: Zhongguo shehuixue chubanshe.

Li Li. 2008. "Kunming liudagongcheng jiasu Dianchi zhili [Six Major Engineering Projects Accelerate the Governance of Lake Dian]." *Yunnan Daily*, October 11. http://special.yunnan.cn/news/content/2008-10/11/content_104129.htm.

Li Peilin. 2002. "Tremendous Changes: The End of Villages–A Study of Villages in the Center of Guangzhou City." *Social Sciences in China*, no. 1: 168–79.

Li Shanghao, Yu Minjuan, Li Guangzhen, Zeng Jimian, Chen Jiayou, Gao Baoyun, and Huang Hongjin. 1963. "Yunnan gaoyuan hubo diaocha [Investigation of Yunnan's High Plateau Lakes]." *Haiyang yu hubo* [Ocean and Limnology] 5, no. 2: 87–114.

Li, Tania. 2007. *The Will to Improve: Governmentality, Development, and the Practice of Politics*. Durham, NC: Duke University Press.

Li Tianwei, Geng Haiqing, Ma Muye, Zhang Hui, Zhu Yuan, and Liu Lei. 2014. "Woguo xinxing chengzhenhua shengtaihongxian guankong tanxi [Analysis of China's New Type Urbanization Ecological Red Line Management and Control]." *Huanjing yingxiang pingjia* [Environmental Impact Assessment] 4: 18–21.

Li, Xiaolin, Annette Janssen, Jeroen de Klein, Carolien Kroeze, Maryna Strokal, Lin Ma, and Yi Zheng. 2019 "Modeling Nutrients in Lake Dianchi (China) and its Watershed." *Agricultural Water Management* 212: 48–59.

Li Wenqing, Wang Fang, Zhu Xiaoman, Yu Xin, and Liu Haibin. 2015. "Chengshi cengmian tuijin shengtai baohu hongxian guanli jizhi duici fenxi [Analysis of Measures to Promote the Red Line Management Mechanisms of Ecological Protection at the City Level]." *Zhongguo huanjing guanli ganbu xueyuan xuebao* [Journal of China Institute of Environmental Management] no. 1: 20–22.

Li Yifei and Judith Shapiro. 2020. *China Goes Green: Coercive Environmentalism for a Troubled Planet*. Cambridge: UK. Polity Press.

Li Yingqing and Wang Ying. 2009. "146 Million for Cleaning Dianchi." *China Daily*, March 17. http://www.chinadaily.com.cn/bizchina/2009-03/17/content_7585732.htm.

Lieberthal, Kenneth, and Michel Oksenberg. 1988. *Policy Making in China*. Princeton, NJ: Princeton University Press.

Liebman, Adam. 2019. "Reconfiguring Chinese Natures: Frugality and Waste Reutilization in Mao era Urban China." *Critical Asian Studies* 51, no. 4: 537–57.

Liebman, Adam. 2021. "Waste Politics in Asia and Global Repercussions. *Education about Asia* 26, no. 1: 35–40.

Lin, George. 2009. *Developing China: Land, Politics and Social Conditions*. London: Routledge.

Lindeman, Eduard. 1940. "Ecology: An Instrument for the Integration of Science and Philosophy." *Ecological Monographs* 10, no. 3: 367–72.

Liu Mingfu and Wang Zhongyuan. 2017. *The Thought of Xi Jinping*. Salt Lake, UT: American Academic Press.

Liu Yun. 2013. "Dianchi huanhu jiewugongcheng quanmianwan gongyongshui [The Dianchi Lake Sewage Interception Project is Fully Completed and Connected]." *China News*, January 16. http://www.chinanews.com/df/2013/01-16/4494538.shtml.

Liu Zhi. 2019. "Land-based Finance and Property Tax in China." *Area Development and Policy* 4, no. 4: 367–81.

Looney, Kristin. 2015. "China's Campaign to Build a New Socialist Countryside: Village Modernization, Peasant Councils, and the Ganzhou Model of Rural Development." *China Quarterly* 224: 909–32.

Lowe, Celia. 2013. *Wild Profusion: Biodiversity Conservation in an Indonesian Archipelago*. Princeton, NJ: Princeton University Press.

Lowenthal, David. 2015. *The Past Is a Foreign Country—Revisited*. Cambridge: Cambridge University Press.

Lu Jing, Wang Haibin, Pan Min, Xia Jing, Xing Wei, and Liu Guihua. 2012. "Using Sediment Seed Banks and Historical Vegetation Change Data to Develop Restoration Criteria for a Eutrophic Lake in China." *Ecological Engineering* 39: 95–103.

Lu Xiaobo. 1997. "The Politics of Peasant Burden in Reform China." *Journal of Peasant Studies* 25, no. 1: 113–38.

Lü Hongdi, Wan Jun, Wang Chengxin, Yu Lei, and Jiang Wenjin. 2014. "Chengshi shengtaihongxian tixi goujian jiqi yu guanli zhidu xianjie de yanjiu [The Construction of Urban Ecological Redline Systems and their Connection with Management Systems]." *Huanjing kexue yanjiu* [Environmental Science and Management] 39, no. 1: 5–11.

Lü Yihe, Ma Zhimin, Zhang Liwei, Fu Bojie, and Gao Guangyao. 2013. "Redlines for the Greening of China." *Environmental Science and Policy* 33: 346–53.

Luo Yu. 2018. "An Alternative to the 'Indigenous' in Early Twenty-First-Century China: Guizhou's Branding of Yuanshengtai." *Modern China* 44, no. 1: 68–102.

Ma Jun. 2007. "Ecological Civilization Is the Way Forward." *China Dialogue*. https://chinadialogue.net/article/1440-Ecological-civilisation-is-the-way-forward.

Ma, Laurence. 2005. "Urban Administrative Restructuring, Changing Scale Relations and Local Economic Development in China." *Political Geography* 24, no. 4: 477–97.

Ma Shijun. 1981. "Shengtai guilü zai huanjingguanlizhong de zuoyong—zhanlüe xiandai huanjing guanli de fazhan chushi [The Role of Ecological Laws in Environmental Management: A Discussion on the Development Trends of Modern Environmental Management]." *Huanjing kexue xuebao* [Journal of Environmental Science] 1, no. 1: 95–100.

Ma Shijun and Wang Rusong. 1984. "Shehui jingji ziran fuhe shengtaixitong [The Social-Economic-Natural Complex Ecosystem]." *Shengtai xuebao* [*Acta Ecologica Sinica*] 4, no. 1: 1–9.

Magubane, Zine. 2003. "Simians, Savages, Skulls, and Sex: Science and Colonial Militarism in 19th-Century South Africa." In *Race, Nature, and the Politics of Difference*, edited by Donald Moore, Jake Kosek, and Anand Pandian, 99–121. Durham, NC: Duke University Press.

Makino, Tomitaro, 1949. *An Illustrated Flora of Japan: With the Cultivated and Naturalized Plants*. Tokyo: Hokuryūkan.

Mann, Michael. 1984. "The Autonomous Power of the State: Its Origins, Mechanisms, and Results." *European Journal of Sociology/Archives européennes de sociologie* 25, no. 2: 185–213.

Mao Zedong. 1927. "Report on an Investigation of the Peasant Movement in Hunan." *Selected Works of Mao Zedong*, 1: 23–59.

Mao Zedong. 1956. *Analyses of the Classes in Chinese Society*. Beijing: Foreign Language Press.

Marston, Andrea. 2020. "Vertical Farming: Tin Mining and Agro-mineros in Bolivia." *Journal of Peasant Studies* 47, no. 4: 820–40.

Marston, Andrea. 2021. "Of Flesh and Ore: Material Histories and Embodied Geologies." *Annals of the American Association of Geographers* 111, no. 7: 2078–95.

Martin, Laura. 2018. "Proving Grounds: Ecological Fieldwork in the Pacific and the Materialization of Ecosystems." *Environmental History* 23, no. 3: 567–92.

Martin, Laura. 2022. *Wild by Design: The Rise of Ecological Restoration*. Cambridge, MA: Harvard University Press.

Marx, Karl. 1976 [1867]. *Capital: A Critique of Political Economy*. London: Penguin.

Marx, Karl. 2005 [1939]. *Grundrisse: Foundations of the Critique of Political Economy*. New York: Vintage Books.

Massey, Doreen. 2005. *For Space*. London: Sage.

Massey, Doreen. 2009. "Concepts of Space and Power in Theory and in Political Practice." *Documents d'anàlisi geogràfica* 55: 15–26.

Massey, Doreen. 2013. *Space, Place, and Gender*. Oxford: Polity Press.

Matsumura, Jinzo, and Manabu Miyoshi. 1900. *Cryptogamae Japonicae Iconibus Illustratae: or Figures with Brief Descriptions and Remarks of the Musci, Hepaticae, Lichenes, Fungi and Algae of Japan*. Tokyo: Keigyosha.

Mattingly, Daniel. 2019. *The Art of Political Control in China*. Cambridge: Cambridge University Press.

McGee, Terry. 2015. "The Emergence of Desakota Regions in Asia: Expanding a Hypothesis." In *Implosions/Explosions*, edited by Neil Brenner, 121–37. Berlin: Jovis.

McIntosh, Robert. 1986. *The Background of Ecology: Concept and Theory*. Cambridge: Cambridge University Press.

Meisner, Maurice. 1970. *Li Ta-chao and the Origins of Chinese Marxism*. New York: Atheneum.

Meisner, Maurice. 1978. "Dazhai: The Mass Line in Practice." *Modern China* 4, no. 1: 27–62.

Mertha, Andrew. 2005. "China's 'Soft' Centralization: Shifting Tiao/kuai Authority Relations." *China Quarterly* 184: 791–810.

Mertha, Andrew. 2009. "'Fragmented Authoritarianism 2.0': Political Pluralization in the Chinese Policy Process." *China Quarterly* 200: 995–1012.

Ministry of Ecology and Environment. 2017. *Guidance on Promoting Green Belt and Road*. http://english.mee.gov.cn/Resources/Policies/policies/Frameworkp1/201706/t20170628_416864.shtml.

Mitchell, Timothy. 1991. "The Limits of the State: Beyond Statist Approaches and Their Critics." *American Political Science Review* 85, no. 1: 77–96.

Mitsch, William. 2012. "What Is Ecological Engineering?" *Ecological Engineering* 45: 5–12.

Miyoshi. Manabu. 1890. "Notes on Pinguicula Ramosa, with Plate XI." *Botanical Magazine, Shokubutsugaku Zasshi* 4: 1–3.

Miyoshi, Manabu. 1905. *Atlas of Japanese Vegetation: Phototype Reproductions of Photographs of Wild and Cultivated Plants as well as the Plant-landscapes of Japan. With Explanatory Text*. Tokyo: The Maruzen Kabushiki Kaisha.

Miyoshi, Manabu. 1912. *Saishin shokubutsugaku kōgi* [Plant Ecology and Beauty]. Zōtei kaihan. Tōkyō: Fuzanbō.

Miyoshi, Manabu. 1921. *Shiseki meishō tennen kinenbutsu hozon yōmoku kaisetsu: shokubutsu no bu* [Explanations on the Conservation of Natural Monuments and Historic Sites: Plant Department]. Tōkyō: Naimushō, Taishō.

Moise, Edwin. 2013. *Modern China*. London: Routledge.

Moore, Donald, Jake Kosek, and Anand Pandian, eds. 2003. *Race, Nature, and the Politics of Difference*. Durham, NC: Duke University Press.

Moore, Scott. 2014. "Modernisation, Authoritarianism, and the Environment: The Politics of China's South–North Water Transfer Project." *Environmental Politics* 23, no. 6: 947–64.

Morgan, Lewis Henry. 1877. *Ancient Society; or, Researches in the Lines of Human Progress from Savagery, through Barbarism to Civilization*. New York: Henry Holt.

Muldavin, Joshua. 2007. "The Politics of Transition: Critical Political Ecology, Classical Economics, and Ecological Modernization Theory in China." In *The Political Geography Handbook*, edited by Kevin Cox, Murray Low, and Jenny Robinson, 247–62. London: Sage.

Muldavin, Joshua. 2015. "Using Cities to Control the Countryside: An Alternative Assessment of the China National Human Development Report 2013." *Development and Change* 46, no. 4: 993–1009.

Nadkarni, Maya, and Olga Shevchenko. 2004. "The Politics of Nostalgia: A Case for Comparative Analysis of Post-socialist Practices." *Ab imperio* 2: 487–519.

Nathan, Andrew. 2001. "The Tiananmen Papers." *Foreign Affairs* 80, no. 1: 2–48.

Nathan, Andrew. 2017. "China's Changing of the Guard: Authoritarian Resilience." In *Critical Readings on the Communist Party of China*, edited by Kjeld Brodsgaard, 86–99. Leiden, Netherlands: Brill.

National New-Type Urbanization Plan (2014–2020). 2014. http://www.gov.cn/zhuanti/xxczh/.

National Research Council and Committee on Restoration of Aquatic Ecosystems-Science and Policy (NRC). 1992. *Restoration of Aquatic Ecosystems: Science, Technology, and Public Policy*. Washington, DC: National Academies Press.

Naughton, Barry. 1995. *Growing Out of the Plan: Chinese Economic Reform, 1978–1993*. New York: Cambridge University Press.

Needham, Joseph. 1954. *Science and Civilization in China*. Vol. 1. *Introductory Orientations*. Cambridge: Cambridge University Press.

Neumann, Roderick. 1998. *Imposing Wilderness: Struggles over Livelihood and Nature Preservation in Africa*. Berkeley: University of California Press.

Noy, Chaim. 2008. "Sampling Knowledge: The Hermeneutics of Snowball Sampling in Qualitative Research." *International Journal of Social Research Methodology* 11, no. 4: 327–44.

Oakes, Tim. 2005. *Tourism and Modernity in China*. London. Routledge.

Oakes, Tim. 2019. "China's Urban Ideology: New Towns, Creation Cities, and Contested Landscapes of Memory." *Eurasian Geography and Economics* 60, no. 4: 400–421.

Odum, Eugene. 1959. *Fundamentals of Ecology*. Philadelphia: W. B. Saunders.

Odum, Howard, and Bill Odum. 2003. "Concepts and Methods of Ecological Engineering." *Ecological Engineering* 20, no. 5: 339–61.

Oi, Jean. 1992. "Fiscal Reform and the Economic Foundations of Local State Corporatism in China." *World Politics* 45, no. 1: 99–126.

Oi, Jean. 1999. *Rural China Takes Off: Institutional Foundations of Economic Reform*. Berkeley: University of California Press.

Ostrom, Elinor. 1990. *Governing the Commons: The Evolution of Institutions for Collective Action*. Cambridge. Cambridge University Press.

Ouyang Zhiyun, Zheng Hua, Xiao Yi, Stephen Polasky, Liu Jianguo, Xu Weihua. 2016. "Improvements in Ecosystem Services from Investments in Natural Capital." *Science* 352, no. 6292: 1455–59.

Palmer, Meredith Alberta. 2020. "Rendering Settler Sovereign Landscapes: Race and Property in the Empire State." *Environment and Planning D: Society and Space* 38, no. 5: 793–810.

Pan Jiahua. 2013a. *China's Environmental Governing and Ecological Civilization*. Berlin: Springer.

Pan Jiahua. 2013b. "Ensuring Ecological Security by Adapting to Carrying Capacity." *Social Sciences in China* 34, no. 4: 154–61.

Pan Jiahua, Gao Shiji, Li Qingqui, Wang Jinnan, Wu Dekui, and Huang Chengliang, eds. 2021. *Beautiful China: 70 Years since 1949 and 70 People's Views on Eco-civilization Construction*. New York: Springer and China Environment Publishing.

Park, Choong-Hwan. 2014. "Nongjiale Tourism and Contested Space in Rural China." *Modern China* 40, no. 5: 519–48.

Perdue, Peter. 1987. *Exhausting the Earth: State and Peasant in Hunan, 1500–1850*. Cambridge, MA: Harvard University Press.

Pow, Choon-Piew. 2018. "Building a Harmonious Society through Greening: Ecological Civilization and Aesthetic Governmentality in China." *Annals of the American Association of Geographers* 108, no. 3: 864–83.

Pu Riguo. 2012. "'Situisanhuanyihu' zhudianchi shui bianqing fanglangdi jiangquanzhaichu ['Four Removals, Three Returns, for One Protection' to Help Purify Lake Dian, the Breakwater Will be Completely Removed]." *Kunming Daily*, November 3.

Qian, Linda. 2017. "The Political Economy and Cultural Politics of Rural Nostalgia in Xi-Era China: The Case of Heyang Village." *International Journal of Communication* 11: 4423–42.

Qu Zhongxiang and Li Heng. 1983. *Dianchi zhiwu qunluo yu wuran Dianchi wuran yu Shuishengwu* [Pollution Control in Lake Dian and Aquatic Organisms]. Kunming: Yunnan renmin chubanshe.

Ramzy, Austin. 2014. "8 Killed in Clash over Development in Southwest China." *New York Times,* October 15. https://sinosphere.blogs.nytimes.com/2014/10/15/8-killed-in-clash-over-development-in-southwestern-china/.

Rancière, Jacques. 2013. *The Politics of Aesthetics: The Distribution of the Sensible*. Translated by Gabriel Rockhill. London: Bloomsbury.

Ribot, Jesse, and Nancy Peluso. 2003. "A Theory of Access." *Rural Sociology* 68, no. 2: 153–81.

Robbins, Paul. 2011. *Political Ecology: A Critical Introduction*. Hoboken, NJ: Blackwell.

Robinson, Cedric. 2000. *Black Marxism: The Making of the Black Radical Tradition*. Chapel Hill: University of North Carolina Press.

Robinson, Jennifer, and Ananya Roy. 2016. "Debate on Global Urbanisms and the Nature of Urban Theory." *International Journal of Urban and Regional Research* 40, no. 1: 181–86.

Rodenbiker, Jesse. 2017. "Superscribing Sustainability: The Production of China's Urban Waterscapes." *UPLanD-Journal of Urban Planning, Landscape and Environmental Design* 2, no. 3: 71–86.

Rodenbiker, Jesse. 2019. "Uneven Incorporation: Volumetric Transitions in Peri-urban China's Conservation Zones." *Geoforum* 104: 234–43.

Rodenbiker, Jesse. 2020. "Urban Ecological Enclosures: Conservation Planning, Peri-urban Displacement, and Local State Formations in China." *International Journal of Urban and Regional Research* 44, no. 4: 691–710.

Rodenbiker, Jesse. 2021. "Making Ecology Developmental: China's Environmental Sciences and Green Modernization in Global Contexts." *Annals of the American Association of Geographers* 111, no. 7: 1931–48.

Rodenbiker, Jesse. 2022a. "Adapting Participatory Research Methods for Reflexive Environmental Management." *Qualitative Research* 22, no. 4: 559–77.

Rodenbiker, Jesse. 2022b. "Geoengineering the Sublime: China and the Aesthetic State." *Made in China Journal* 7, no. 2: 140–45.

Rodgers, Dennis, and Bruce O'Neill. 2012. "Infrastructural Violence: Introduction to the Special Issue." *Ethnography* 13, no. 4: 401–12.

Røpke, Inge. 2004. "The Early History of Modern Ecological Economics." *Ecological Economics* 50, nos. 3–4: 293–314.

Rose, Nikolas. 1999. *Powers of Freedom: Reframing Political Thought*. Cambridge: Cambridge University Press.

Roy, Ananya. 2009. "The 21st-Century Metropolis: New Geographies of Theory." *Regional Studies* 43, no. 6: 819–30.

Roy, Ananya. 2016. "What Is Urban about Critical Urban Theory?" *Urban Geography* 37, no. 6: 810–23.

Sayre, Nathan. 2008. "The Genesis, History, and Limits of Carrying Capacity." *Annals of the Association of American Geographers* 98, no. 1: 120–34.

Sayre, Nathan. 2010. "Climax and Original 'Capacity': The Science and Aesthetics of Ecological Restoration in the Southwestern USA." *Ecological Restoration* 28, no. 1: 23–31.

Schein, Louisa. 1997. "Gender and Internal Orientalism in China." *Modern China* 23, no. 1: 69–98.

Schiller, Friedrich. 2016 [1795]. *On the Aesthetic Education of Man*. London: Penguin.

Schleicher, Judith, Julie G. Zaehringer, Constance Fastré, Bhaskar Vira, Piero Visconti, and Chris Sandbrook. 2019. "Protecting Half of the Planet Could Directly Affect over One Billion People." *Nature Sustainability* 2, no. 12: 1094–96.

Schmalzer, Sigrid. 2016. *Red Revolution, Green Revolution: Scientific Farming in Socialist China*. Chicago: University of Chicago Press.

Schmitt, Edwin. 2018. "Living in an Ecological Civilization: Ideological Interpretations of an Authoritarian Mode of Sustainability in China." *Critical Approaches to Discourse Analysis across Disciplines* 10, no. 2: 69–81.

Schneider, Mindi. 2015. "What, Then, Is a Chinese Peasant? Nongmin Discourses and Agroindustrialization in Contemporary China." *Agriculture and Human Values* 32, no. 2: 331–46.

Schneider, Mindi. 2017a. "Wasting the Rural: Meat, Manure, and the Politics of Agroindustrialization in Contemporary China." *Geoforum* 78: 89–97.

Schneider, Mindi. 2017b. "Dragon Head Enterprises and the State of Agribusiness in China." *Journal of Agrarian Change* 17, no. 1: 3–21.

Schumacher, Ernst. 1975. *Small Is Beautiful: Economics as if People Mattered*. New York: Harper and Row.

Scott, James. 1998. *Seeing Like a State: How Certain Schemes to Improve the Human Condition Have Failed*. New Haven, CT: Yale University Press.

Selden, Mark. 1993. *The Political Economy of Chinese Development*. New York: M. E. Sharpe.

Sen, Amartya. 1993. "Positional Objectivity." *Philosophy and Public Affairs* 22, no. 2: 126–45.

Shapiro, Judith. 2001. *Mao's War against Nature: Politics and the Environment in Revolutionary China*. Cambridge: Cambridge University Press.

Shen, Grace. 2014. *Unearthing the Nation: Modern Geology and Nationalism in Republican China*. Chicago: University of Chicago Press.

Shen Yongdong and Anna Ahlers. 2019. "Blue Sky Fabrication in China: Science-Policy Integration in Air Pollution Regulation Campaigns for Mega-Events." *Environmental Science and Policy* 94: 135–42.

Shi, Tian. 2002. "Ecological Economics in China: Origins, Dilemmas and Prospects." *Ecological Economics* 41, no. 1: 5–20.

Shue, Vivienne. 1988. *The Reach of the State: Sketches of the Chinese Body Politic*. Stanford, CA: Stanford University Press.

Simone, AbdouMaliq. 2004. "People as Infrastructure: Intersecting Fragments in Johannesburg." *Public Culture* 16, no. 3: 407–29.

Smith, Adam. 1937 [1776]. *The Wealth of Nations*. New York: Modern Library.

Smith, Nick. 2021. *The End of the Village: Planning the Urbanization of Rural China*. Minneapolis: University of Minnesota Press.

Song Cheng, Huang Dong, Bing Shu, and Cheng Peng. 1947. "Yunnan Dianchi quyu zhi diliyong [Land Use in the Yunnan Lake Dian Area]." *Dili xuebao [Acta Geographica Sinica]* 14, no. 2: 11–33.

Spence, Mark. 1999. *Dispossessing the Wilderness: Indian Removal and the Making of the National Parks.* Oxford: Oxford University Press.

Stafleu, Frans, and Richard Cowan. 1981. *Taxonomic Literature a Selective Guide to Botanical Publications and Collections with Dates, Commentaries and Types.* Vol. 3. *Lh-O.* The Hague: Holkema Publishers.

Stepan, Nancy. 1991. *The Hour of Eugenics: Race, Gender, and Nation in Latin America.* Ithaca, NY: Cornell University Press.

Su Biwei, Heshmati Almas, Geng Yong, and Yu Xiaoman. 2013. "A Review of the Circular Economy in China: Moving from Rhetoric to Implementation." *Journal of Cleaner Production* 42: 215–27.

Summers, Brandi. 2019. *Black in Place: The Spatial Aesthetics of Race in a Post-Chocolate City.* Chapel Hill: University of North Carolina Press.

Svolik, Milian. 2012. *The Politics of Authoritarian Rule.* Cambridge: Cambridge University Press.

Szamosszegi, Andrew, and Kyle Cole. 2011. *An Analysis of State-Owned Enterprises and State Capitalism in China.* Vol. 52. *Capital Trade.* Washington, DC: US-China Economic and Security Review Commission.

Sze, Julie, ed. 2018. *Sustainability: Approaches to Environmental Justice and Social Power.* New York: New York University Press.

Tanaka, Takshi, Takahiro Sato, Kazuo Watanabe, Wang Ying, Dan Yang, Hiromo Inoue, and Tatsuya Inamura. 2013. "Irrigation System and Land Use Effect on Surface Water Quality in River, at Lake Dianchi, Yunnan, China." *Journal of Environmental Sciences* 25, no. 6: 1107–16.

Tang Bebei. 2015. "Not Rural but Not Urban: Community Governance in China's Urban Villages." *China Quarterly* 223: 724–44.

Tansley, Arthur. 1935. "The Use and Abuse of Vegetational Concepts and Terms." *Ecology* 16, no. 3: 284–307.

Teets, Jessica. 2014. *Civil Society under Authoritarianism: The China Model.* Cambridge: Cambridge University Press.

Tilly, Charles. 2010. *Regimes and Repertoires.* Chicago: University of Chicago Press.

Tomba, Luigi. 2014. *The Government Next Door: Neighborhood Politics in Urban China.* Ithaca, NY: Cornell University Press.

Tong, Christopher. 2019. "The Paradox of China's Sustainability." In *Chinese Environmental Humanities,* edited by Chang Chia-Ju, 239–70. New York: Palgrave Macmillan.

Turner, Monica, Robert Gardner, and Robert O'Neill. 2001. *Landscape Ecology in Theory and Practice.* New York: Springer.

Trotsky, Leon. 2008 [1930]. *History of the Russian Revolution.* Translated by Max Eastman. Chicago, IL: Haymarket Books.

Trotsky, Leon. 2010 [1931]. *The Permanent Revolution & Results and Prospects.* Seattle: Red Letter Press.

Ueda, Makoto. 2015. "The History of Ecological Environment: Ideas Derived from Chinese Research." In *Economic History of Energy and Environment,* edited by S. Sugiyama, 69–83. Tokyo: Springer.

UNDP. 2013. *Sustainable and Livable Cities: Toward Ecological Civilization.* Human Development Report. http://hdr.undp.org/en/content/sustainable-and-liveable-cities-toward-ecological-civilization.

UNEP. 2019. "Building an Ecological Civilization: Theme for 2020 UN Biodiversity Conference Announced." Sept 10, 2019. https://www.unep-wcmc.org/news/building-an-ecological-civilization--theme-for-2020-un-biodiversity-conference-announced.

UNEP. 2020. "Update of the Zero Draft of the Post-2020 Global Biodiversity Framework. Convention on Biological Diversity." Released August 17, 2020.

UNEP. 2021. "First Draft of the Post-2020 Global Biodiversity Framework. Convention on Biological Diversity." Released July 5, 2021.

Urry, John. 2002. *The Tourist Gaze*. London. Sage.

Verdery, Katherine. 2003. *The Vanishing Hectare: Property and Value in Postsocialist Transylvania*. Ithaca, NY: Cornell University Press.

Volkov, Vadim. 2016. *Violent Entrepreneurs: The Use of Force in the Making of Russian Capitalism*. Ithaca, NY: Cornell University Press.

Wade, Robert. 2004. *Governing the Market: Economic Theory and the Role of Government in East Asian Industrialization*. Princeton, NJ: Princeton University Press.

Walder, Andrew. 2015. *China under Mao: A Revolution Derailed*. Cambridge, MA: Harvard University Press.

Walker, Richard. 2009. *The Country in the City: The Greening of the San Francisco Bay Area*. Seattle: University of Washington Press.

Walsh, Katie. 2009. "Methods: Participant Observation." In *International Encyclopedia of Human Geography*, edited by Nigel Thrift and Rob Kitchin, 77–81. London: Elsevier.

Wan Jun, Yu Lei, Zhang Peipei, Wang Chengxin, and Zhang Nannan. 2015. "Chengshishengtai baohuhongxian huading fangfa yu shijian [Methods and Practices for Delineating Urban Ecological Redlines]." *Huanjing baohu kexue* [Environmental Science] 41, no. 1: 6–11.

Wang Aiehe. 2006. *Cosmology and Political Culture in Early China*. Cambridge: Cambridge University Press.

Wang, Caroline, and Mary Ann Burris. 1997. "Photovoice: Concept, Methodology, and Use for Participatory Needs Assessment." *Health Education and Behavior* 24, no. 3: 369–87.

Wang Chengxin, Xu Yanying, Yu Lei, and Wang Yi. 2017. "Chengshi shengtaibaohuhongxian yu shengtaikongzhixian hexiexing yanjiu [Research on the Coordination of Urban Ecological Protection Redlines and Ecological Control Lines]." *Zhongguo huanjing guanli* [Chinese Environmental Management] 9, no. 1: 69–74.

Wang Jin. 1986. "Shengtaixue Makesizhuyi he shengtaishehuizhuyi [Ecological Marxism and Ecological Socialism]." *Jiaoxueyuyanjiu* [Research in Teaching] 6: 39–44.

Wang Rusong. 1999. "Cong nongye wenming dao shengtai wenming—zhuanxingqi nongcun kechixu fazhan de shengtaixue fangfa [From Agricultural Civilization to Ecological Civilization—Ecological Methods for Sustainable Rural Development in Transition]." *Renwen zazhi* [Journal of Humanities] 6: 53–59.

Wang Rusong and Ouyang Zhiyun. 2012. "Shehui-jingji-ziran fuhe shengtaixitong yu kechixufazhan [Social-Economic-Natural Complex Ecosystems and Sustainable Development]." *Nian kechixu fazhan 20 nian xueshu yantohui* [20 Year of Sustainable Development Symposium]. DOI:10.3969/j.issn.1000-3045.2012.03.012, 337–45.

Wang Yaping and Zhao Min. 2009. "Urban Spill Over vs. Local Urban Sprawl: Entangling Land-use Regulations in the Urban Growth of China's Megacities." *Land Use Policy* 26, no. 4: 1031–45.

Wang Zhihe. 2012. "Ecological Marxism in China." *Monthly Review* 63, no. 9: 36.

Watts, Jonathan. 2020. "China Plans Rapid Expansion of 'Weather Modification Efforts.'" *The Guardian*. December 3. https://www.theguardian.com/world/2020/dec/03/china-vows-to-boost-weather-modification-capabilities.

Watts, Michael. 2012. "A Tale of Two Gulfs: Life, Death, and Dispossession along Two Oil Frontiers." *American Quarterly* 64, no. 3: 437–67.

Weizman, Eyal. 2007. *Hollow Land: Israel's Architecture of Occupation*. London: Verso.

Wen Tiejun. 2001. "Reflections at the Turn of the Century on 'Rural Issues in Three Dimensions.'" *Inter-Asia Cultural Studies* 2: 187–295.

Wen Tiejun. 2008. "Four Stories in One: Environmental Protection and Rural Reconstruction in China." *positions: east asia cultures critique* 16, no. 3: 491–505.

Wen Tiejun. 2021. *Ten Crises: The Political Economy of China's Development (1949–2020)*. New York: Palgrave Macmillan.

Wen Tiejun, Lau Kinchi, Cheng Cunwang, He Huili, and Qiu Jiansheng. 2012. "Ecological Civilization, Indigenous Culture, and Rural Reconstruction in China." *Monthly Review* 63, no 9: 29–35.

Weng Xiaoxue, Dong, Zhanfeng, Wu Qiong, and Qin Ying. 2015. *China's Path to a Green Economy. Decoding China's Green Economy Concepts and Policies*. London. International Institute for Environment and Development.

West, Paige, James Igoe, and Dan Brockington. 2006. "Parks and Peoples: The Social Impact of Protected Areas." *Annual Review of Anthropology* 35: 251–77.

Wilczak, Jessica. 2017. "Making the Countryside More Like the Countryside? Rural Planning and Metropolitan Visions in Post-quake Chengdu." *Geoforum* 78: 110–18.

Williams, Dee Mack. 1997. "The Desert Discourse of Modern China." *Modern China* 23, no. 3: 328–55.

Williams, Raymond. 1980. *Problems in Materialism and Culture: Selected Essays*. New York: Verso.

Williams, Raymond. 1995. "Socialism and Ecology." *Capitalism Nature Socialism* 6, no. 1: 41–57.

Williams, Raymond. 2011 [1973]. *The Country and the City*. Nottingham, UK: Spokesman Books.

Woon Chih Yuan and Klaus Dodds. 2021. "Subterranean Geopolitics: Designing, Digging, Excavating, and Living." *Geoforum* 127: 349–55.

Wortley, Liana, Jean-Marc Hero, and Michael Howes. 2013. "Evaluating Ecological Restoration Success: A Review of the Literature." *Restoration Ecology* 21, no. 5: 537–43.

Wu Fulong. 2007. "Re-orientation of the City Plan: Strategic Planning and Design Competition in China." *Geoforum* 38, no. 2: 379–92.

Wu Huifang and Jingzhong Ye. 2016. "Hollow Lives: Women Left Behind in Rural China." *Journal of Agrarian Change* 16, no. 1: 50–69.

Wu Ruidong, Long Yongcheng, George Malanson, Paul Garber, Zhang Shuang, Li Diqiang, Peng Zhao, Wang Longzhu, and Duo Hairui. 2014. "Optimized Spatial Priorities for Biodiversity Conservation in China: A Systematic Conservation Planning Perspective." *PLoS One* 9, no. 7: e103783.

Xi Jinping. 2017. *Speech at 199th CCP National Congress*. https://www.chinadaily.com.cn/china/19thcpcnationalcongress/2017-11/04/content_34115212.htm.

Xiao Yuan. 2014. "Making Land Fly: The Institutionalization of China's Land Quota Markets and Its Implications for Urbanization, Property Rights, and Intergovernmental Politics." PhD diss., Massachusetts Institute of Technology.

Xinhua. 2017. "CPC Incorporates 'Beautiful China' into Two-stage Development Plan." October, 18. https://www.chinadaily.com.cn/china/2017-10/18/content_33404172.htm.

Xinhua. 2021. "25 Pct of China's Land Area Demarcated for Ecological Protection." http://www.xinhuanet.com/english/2021-07/07/c_1310047714.htm.

Xun Lili and Bao Z. 2007. "Environmental Policies Based on Government Mobilization and their Local Implementation: A Sociological Analysis of Ecological Migration at S Banner in Inner Mongolia." *Social Sciences in China* 5: 114–28.

Yang Guobin. 2016. *The Red Guard Generation and Political Activism in China*. New York: Columbia University Press.

Yang Jun-Xing, Shu Shu-Sen, and Chen Xiao-Yong. 2013. "Effect of Grass Carp Introduction of the Extinction of Ottelia acuminata in Dianchi Lake." *Zoological Research* 34, no. 6: 631–35.

Yang Yongjin. 2007. *Nong jia le: Lüyou jingying zhinan* [Tourism Operation Guidebook]. Beijing: Nongye chubanshe.

Ye Qianji. 1982. "Shengtai nongye [Ecological Agriculture]." *Nongyejingji wenti* [Issues in Agricultural Economy] 11: 3–10.

Ye Qianji. 1987. "Shengtainongyefazhande zhanlüe wenti [Strategic Problems of Developing Ecological Agriculture]." *Xinan nongye daxue xuebao* [Journal of Southwest Agricultural University] 9, no. 1: 1–8.

Ye Qianji. 1988. *Shengtai nongye: Nongye de weilai* [Ecological Agriculture: The Future of Agriculture]. Chongqing: Chongqing chubanshe.

Yeh, Emily T. 2009. "Greening Western China: A Critical View." *Geoforum* 40, no. 5: 884–94.

Yeh, Emily T. 2013a. *Taming Tibet: Landscape Transformation and the Gift of Chinese Development*. Ithaca, NY: Cornell University Press.

Yeh, Emily T. 2013b. "The Politics of Conservation in Contemporary Rural China." *Journal of Peasant Studies* 40, no. 6: 1165–88.

Yeh, Emily, and Christopher Coggins, eds. 2014. *Mapping Shangrila: Contested Landscapes in the Sino-Tibetan Borderlands*. Seattle: University of Washington Press.

Yuan Zhengwen, Bi Jun, and Yuichi Moriguichi. 2006. "The Circular Economy: A New Development Strategy in China." *Journal of Industrial Ecology* 10, no. 1–2, 4–8.

Yunnan News. 2017. "Kunming 5,000 yuming shimin chengwei jiaotong zhiyuanzhe changdao wenming chuxing [More than 5,000 Citizens of Kunming Became Transportation Volunteers, Initiating Civilized Travel]." May 27. http://news.163.com/17/0527/13/CLEPDH8S000187VG.html.

Zee, Jerry. 2020. "Machine Sky: Social and Terrestrial Engineering in a Chinese Weather System." *American Anthropologist* 122, no. 1: 9–20.

Zhang Ge. 2013. "Dali tuijin shengtai wenming nuli jianshe meili Zhongguo [Vigorously Promoting Ecological Civilization and Striving to Build a Beautiful China]." *Qiushi* 24: 3–11.

Zhang Lei, Arthur Mol, and David Sonnenfeld. 2007. "The Interpretation of Ecological Modernisation in China." *Environmental Politics* 16, no. 4: 659–68.

Zhang Li. 2010. *In Search of Paradise: Middle-Class Living in a Chinese Metropolis*. Ithaca NY: Cornell University Press.

Zhang Qian F. 2015. "Class Differentiation in Rural China: Dynamics of Accumulation, Commodification, and State Intervention." *Journal of Agrarian Change* 15, no. 3: 338–65.

Zhang Qian F., and John Donaldson. 2010. "From Peasants to Farmers: Peasant Differentiation, Labor Regimes, and Land-Rights Institutions in China's Agrarian Transition." *Politics and Society* 38, no. 4: 458–89.

Zhang Qian F., Carlos Oya, and Ye Jingzhong. 2015. "Bringing Agriculture Back In: The Central Place of Agrarian Change in Rural China Studies." *Journal of Agrarian Change* 15, no. 3: 299–313.

Zhang Qian F., and Wu Jianliang. 2017. "Political Dynamics in Land Commodification: Commodifying Rural Land Development Rights in Chengdu, China." *Geoforum* 78, 98–109.

Zhang Shan. 1985. "Zai chengshu shehui zhuyi tiaojian xia peiyang geren shengtai wenming de tujing [Ways of Cultivating Personal Ecological Civilization under Mature Socialist Conditions]." February 18. *Guangming Daily*. Reproduced from Scientific Communism Conference, Moscow.

Zhang Xunhua and Wang Yan. 2013. "Essentials of the Construction of an Ecological Civilization." *Social Sciences in China* 34, no. 4: 180–92.

Zhang Yong. 2008. *Large Chinese State-Owned Enterprises: Corporatization and Strategic Development*. New York: Palgrave Macmillan.

Zhao Jijun and Jan Woudstra. 2007. "'In Agriculture, Learn from Dazhai': Mao Zedong's Revolutionary Model Village and the Battle Against Nature." *Landscape Research* 32, no. 2: 171–205.

Zhao Jingzhu. 2011. *Towards Sustainable Cities in China: Analysis and Assessment of Some Chinese Cities in 2008*. New York: Springer.

Zheng Jinran. 2016 "Project Aims to Divert Water through the Sky." *China Daily*, September 14. http://www.chinadaily.com.cn/china/2016-09/14/content_26793165.htm.

Zhou D. Q. and Edward Grumbine. 2011. "National Parks in China: Experiments with Protecting Nature and Human Livelihoods in Yunnan Province, Peoples' Republic of China (PRC)." *Biological Conservation* 144, no. 5: 1314–21.

Zhou Guomei. 2018. "Green 'One Belt, One Road' Will Bring Three Business Opportunities." *China Finance Information Network*. December 3. http://greenfinance.xinhua08.com/a/20181203/1787766.shtml.

Zhou Yanwen. 1998. *Zhang Jingsheng wenji* [Collected Works by Zhang Jingsheng]. Guangzhou: Guangzhou chubanshe.

Zimmerer, Karl. 1994. "Human Geography and the New Ecology: The Prospect and Promise of Integration." *Annals of the Association of American Geographers* 84, no. 1: 108–25.

Zinda, John. 2012. "Hazards of Collaboration: Local State Co-optation of a New Protected-Area Model in Southwest China." *Society and Natural Resources* 25, no. 4: 384–99.

Zinda, John, Christine Trac, Deli Zhai, and Stevan Harrell. 2017. "Dual-function Forests in the Returning Farmland to Forest Program and the Flexibility of Environmental Policy in China." *Geoforum* 78: 119–32.

Index

Page numbers followed by italicized f and t refer to figures and tables, respectively.